The Logic of Images in
International Relations

Written under the auspices of the
CENTER FOR INTERNATIONAL AFFAIRS
Harvard University

The Logic of Images
in International Relations

ROBERT JERVIS

PRINCETON UNIVERSITY PRESS

1970

To My Parents

Acknowledgments

As WILL BE CLEAR to anyone who reads beyond these acknowledgments, my greatest intellectual debts are to Erving Goffman and Thomas Schelling. Not only did my approach to the subject develop out of their work, but they read several drafts of the manuscript, pointed out numerous pitfalls and problems, and supplied frequent encouragement. I have also benefited from comments by Alexander George, Ernst Haas, James Schlesinger, and Aaron Wildavsky. The reader and the author owe thanks to William J. Mc-Clung of Princeton University Press for his extensive and invaluable editorial assistance.

The Harvard Center for International Affairs supplied not only financial support but also a fine blend of intellectual stimulation and freedom from distractions, which made my work more enjoyable. Jeanette Asdourian, Marcessia Gelowtski, Elizabeth Harris and Stephanie Whitlock receive my grateful thanks for deciphering my original manuscript and making numerous editorial improvements.

Finally, I would like to thank my wife Kathe for keeping me in good spirits.

R.J.

Cambridge, Mass.
September, 1969

Contents

Acknowledgments vii

CHAPTER ONE Introduction 3

CHAPTER TWO Signals and Indices 18

Signals 20

Indices 26
 Too Important to be Used for Deception 28
 Causes and Correlations 29
 Samples 30
 Personal Characteristics 32
 Domestic Events 34
 Statements as Indices 35
 Capability Indices 38

CHAPTER THREE The Manipulation of Indices 41

Varieties of Manipulation 43
 Necessary Conditions as Indices 53

The Discovery That an Index Can Be Manipulated 55
 Multiple Cycles of Manipulation 57
 Transformation of Indices Into Signals 60
 Getting Caught Manipulating Indices 61

Nonmanipulatable Indices 64

CHAPTER FOUR Signals and Lies 66

Restraints on Lying 70
 Moral Restraints 70
 Stake in the International System 71
 Changing the International Environment 73
 Internal Restraints 74
 Signaling Reputation 78
  AVOIDING THE REPUTATION OF LIAR 83
  ADVANTAGES OF BEING KNOWN TO LIE 84

CONTENTS

Incentives for Lying   88
    Signaling in Crises   90
    Unexpected Belief in Signals   96

Debasing   102

Treaties of Alliance   110

CHAPTER FIVE   Signals and Ambiguity   113

Codes and the Protection of Images   113

The Utility of Ambiguity   123

Costs and Risks of Ambiguity   130

Methods of Creating Ambiguity   135

CHAPTER SIX   Coupling and Decoupling of Signals   139

The Conventional Nature of Signals   139

Coupling and Decoupling   142
    Impact of Different Signals on Conflicts   145
    Multilateral Decoupling   147
    Unilateral Decoupling   152
        DECOUPLING AND DECOMMITTING   155

Coupling   165

CHAPTER SEVEN   Coupling and Decoupling of
               Indices   174

Affecting the Interpretation of Indices   174
    Coupling and Decoupling of Signals and Indices   179
    The Likelihood of Successful Coupling
      and Decoupling   187
    Decoupling and Avoiding Challenges 190
    Alternative Explanations for Retreats   197
    Victory Claims   201
    Claims About Images of Others   204
    Challenges Avoided or Created by Claims About
      One's Own Motives   207

Expectations   216

Conclusion   223

CHAPTER EIGHT   Signals and Indices in
                the Nuclear Era   225

Lack of Capability Indices   226

Doctrine and Reality   230
    The Strategic Dialogue and Limited War   232
    The Transformation of the Threat That Leaves
    Something to Chance   237
        RISKS AND TWO WAYS TO PREVAIL IN A CRISIS   242

Images and "Security Areas" in
    the Nuclear Era   244

Sacrificing Values as an Index   250

CHAPTER NINE   Application   254

Images, Signals, and Indices in the Vietnam Conflict   254

Index   277

The Logic of Images in
International Relations

"[An] individual who presents himself before [others] . . . may wish them to think highly of him, or to think that he thinks highly of them, or to perceive how in fact he feels toward them, or to obtain no clear-cut impression; he may wish to ensure sufficient harmony so that the interaction can be sustained, or to defraud, get rid of, confuse, mislead, antagonize, or insult them. Regardless of the particular objective which the individual has in mind and of his motive for having this objective, it will be in his interest to control the conduct of others, especially their responsive treatment of him. This control is achieved largely by influencing the definition of the situation which the others come to formulate, and he can influence this definition by expressing himself in such a way as to give them the kind of impression that will lead them to act voluntarily in accordance with his own plan."

"Whether an honest performer wishes to convey the truth or whether a dishonest performer wishes to convey a falsehood, both must take care to enliven their performances with appropriate expressions, exclude from their performances expressions that might discredit the impressions being fostered, and take care lest the audience impute unintended meanings."

Erving Goffman
The Presentation of Self in Everyday Life

CHAPTER ONE Introduction

THE SUBJECT of this book is a little-discussed aspect of international politics, the ways states can affect the images others have of them and thereby exercise influence without paying the high cost of altering their own major policies. Military and economic resources, the main instrumentalities of power, have been widely studied. Less has been written about the role of diplomatic skill, and the authors of this literature have rarely focused on the full range of techniques by which a state can influence the inferences others are making about it and have not explored in any detail the ways desired images, which may be accurate or inaccurate, not only supplement the more usual forms of power, but are indispensable for reaching certain goals.

This study is designed to begin to fill this serious gap in understanding international interactions.[1] My purpose is to look at policies and events in terms of such questions as: How do actors draw inferences from others' behavior? How can actors influence the inferences others are drawing? How can a desired image be maintained by an actor who wants to act in a way that contradicts that image.[2] How, in short, can an actor influence beliefs about himself and lead others to make predictions about his behavior that will contribute to his reaching his goals? How can he do this whether or not these predictions are accurate (i.e. whether the actor is being honest or deceptive)?[3] And I

[1] While I am concerned here largely with international relations, many of the principles to be discussed also apply to interorganizational, and interpersonal, conflict. Examples from other arenas will thus sometimes be used and possible applications of the argument to other fields will be briefly treated. But I have not attempted to discuss systematically the degree to which all kinds of conflicts can be fruitfully examined in the framework elaborated here.

[2] Two books titled *The Image* [Kenneth Boulding, *The Image* (Ann Arbor: University of Michigan Press, 1956) and Daniel Boorstin, *The Image* (New York: Atheneum, 1962)] are less relevant to my concerns than their titles would indicate.

[3] Deception, incidentally, is impossible in some primitive communi-

3

will only be concerned about how actors can do this without paying a high price in terms of resources used, risks run, and other goals sacrificed; in other words, with how actors can project images "on the cheap."[4] This restriction on the scope of the analysis permits us to single out a small subset of behavior rather than treating the entire range of variables that influence images.

It is now almost a truism to argue that what men do cannot be explained without some reference to or assumptions about their views about the nature of the world. Herbert Blumer points out that an individual's behavior "is not a result of such things as environmental pressures, stimuli, motives, attitudes, and ideas, but arises instead from how he interprets and handles these things in the action which he is constructing."[5] And Harold and Margaret Sprout have argued that while the outcomes of state behavior can be understood largely in terms of the decision-makers' "operational environment"—the capabilities and intentions of relevant actors—the decisions themselves must be understood in terms of the decision-makers' "psychological environment"—their beliefs about the world and other actors.[6] And the decision-maker's image of a specific other actor is al-

---

cation systems. "Bees, for example . . . on returning to a hive leave traces which serve as directions to other bees as to the location of pollen-bearing flowers. . . . [T]his process resembles symbol usage in human communication only superficially. Someone has shrewdly observed that the bees cannot lie." Franklin Fearing, "Human Communication," in L. A. Dexter and D. M. White, eds., *People, Society and Mass Communication* (New York: Free Press, 1964), 61.

[4] I will generally use the phrase "projecting images" without including the modification "on the cheap," but it should be understood to be implied.

[5] Herbert Blumer, "Society as Symbolic Interaction," in Arnold Rose, ed., *Human Behavior and Social Processes* (Boston: Houghton Mifflin, 1962), 183.

[6] "Environmental Factors in the Study of International Politics," *Journal of Conflict Resolution* 1 (December 1957), 318. Also see Harold and Margaret Sprout, *Man-Milieu Relationship Hypotheses in the Context of International Politics* (Princeton: Center for International Studies, 1956).

most always an important component of this environment,[7] and it is this component with which we will be concerned in this book. A decision-maker's image of another actor can be defined as those of his beliefs about the other that affect his predictions of how the other will behave under various circumstances.

The importance of images in international relations may be illustrated briefly. In October 1962, the United States changed the Russian estimate of the risks the United States was willing to run to keep surface-to-surface missiles out of Cuba and thereby greatly influenced the costs the Soviets perceived were involved in continuing their policy. A major change in Soviet policy resulted from this change of image. A change in a state's policy also can be produced by a change in its perception of another's goals, as was the case with the reversal of British foreign policy in mid-March 1939 after the German take-over of Czechoslovakia.[8] As this example shows, an incident can lead to changes in a state's policy way out of proportion to the inherent value or importance of the event itself by altering the state's images of others. Hitler's conquest of the non-German parts of Czechoslovakia was of course a major and dramatic act, but the direct strategic implications were no greater than those of his previous coups, which had not altered British policy. Although "it would have been so much easier to make out a *prima facie* case for appeasing

[7] See pp. 12-13 for a discussion of when this is false or true only in a trivial sense. But I do not mean to imply that other parts of the decision-makers' psychological environments—which include the decision-makers' beliefs about the physical laws of the universe, their general theories of international relations, and their beliefs about ability and willingness of their own country to undertake given endeavors—are either unimportant or always possible to separate from images of specific other actors.

[8] A.J.P. Taylor argues that the impact of this event has been somewhat exaggerated and that the British employed both carrots and sticks throughout the whole period. While it is true that British efforts to reach an accommodation with Germany did not totally cease after March, the change in emphasis in British policy was great enough to merit calling it a reversal. A.J.P. Taylor, *The Origins of the Second World War* (Greenwich, Connecticut: Fawcett, 1966) 2nd Edn., 199-200.

Germany in the case of Poland than had been possible in the case of Czechoslovakia," the conquest of the latter precipitated the British guarantee to Poland, "one of the most remarkable public declarations in the history of British foreign policy."[9] That the British response was disproportionate to the German action can be explained by the fact that this was the first time Hitler had taken land not inhabited by Germans, thus leading Chamberlain to reject his previous belief that Germany only wanted to redress the grievances of the Treaty of Versailles.

These examples serve as a reminder that the image of a state can be a major factor in determining whether and how easily the state can reach its goals. A desired image (the substance of which will depend on the actor's goals and his estimate of the international environment) can often be of greater use than a significant increment of military or economic power. An undesired image can involve costs for which almost no amount of the usual kinds of power can compensate and can be a handicap almost impossible to overcome. Thus the image of Nazi Germany as desiring only the rectification of the Treaty of Versailles enabled Hitler to win peaceful victories out of proportion to his arms. And by convincing the USSR that it would consider an attack on Europe to be the equivalent of an attack on its own territory, the United States can deter a Soviet attack on Europe even though its armies might not be sufficient to defeat such an attack.[10] Similarly, the American blockade of Cuba could not directly force the Soviets to remove the missiles and bombers from the island, but contributed to this end by influencing the Soviet image of America's resolve. The costs of an undesired image are similarly large and obvious. Bismarck's peacekeeping efforts after 1871 were made much more difficult by the fact that other states which shared Germany's interest in

[9] John Wheeler-Bennett, *Munich* (New York: Viking, 1964), 374-375.

[10] For a discussion of the basic difference between defense and deterrence see Glenn Snyder, *Deterrence and Defense* (Princeton: Princeton University Press, 1961), 3-52.

the status quo incorrectly believed that Bismarck had plans for further expansion and could not be trusted. Hitler's image of Norway (the accuracy of which is difficult to determine) as unwilling or unable to defend its neutrality against England was a major factor leading him to the risky attack on that country.[11]

Throughout history, and especially for the great powers since 1945,[12] states have often cared about specific issues less for their intrinsic value than for the conclusions they felt others would draw from the way they dealt with them. This is often not understood. A state may be conciliatory and make sacrifices on a small issue or may not take advantage of the temporary weakness of another state. Observers who pride themselves on their hard-headed realism may claim that such actions are a foolish attempt to gain ephemeral good will at the price of concrete and valuable interests. In other circumstances a state may be willing to pay a high price or take risks to win a minor symbolic victory. Critics may charge that such a policy is a wasteful and unrealistic pursuit of prestige. Or a state may refuse to retreat on a trivial matter. In such instances the actors themselves may speak of the "national honor" and commentators often observe an unfortunate concern with "saving face."

But good will, prestige, and saving face are often not ephemeral goals pursued by politicians courting domestic support or foolish statesmen unappreciative of the vital role of power. Rather these are aspects of a state's image that greatly contribute to its pursuit of other goals. If state A can convince B of its good will, that is, of its friendly intentions toward B, B may be more willing to cooperate since it will not fear that A is trying to draw it into a trap.[13]

[11] F. H. Hinsley, *Hitler's Strategy* (Cambridge: Cambridge University Press, 1951), 48-59, and Annette Baker Fox, *The Power of Small States* (Chicago: Chicago University Press, 1959), 100-1.

[12] See Chapter 8 for a discussion of this point.

[13] The way B reacts to its belief in A's good will depends in part on B's intentions. A's policy is apt to produce unintended and undesired consequences if its beliefs about B are incorrect, as was the

A symbolic victory can lead others to see high resolve and risk-taking in a state's behavior. This image is apt to make other states retreat or act cautiously in conflicts with the first state. Similarly, saving face can contribute to later successes. If in a major defeat a state salvages enough to credibly claim that its efforts were not wasted or its policies completely mistaken, others will not be able to count on the state's avoiding similar situations. This image can then provide the state with a significant degree of deterrence.

This of course is not to deny that efforts to gain good will, prestige, or to save face may fail, be unnecessary, or involve inordinate risks. But they cannot be dismissed merely as efforts that sacrifice valuable resources to win domestic votes or the short-term approval of foreign opinion. For if they succeed they can bring rewards all out of proportion to their costs by influencing the psychological environments and policies of other decision-makers.

But even if it is acknowledged that the image of a state is a major factor in determining other states' policies toward it and that states therefore have good reason to try to project desired images, it can still be argued that there are no special ways the state can do this. To get others to believe an image a state must fully act out that image; any reputation must be earned by the fairly narrow behavior it specifies and predicts. To project the image of a basically status quo power a state would in fact have to be such a power. And to seem unwilling to retreat under pressure a state would have to always, or almost always, stand firm. This view implies that states can, and to project desired images must, give proof that the image is accurate. If this were so—and the rest of this study will attempt to show why it is not—a state's image would be completely dependent on the major actions it took. Not only would there be no interesting category of "projecting images on the cheap" to examine, but the whole study of images would be a waste of time because, while they would still in some im-

---

case in the 1930s when Britain convinced Germany that she wanted cooperation between the powers.

mediate sense cause behavior, images would be explained by and predictably linked to fairly standard patterns of behavior.[14]

But the link between actions and images is less firm and immutable than this. While a state's intentions may be obvious in retrospect, they are often obscure at the time. A look at the information available to decision-makers as they draw inferences about other states must make us less harsh on those whose judgments prove to be incorrect. Few actions are unambiguous. They rarely provide anything like proof of how the state plans to act in the future. This is shown, first, by historical examples of successful attempts to project inaccurate, and even wildly inaccurate, images. Aggressive states have convinced others they were peaceful. As so often, Hitler's policies provide clear examples of this. And states have convinced others that they were willing to fight when in fact they were ready to retreat. The British successfully projected such a false image to the United States in 1812, and only slow communications prevented them from making the concessions they were willing to make to keep peace.[15] Second, the at least partial independence of images from reality is revealed by the opposite phenomenon—the frequent instances of states *unable* to convey to others their intentions.[16] Thus in the spring and summer of 1939 Britain could not make Germany believe it would enter, and stay in, a war in response to further German aggression. And China could not convince the United States she would fight if United Nations forces

[14] For a view which might be understood to contradict this see Fred Greenstein, "The Impact of Personality on Politics," *American Political Science Review* 61 (September 1967), 631-32. I agree with the position stated by Abraham Kaplan that an explanation does not require a spelling out of all the linkages between independent and dependent variables. Abraham Kaplan, "Non-Causal Explanation," in Daniel Lerner, ed., *Cause and Effect* (New York: Free Press, 1965), 146.

[15] Bradford Perkins, *Prologue to War* (Berkeley and Los Angeles: University of California Press, 1961), passim.

[16] I have discussed the general topic of misperception in "Hypotheses on Misperception," *World Politics* xx (April 1968), 454-79.

9

crossed the 38th parallel in Korea. Finally, since validation of the threat of nuclear war employed by the superpowers would be suicidal, anything like complete proof of this intention is impossible.

The absence of a one-to-one correspondence between a state's behavior and its image makes it possible for a state to consciously influence others' images of it without paying the price of altering its basic behavior and sacrificing other goals, including the goals these images are designed to serve. It is true, but hardly interesting to statesmen or scholars, that a state can usually project an image of being a status quo power by never menacing its neighbors. But a state with limited claims that may lead others to suspect wider ambitions, and a state with unlimited ambitions to obscure, need to convince others that they are committed to the essential of the status quo without giving up their substantive goals. Similarly, a state can usually convince others of its willingness to defend its vital interests by frequently fighting for interests others believe it feels are less than vital, but a state wishing to avoid the cost of this policy and still project the desired image must seek other ways of reaching this goal.

Much of what I will be discussing constitutes the foundations for a theory of deception in international relations. This subject has been treated only tangentially in the existing literature. Schelling's work is a partial exception to this statement,[17] but he has not singled this subject out for special consideration, and, as I shall discuss later, some of his arguments are undermined by the ability of states to cheaply influence images. While diplomatic historians usually mention major instances of deception, they devote no systematic attention to the topic. It is only in books on spying and espionage that concentrated attention is paid to deception, and while these provide useful data, they are

[17] Thomas Schelling, *The Strategy of Conflict* (New York: Oxford University Press, 1963), and *Arms and Influence* (New Haven: Yale University Press, 1966).

barren of theory.[18] This study is, I think, the first attempt to treat deception as an integral part of international relations and to try to develop concepts and principles from which a theory of deception might be developed.[19]

If, almost by definition, deception involves minor and relatively cheap (although often not easy) changes in behavior to project a desired image, not all projections of images are deceptions. Accurate images are not automatically accepted, especially when the perceiver has reason to believe a state would like an image accepted whether it is accurate or not. Sometimes a state can provide the kind of evidence about its intentions which a deceiver could not. For example, a state could prove it was peaceful by totally and unilaterally disarming. But, as this example illustrates, this option, when it is available, is apt to be costly or risky. When it is not available or when states feel they cannot afford to take it, states wishing to project an accurate image must weigh the same considerations as deceivers.

The study of how states can cheaply project desired images is only a small portion of the study of international relations. Images of a state are only one of the many elements that influence the predictions other states make about how it will behave and such predictions are in turn only one of the many elements that influence their foreign policies. One approach to the study of international relations —system-oriented systems theory[20]—ignores the area of decision-making, and so does not consider the possibility that images influence basic policies. Thus Kaplan claims that the main outlines of actor behavior are specified by the

[18] For an exception see Ewan Montagu, *The Man Who Never Was* (Philadelphia: Lippincott, 1954).

[19] Erving Goffman has developed a perspective on communication, interaction, and deception which lays a similar groundwork. See his *Strategic Interaction* (Philadelphia: University of Pennsylvania Press, 1969). I have found the work of earlier sociologists of the symbolic-interaction school, such as George Herbert Mead and W. I. Thomas, relatively unhelpful because of their lack of concern with deception.

[20] Ernst Haas, *Beyond the Nation-State* (Stanford: Stanford University Press, 1964), 55-56, 63-65.

international system and certain general characteristics of the actor's internal system (i.e., directive or nondirective, system dominant or subsystem dominant).[21] To the extent that such theories can account for behavior without treating the specific predictions states make about other states' behavior, images need not be studied.[22] But in the absence of applications of such theories,[23] we cannot be sure whether, or under what circumstances, or for what types of behavior,[24] this is true.

A greater limitation on the importance of studying images is apparent when we descend from the systemic to the decision-making level. First, a state's policy is influenced by factors other than its perception of its external environment. These include its goals, the risks it is willing to run, its beliefs about its own military and diplomatic capabilities, and its beliefs about what is domestically feasible and popular. Second, actors have "operational codes"[25] —beliefs about what behavior will lead actors, or classes of actors, to respond in specified ways. Confidence in the validity of the means-ends chains which such a code provides makes it unnecessary for the actor to have a detailed

[21] Morton Kaplan, *System and Process in International Politics* (New York: Wiley, 1957), 1-85.

[22] This, of course, is part of the level-of-analysis problem. See, for example, J. David Singer, "The Level-of-Analysis Problem in International Relations," in Klaus Knorr and Sidney Verba, eds., *The International System* (Princeton: Princeton University Press, 1961), 77-92; Kenneth Waltz, *Man, The State, and War* (New York: Columbia University Press, 1957); James Rosenau, "Pre-Theories and Theories of Foreign Policy," in R. Barry Farrell, ed., *Approaches to Comparative and International Politics* (Evanston, Ill.: Northwestern University Press, 1966), 27-52.

[23] Kaplan's students have produced two applications—Hsi-sheng Chi, "The Chinese Warlord System as an International System," in Morton Kaplan, ed., *New Approaches to International Relations*, (New York: St. Martin's 1968), 405-25, and Winfried Franke, "The Italian City-State as an International System," 426-58. The only book-length application is even less successful—see William Garner, *The Chaco Dispute* (Washington: Public Affairs Press, 1966).

[24] See Kaplan's introduction in *New Approaches . . .*, vi-vii, and his "Strategy of Survival," *Survey*, 58 (January 1966), 87.

[25] Nathan Leites, *A Study of Bolshevism* (Glencoe, Ill.: Free Press, 1953), 27-63.

image of the other state in order to believe he can predict its behavior.

Third, actors do not pay careful attention to the images they have of other states—or the images they project—in periods when they believe everyone has the same goals and view of the world and so will behave similarly.[26] In these cases a decision-maker believes he can at least tentatively predict another's behavior by asking himself what he would do if he were in the other state's position. Introspection may also be used when decision-makers believe the domestic, or, more commonly, the international, environment exercises a high degree of "compulsion"[27] which leads statesmen who have different values and perceptions to behave similarly. However, decision-makers are rarely content to rely heavily on introspection. Even if they think they share the general values and "psychological environment" of their opposite numbers, they are not apt to have faith that their knowledge of the other and his situation is detailed enough to permit accurate predictions by this method.

Fourth, even when decision-makers believe that uniform rules are insufficient for the prediction of another's behavior and feel that specific images of the other are needed, there may still be little a state can do to get others to accept a desired image. Many factors about a state that contribute heavily to its image are permanent or semipermanent and thus beyond the control of its decision-makers. A state's geography and history and to a large extent its internal political, economic, and social systems are beyond manipulation. A state's objective needs and the ways it and others like it have previously tried to meet them often provide at least general guidelines for predicting the state's behavior. While we will discuss in Chapter 7 the ways some of these beliefs can be cheaply influenced by the state being observed, in many cases the previous patterns of behavior seem so clear and so deeply rooted that the state cannot affect the predictions others make about it.

[26] Arnold Wolfers, *Discord and Collaboration* (Baltimore: Johns Hopkins Press, 1962), 6.
[27] *Ibid.,* 13-15.

13

Thus the images states can cheaply project are limited. A nation that has always coveted a part of its neighbor's territory will find it difficult to convince others that it has renounced this desire. A country that has never been willing to run high risks cannot suddenly make others believe it will undertake audacious actions unless its demands are met. In other words reality, or rather states' beliefs about reality, often can only be altered to some extent, and can be cheaply altered to an even smaller extent.

Further limitations on the projection of desired images derived from the fact that states are not unitary actors and that they must usually take more than one audience into account. Although some of the ways a state can use internal divisions and multiple audiences to project a credible image are discussed in later chapters, these considerations usually reduce the ability of a state to control and manipulate its behavior to influence selected foreign audiences. Finally, the tendency for decision-makers to interpret incoming information to conform with their existing images means that they are often impervious to behavior which in retrospect seems hard to reconcile with the prevailing view.[28] However three considerations modify the extent to which this limits the successful projection of images. First, these efforts may begin before observers develop a fixed image of the actor. Hitler, for example, sought from the beginning to convince others that he desired peace and wanted only to see Germany regain what had unjustly been taken by the Treaty of Versailles. Second, the image a state wants to project is sometimes consistent with the views others already have of it. In these cases the tendency for observers to perceive what they expect to perceive makes it easier for the actor to project a desired image. Third, while the basic elements of an image may be difficult to alter, detailed aspects of it, which may strongly influence the way the perceiver acts, are more susceptible to change. Beliefs about the specific issues on which a state will fight,

[28] I have discussed this tendency in Jervis, "Hypotheses on Misperception," 455-62.

14

its flexibility in any given negotiation, and the special reasons a state acted in an unusual way in a particular situation are generally subject to influence.

In this study I will generally assume that the limitations discussed in the previous several pages are not operative. These simplifying assumptions are made to more fully and clearly highlight how images can be cheaply projected. Further research may indicate that once these assumptions are dropped some of the phenomena discussed here are less significant than they appear. But at this point I believe there is value in examining the projection of images in relative isolation.

By concentrating on how states cheaply project desired images I will not give a balanced view of international interaction. Rather I will try to direct a sharp, and admittedly narrow, light on the subject. Even if the analysis were faultless this light would cover only a small portion of international relations, and, if it were seen only in this light, would be greatly distorted. However, since no systematic efforts have been made to see the techniques of influence in this way, it is worth at least a tentative attempt to see what this narrow light reveals.

This perspective involves proceeding from the assumption that rational actors try to project desired images, whether accurate or not, and skeptically view the images projected by others. Deductively tracing the consequences of this assumption involves asking an unusual set of questions about interactions and seeing what the world looks like when a few variables are singled out. Thus I will constantly be concerned with the question of why rational actors should believe what others say, why they should draw certain inferences from others' behavior, and what status as evidence of an actor's capabilities and intentions his statements and actions have.

I shall not consider a long list of variables that clearly influence how the sender projects images and the receiver perceives and weighs evidence. I have done this in the belief that one of the best routes to international relations

15

theory does not lie in an attempt to deal with all the significant variables operating in any case, but rather in the attempt to see what the world would look like if only a few dominant influences were at work. As Anatol Rapoport has pointed out, one can never understand the operation and patterns of waves by looking at the ocean all his life.[29] Understanding often progresses by adopting a view of the "Natural Order" of the world far removed from that observed in everyday life.[30] We all know that in the world around us all objects do not fall with equal speed and that an object set in motion does not continue on a straight line indefinitely. But taking this as what would happen "all else being equal" has proven immensely fruitful. Efforts proceeding along these lines do not provide richness of detail and do not add to the store of facts available for future theorizing. For these sacrifices to be worthwhile, the study must produce insights not readily available by other methods of theorizing, must relate these insights to one another and to the basic framework of the analysis, and must lead to other interesting questions.

Of course for the analysis to be of value it must also bear some relation to empirical events. The examples provided throughout this book are designed to meet this requirement. The worth of a new approach is often demonstrated by its ability both to show that previous explanations are inadequate and to provide parsimonious and satisfying accounts of a wide variety of events.[31] The value of the

[29] Anatol Rapoport, "Various Meanings of 'Theory'," in James Rosenau, ed., International Politics and Foreign Policy (New York, 1961) 1st edn., 52.

[30] Stephen Toulmin, Foresight and Understanding (New York: Harper and Row, 1963), 56.

[31] My indebtedness to Toulmin, ibid., Michael Polanyi, Personal Knowledge (London: Routledge and Kegan Paul, 1958), Polanyi, Science, Faith, and Society, (Chicago: University of Chicago Press, 1964), and Thomas Kuhn, The Structure of Scientific Revolutions (Chicago: University of Chicago Press, 1962) is great. My temptation to adopt Kuhn's concept and call my perspective a paradigm was resisted because although Kuhn is vague about the level of abstraction at which paradigms are conceived, it seems unlikely that

analysis is much greater if the events so explained seemed from other perspectives to be diverse and lacking connections (i.e. if they had previously seemed inexplicable or at best had been accounted for by *ad hoc* hypotheses). I believe the examples supplied in this book thus serve not only to clarify the arguments, but to show the value of the perspective employed. However, it should be clear that they in no sense constitute proof. Indeed they do not show that what I claim should occur given certain assumptions does in fact occur all, or even most of, the time. The variables omitted from consideration here may come into play in many, or almost all, actual interactions and produce behavior different from what this analysis, taken in isolation from other approaches and findings, would lead one to expect. The examples may thus lend support to the argument, but at this point what persuasiveness this study has must be supplied largely by its structure and logic.[32]

most analysis in the social sciences, including that presented here, can be said to constitute a paradigm without doing violence to that concept.

[32] This is true also for formally axiomatic theories such as those of Anthony Downs, *An Economic Theory of Democracy* (New York: Harper, 1957), Mancur Olson, *The Logic of Collective Action* (Cambridge: Harvard University Press, 1965), and William Riker, *The Theory of Political Coalitions* (New Haven: Yale University Press, 1962). Like these studies and game theory, my analysis contains a prescriptive element. See especially Chapters 7 and 9 below.

CHAPTER TWO   Signals and Indices

To INVESTIGATE the world from the perspective of the projection of images, it is useful to divide behavior into two categories, signals and indices, on the basis of the reasons men believe an act is a valid indicator of an actor's intentions.[1] *Signals* are statements or actions the meanings of which are established by tacit or explicit understandings among the actors. As all actors know, signals are issued mainly to influence the receiver's image of the sender. Both the sender and the perceiver realize that signals can be as easily issued by a deceiver as by an honest actor. The costs of issuing deceptive signals, if any, are deferred to the time when it is shown that the signals were misleading.[2] Signals, then, can be thought of as promissory notes. They do not contain inherent credibility. They do not, in the absence of some sort of enforcement system, provide their own evidence that the actor will live up to them.[3] Signals include diplomatic notes, military maneuvers, extending or breaking diplomatic relations, and choosing the shape of a negotiating table.

In contrast to signals, *indices* are statements or actions that carry some inherent evidence that the image projected is correct because they are believed to be inextricably linked to the actor's capabilities or intentions. Behavior that constitutes an index is believed by the perceiver to tap dimensions and characteristics that will influence or predict an actor's later behavior and to be beyond the ability of the actor to control for the purpose of projecting a misleading image. Examples of indices include private mes-

---

[1] For a similar distinction see Goffman, *Strategic Interaction*, 5-6.

[2] As will be discussed later, high costs are often involved if it is later discovered that the actor's signals were designed to be misleading. Indeed, if there were no such costs associated with issuing misleading signals, there would be no reason for receivers to place any faith in them.

[3] One exception to this is the relatively infrequent signals that convey a message only an honest actor would want believed. For example, if a statesman claims he made a commitment to another

sages the perceiver overhears or intercepts; patterns of behavior that disclose, unknown to the actor, important information (e.g. a pitcher's mannerism revealing what he will throw next); and major actions that involve high costs.

While there are some similarities between my categories and the familiar words-versus-deeds distinction, the latter is not useful in this context. In trying to predict how others will behave states often examine the words and deeds of others in much the same way and, as both a cause and an effect of this, in trying to convey a message words and actions often serve the same functions.

Actions are not automatically less ambiguous than words. Indeed, without an accompanying message it may be impossible for the perceiving actor to determine what image the other is trying to project. And rarely is there only one obvious prediction about the actor's future behavior to be made on the basis of his actions. It is often claimed that even when statements and actions are equally ambiguous, some action makes it more likely that the message will be believed. Schelling observes that "words are cheap [and] not inherently credible when they emanate from an adversary. . . . Actions . . . prove something; significant actions usually incur some cost or risk, and carry some evidence of their own credibility."[4]

While this emphasis on cost as contributing to a message's credibility is warranted, words also can be costly, as a gentleman who swears in polite mixed company soon learns.[5] Bethmann Hollweg paid a high price for saying that the Treaty guaranteeing Belgium's neutrality was "just . . . a scrap of paper." Indeed if states did not pay a high price for violating treaties there would be little reason

---

state which he now realizes he would rather not carry out, no one is apt to think he is lying, whereas if he had denied making such a commitment his signals might be suspect. For this reason, in legal proceedings extra weight is apt to be given to the testimony of a witness which is against his own interest.

[4] Schelling, *Arms and Influence*, 150.
[5] Personal communication from Erving Goffman.

19

for states to conclude many of them. Statements of hostility toward another actor, if believed, may also involve costs to the actor making them. Some words (e.g. ultimata) can create impressions that make war more likely. Furthermore, the issuance of many statements is preceded by conflict within the state, and thus the state's decision-makers often pay a price for their words in terms of time, energy, and other political resources.

While it is true that words often fail to convince listeners, many actions are equally ineffectual. The cost of breaking diplomatic relations for example, may not be much higher than that of issuing a statement of hostility. And when the gains of projecting a given image are high, a deceiver as well as an honest actor may be willing to take risky and costly actions. Largely because of the post-war increase in the disparity between the probable gains and losses of a major war, the stakes involved today in many specific conflicts are less concrete possessions, such as money and territory (e.g. Berlin), than images of resolve and intention. Refraining from taking advantage of another's weakness, an example of an action involving a significant loss, can be worthwhile if it convinces others that the actor is trustworthy. The risks involved in standing firm on a minor issue can be worth taking if there is a good probability that this will convince others of the actor's high resolve. Because these actions will be worth taking whether the image the state is trying to project is accurate or misleading, perceivers will not automatically draw the desired inferences from the behavior. This is not to claim that words and actions are interchangeable, that to say one will blockade an island or bomb a city conveys the same impression as doing it. Rather the argument is that since both words and actions are ambiguous, involve costs, and can be used to deceive, other categories will prove more useful in the analysis of how states project and interpret images.

SIGNALS

Signals, to repeat, are statements or actions the meanings of which are established by tacit or explicit understandings among the actors. As all actors know, signals are issued mainly to influence the receiver's image of the sender. Both the sender and the perceiver realize that signals can be as easily issued by a deceiver as by an honest actor. The costs of issuing deceptive signals, if any, are deferred to the time when it is shown that the signals were misleading. Signals, then, can be thought of as promissory notes. They do not contain inherent credibility. They do not, in the absence of some sort of enforcement system, provide their own evidence that the actor will live up to them. Thus a system of signals is in some ways like a language, a consideration which will be explored at greater length in Chapter 6.[6] Signals do not alter the actors' capabilities and therefore do not directly affect the distribution of power among them. Nor do they directly affect the significant interests of the signaling or perceiving actor.

The most obvious examples of signals are a state's direct statements of intention. All secret messages and most public ones are signals, as are diplomatic gestures such as the recall of ambassadors, the breaking of relations, and diplomatic snubs. These signals may involve following an established routine, as in the use of "diplomatic language," or may entail breaking that pattern. For example, in the dispute with France over control of the upper Nile, one of the ways the British Prime Minister made his determination clear was "by publishing a Blue Book on the Fashoda crisis, a most unusual step, since as a matter of courtesy, records of diplomatic negotiations are not generally given to the public until the negotiations with which they are concerned are ended."[7]

Many diplomatic conflicts and agreements are more important as signals than for their substantive alteration of

[6] Some authorities distinguish between language and signaling systems. Although both are established by convention, the former permits the users to send an infinite variety of messages, whereas the latter lacks this flexibility and can only communicate a much narrower set of messages. However for the purposes of this book this distinction is not particularly useful.

[7] J.A.S. Grenville, *Lord Salisbury and Foreign Policy* (London: Athlone Press, 1964), 228.

international relations. The breaking of treaties and tacit agreements, the exacerbation of minor issues, and the refusal to renew trade agreements are essentially signals. All these have, of course, counterparts in signals of friendship. The US-USSR cultural exchange agreement, and possibly the test ban treaty, are more important as signals than as direct influences on significant interests of either side.

Such statements and actions derive their significance from the common understanding as to what impression they are meant to convey. This is also the case, although it is less immediately apparent, for military gestures which would have little impact on the outcome of hostilities should they occur. Some army maneuvers and certain types of limited mobilizations have served signaling functions in the past, and the ostentatious, but relatively harmless, use of nuclear weapons in a future crisis (such as exploding a warhead high over an enemy country) could be an addition to this category. Moves of this type, which have some military significance, but not enough to account for their full impact, are partially signals. For example, the demonstration of a new weapon, enlargement of the armed forces, or the start of a civil defense program usually have a strong signaling component although they also have direct military effects.

The blockade of Cuba during the missile crisis was partially a signal. While it exerted direct pressure on the Soviet Union not to send further offensive weapons to the island, it helped induce the Russians to withdraw the missiles and bombers already in place by influencing the Soviet image of American resolve. Since the blockade revealed an American willingness to run some risks in opposing the Soviet venture it was partly an index (indices will be discussed below). But it also constituted a clear signal which could have been a bluff and did not involve any strong proof of American willingness to take the much higher risks which would have been necessary to secure American goals had Russia not retreated.

Similarly, in the summer of 1961 President Kennedy wanted to demonstrate his determination not to be forced out of Berlin. Then, as during the missile crisis, he felt that Khrushchev "won't pay any attention to words. He has to see you move."[8] But the actions the President chose—an increase in the defense budget, the calling up of some Reserve and National Guard units, and an expansion of the civil defense program—were largely signals. They did not put the US in an appreciably better military position and they were cheap compared with the gains that would accrue if the Russians believed America would stand firm. Thus one of the functions performed by the blockade, and the main function performed by the actions outlined in the President's Berlin speech, was the same as that accomplished by the delivering of a very stiff note in previous eras. As the Russians presumably considered, an America which was not willing to go much further on the road to war, as well as an America which was willing to do this, could have taken these actions.

Since signals make so few changes in the material situation and since their purpose is known to be that of influencing images, receivers can be expected to at least partially discount them and one might therefore expect signals to be relatively rare or unimportant. But in fact a great deal of modern international relations consists of signals. For example, Marshall Shulman describes the Soviet response to the West's preparations to forming NATO as follows:

> In diplomatic notes the Soviet government threatened to annul its wartime treaties of alliance with France and Great Britain. . . . The Soviet press revived memories of the Allied intervention during the civil war thirty years before and anti-Americanism reached a new and more virulent extreme. . . . Charges of espionage were raised against some American newspapermen. The jamming of the Voice of America was increased. The Soviet Union ordered its consulates in Italy closed. Further re-

[8] Quoted in Arthur Schlesinger, *A Thousand Days* (Boston: Houghton Mifflin, 1965), 391.

ports of troop movements on the borders of Yugoslavia were circulated in West Europe, and the Soviet Union revived the Macedonian question as a threat to both Greece and Yugoslavia. Border incidents with Iran increased, and the Iranian consulate in Baku was closed.[9]

Most of these activities were on the order of tokens and promissory notes, relatively cheaply undertaken and providing little inherent evidence of the Soviets' willingness to take stronger actions if pressed.

In analyzing signals, the receiver has to make inferences at two levels. First, he must determine what message the sender is trying to convey. Second, the receiver must estimate whether this accurately reflects what the sender will do in the future (e.g., whether he is bluffing). This distinction is similar to that made by Herbert Feigl when he says "there are two questions with which we are (or at least should be) concerned in any cognitive enterprise: 'What do we mean by the words or symbols we use?' and 'How do we know what we assert in these terms is true. . . ?' "[10]

Getting a message understood at the first, or what I will call the semantic, level does not guarantee getting it accepted on the second level. Knowing what the other is saying and believing him are different. Scholars who stress misunderstandings as an important cause of conflicts often do not sufficiently appreciate this point. Dean Pruitt, for example, argues that since multiple channels of communication "can be used to transmit information about capabilities and intentions . . . there is less guesswork for the other side."[11] But the most crucial portion of the guesswork usually remains, because even if the perceiving state knows

[9] Stalin's Foreign Policy Reappraised (New York: Atheneum, 1965), 63.

[10] "Operationism and Scientific Method," in Herbert Feigl and Wilfrid Sellers, Readings in Philosophical Analysis (New York: Appleton-Century-Crofts, 1949), 498.

[11] "Definition of the Situation as a Determinant of International Action," Herbert Kelman, ed., International Behavior (New York: Holt, Rinehart and Winston, 1965), 406.

what image the other is trying to project, it still has to estimate how the other will, in fact, act. Extra channels of communication may not make this task easier.

The similar argument is sometimes made that some techniques of diplomacy, such as summit meetings, are useful because they allow the actors to convey messages more clearly than is possible through normal channels. However it is not enough to argue that summit conferences, because of the opportunities for informal contact, probing, and feedback, enable decision-makers to get a more accurate view of the images others are trying to project. This only deals with the semantic level. It remains to be shown that summit meetings are useful for convincing the other side that one's signals are accurate. Sorensen misses this point when he says that Kennedy's advisors favored the Vienna meeting because they believed "it would be useful . . . for the President . . . to make more clear and precise than his letters could do . . . the vital interests for which this nation would fight."[12] This fails to explain why Khrushchev should have been more apt to believe messages conveyed by Kennedy in person than those sent through normal channels. What could Kennedy say when talking to Khrushchev that could not be said by a deceiving Kennedy who wanted to mislead the Soviet leader?[13] In fact, later Soviet behavior indicates Khrushchev did not believe the image of resoluteness Kennedy tried to project. Sorensen's and Schlesinger's discussion of the increased "understanding" of Khrushchev which Kennedy supposedly gained at the meetings similarly misses the crucial difference between merely knowing what signals the other is trying to convey and estimating what relation these signals have to future action.[14]

[12] Sorensen, *Kennedy*, 542.

[13] As I will argue in Chapter 4, messages conveyed in person may stake more of the state's reputation on a signal than normal diplomatic communications. But Sorensen does not seem to have this in mind.

[14] *Ibid.*, 543-58; Schlesinger, *A Thousand Days*, 358-74.

INDICES

As indicated before, indices are statements or actions that carry some inherent evidence that the image projected is correct because they are believed to be inextricably linked to the actor's capabilities or intentions. Behavior that constitutes an index is believed by the perceiver to tap dimensions and characteristics that will influence or predict an actor's later behavior and to be beyond the ability of the actor to control for the purpose of projecting a misleading image.

Of course the observer does not have to believe the correlation between an index and later behavior will be perfect, but only that it is high enough to be of use. Furthermore, the actor being observed may not know what behavior the observer believes constitutes indices and what inferences the observer is drawing from these indices. Indeed, he may believe the theories that underlie the interpretations are faulty.

Of course if these theories are in fact incorrect, the actor's inferences will be inaccurate. Regularities in behavior over a period of time may depend on a variable which, unknown to the observer, is changing.[15] Thus by the end of 1939 members of the foreign office of many European countries noticed that Nazi Germany always issued an ultimatum before attacking, and they assumed this pattern rested on constant traits of Nazi behavior. This was one reason why they were taken by surprise when Hitler, who found it convenient to alter his behavior under wartime conditions, struck at Denmark and Norway without warning. Similarly, Allied intelligence analysts were unable to draw valid inferences about Nazi perceptions and intentions directly from Nazi propaganda. Other intervening variables, such as Nazi propaganda strategy, changed too frequently to be ignored.[16]

[15] This possibility is, of course, an impediment to the development of any theory. Social and physical scientists, as well as decision-makers, also have to take account of it.

[16] Alexander George, *Propaganda Analysis* (Evanston, Ill.: Row, Peterson, & Company, 1959), passim.

Behavior that constitutes an index is usually thought by the perceiver to be a test of some important aspect of the actor's capability or intention. And indices and tests share a central characteristic—the person drawing conclusions from them believes the actor being judged is either not aware of what aspect of his behavior is being observed (and may not even know he is being observed at all) or, more frequently, is not able to control that aspect of his behavior to give a desired, but misleading, impression. The whole point of tests is that the person taking them lacks either the information (as in academic tests) or the self-control (as in lie-detector tests) to use them to deceive, even though he knows what image he wants to project. And since observers believe that indices cannot or at least are not being used for deception, they often rely heavily on them when signals are suspect.

Indices are also used in interpersonal perception and judgment. People develop "implicit personality theories" that involve beliefs about the way various personal characteristics are linked. Although the discipline of physiognomics lost most of its scholarly adherents when it was shown that visible physical features do not provide reliable cues to personality, many people still use physical characteristics as indices—e.g. the widely held belief that fat people tend to be jolly. There are a wide variety of nonphysical attributes employed as indices, and for many people one of the most powerful is the judgment as to where the other falls along a "warm-cold" dimension.[17] The beliefs underlying the use of these indices generally are implicit, and, while they are often at least partially accurate, actors generally make few self-conscious efforts to verify them.

The line between indices and signals is often difficult to draw. Many actions have significant costs and seem to tap

[17] Ash, "Forming Impressions of Persons," *Journal of Abnormal and Social Psychology* 41 (1946), 258-90; and Kelley, "The Warm-Cold Variable in First Impressions of Persons," *Journal of Personality* 18 (1950), 431-39. Halo effects—the impact of the belief that a person ranks favorably on one dimension on the image of other characteristics of the person—can be seen in these terms.

27

the dimension of a major characteristic. But if it is generally known that impressions are being derived from that behavior and that the costs of the behavior are much less than the gains of having the other accept the desired impressions, the action will usually be more a signal than an index. Examples of behavior in this category are engaging in a lengthy debate over the agenda for negotiations, refusing to meet with one's opponent, or making concessions on a minor issue.

To more completely understand the nature of indices, why they are relied on, and how (when one or more of the perceiver's critical assumptions are incorrect) they can be used by the actor to cheaply project a desired image, we should examine the various types of behavior that can be used as indices. As this analysis shall make clear, while all indices are seen as being linked to a characteristic of the actor in a way that allows the observer to predict the actor's behavior, the nature of this perceived link varies in ways that are related to the possible uses of indices for deception.

Too Important To Be Used for Deception

Behavior that is felt to be too important or costly in its own right to be used for other ends is an index, and such behavior tends to make the greatest impact on observers. Many of the interactions that result in major changes in the distribution of values reveal things about the actors that are helpful in predicting future behavior. Thus a state that attacks one of its neighbors will generally be predicted to be aggressive in the future. A state that is willing to sacrifice major values rather than fight will be thought weak in capability or resolve. A state that runs very high risks in one situation will be thought to be willing to run risks under similar circumstances. In these situations, unlike those involving signals, the actors cannot manipulate their behavior to give the desired image without incurring prohibitive costs to the values the image is supposed to serve.[18] For

[18] The possibility that the actor, while unable to manipulate his

example, to engage in a major war merely to show that one has a great deal of resolve is unusual because the costs are apt to outweigh the gains. Thus few people suspected deception when a Cuban killed himself in order to expose the falseness of the charge that he was a selfish politician who was seeking personal gain from the revolution.[19]

Causes and Correlations

Indices can be provided by behavior thought to be a cause of future action. A state deprived of one source of vital raw materials may be expected to try to gain control over another source. Events thought to be causes of or major influences on future policy will be taken as relatively trustworthy indices because of the regularity with which the predicted behavior has followed from the event and because it seems impossible for the actor to employ these indices to deceive. But since decision-makers, unlike scientists,[20] need only to be able to predict how others will act, not understand why they act as they do, knowledge of correlation could be an adequate substitute for knowledge of causation. Although J. David Singer has argued that it is often easier to predict an event than to explain it,[21] decision-makers rarely look for correlations unless they can also see some causal links that satisfy them that the index is valid. Usually decision-makers have some ideas about why behaviors that appear to be correlated do go together, even if these beliefs are vague and not subject to careful scrutiny. Thus many theories of foreign-policy making could lead a decision-maker to believe that the internal unrest plaguing its neighbor will probably lead the latter to develop a belligerent foreign policy. Or the fact that a

behavior in these situations, may be able to influence the interpretations others hold is discussed in Chapter 7.

[19] This has been reported by Roberta Wohlstetter. Personal Communication from Thomas Schelling.

[20] See Toulmin, *Foresight and Understanding*, 18-43.

[21] J. David Singer, "The Level-of-Analysis Problem in International Relations," in Knorr and Verba, eds., *The International System*, 88.

negotiator always gets mad when he has no more concessions to make and flustered when presented with an argument he cannot rebut can be understood in terms of the individual's psychology, even if the exact linkages are not completely known.

A subcategory of those events that are believed to be indices because they are felt to be a cause of a future policy are events believed to be a necessary, but not a sufficient, condition for a policy to be implemented. In the next chapter I shall discuss how this kind of index has been used to project a misleading image.

Samples

Indices do not have to be major events. Instead they can be samples of important categories of behavior—"straws in the wind" believed to reflect the strength of various forces that will determine or heavily influence future interactions. In this way a small victory or defeat can have impact all out of proportion to its intrinsic importance, an impact sometimes mistakenly attributed to the event's "symbolic" or "psychological" effect. Just as politicians can draw far-reaching conclusions from the results of a primary election in a small and unimportant state, so statesmen can get a great deal of information from an incident that may be *representative* of an important class of events even if it does not itself *change* the likely outcome of those events. This makes the French reaction to the battle of Dienbienphu more comprehensible than it seemed to the United States government at the time.

> As the United States saw it, the military value of the fortress had been magnified beyond reality. Washington viewed this development with extreme regret because it knew that the French, from every objective standpoint, could sustain the loss of the garrison and continue fighting. . . . On the other hand, it was also clear to the Administration that the extinction of the garrison and its defenders would make French determination to pull out of Indochina and accept a cease-fire insurmountable.

Dulles revealed the frustration inherent in discussing the Dienbienphu situation with the French when he wrote the President: "There is, of course, no military or logical reason why loss of Dien Bien Phu should lead to collapse of French will. . . . Dien Bien Phu has become a symbol out of all proportion to its military importance."[22]

However Dulles's analysis completely ignores the degree to which the French and others could unemotionally take the results of this siege as an index of the ability of the French to win the war. The battle had been sought by the French since they felt it was the type they could fight best. It was then not unreasonable for them to conclude from their defeat that they could no longer hope for victory in the other aspects of the war in which the Vietminh had even greater relative advantages.

Similarly, a minor issue can lead to a large increase in conflict between two actors if one or both of them take it as an index that reveals the hostile intentions of the other side. For example, some of the restrictions on neutrals' trade with France that Britain imposed during the Napoleonic wars had little effect on the volume of American trade. Yet since these measures were taken as evidence "that Britain intended to act without concern for precedent or American sensibilities,"[23] they resulted in a significant hardening of the American attitude toward England. A contemporary example is provided by the inferences many American leaders are drawing from the Soviet development of a Fractional Orbiting Bombardment System (FOBS). This expensive weapon has advantages over conventional missiles only in missions in which it is important to reduce the adversary's warning time. A first strike against bomber bases is the only task that fits this requirement. The deployment of FOBS may thus be taken as an index of Soviet aggressiveness and the United States could react strongly

[22] Melvin Gurtov, *The First Vietnam Crisis* (New York: Columbia University Press, 1967), 105-6.
[23] Bradford Perkins, *Prologue to War* (Berkeley and Los Angeles: University of California Press, 1961), 81-82.

even though the system's direct military effects are slight.

This type of index can also be provided in a somewhat different way. The attitudes and behavior of an individual can constitute an index to a state's intentions if it is a sample of the characteristics of those in power. Thus a decision-maker's desire to select an ambassador who embodies values prevalent in his country may spring from more than national egotism or the naive belief that the envoy will convert everyone he meets. In those cases where there is strong antipathy between a decision-maker and another state's ambassador, the former would be wise to estimate whether the ambassador is a representative in only a formal sense or whether his attitudes predict those of the leaders of his country. Thus an untrained ambassador who lets his feelings show may reveal more about his country than a professional at pains to give off only controlled impressions.[24] It has been noted of William Dodd, American ambassador to Germany in the 1930s, that while his inability to disguise his loathing of Nazism made him by most standards unsuitable for his post, he was "a singularly honorable example of American idealism. . . . Had the Nazis studied his reactions more carefully, they would have spared themselves many a disagreeable surprise in store for them." And Hugh Wilson, who replaced Dodd, concealed his personal feelings (which were the same as Dodd's) as a good diplomat is supposed to, and may thereby have inadvertently contributed to the Nazis' inaccurate image of the United States.[25]

Personal Characteristics

When an actor is able to directly observe one of his adversaries he will not only try to understand the other's

---

[24] Whether this will benefit either state will be determined by the details of the situation.

[25] The remark was by André François-Poncet, a former French ambassador in Berlin, quoted in James Compton, *The Swastika and the Eagle* (Boston: Houghton Mifflin, 1967), 71. Dodd was aware of this function of his behavior. See Robert Dallek, *Democrat and Diplomat* (New York: Oxford University Press, 1968), 295.

general outlook, but also scrutinize those presumably uncontrolled aspects of personal behavior that are indices to
the adversary's goals, estimate of the situation, and resolve.
The desire to obtain information in this way can be one
motive for summit conferences,[26] a motive strengthened
for many decision-makers by their belief that their rise to
power was partly dependent on a keen ability to judge
others.

Personal behavior is especially apt to be examined if
the circumstances make it unlikely that the actor will be
able to exercise complete control over his emotions and
reactions and so cannot put on displays meant to impress
the observer. This is apt to be the case, for example, during
prolonged and intense negotiations. "Through the days of
severe strain [during the Russo-Japanese negotiations that
ended the war of 1905] . . . the delegates would be able to
observe each other carefully, watching for signs of nervous-
ness or of any declining resistance as the issues became
more clearly defined. . . . The leading Japanese negotiator
showed his displeasure by the force with which he knocked
the ashes from his cigarette, by hitting the table, and by
speaking more shortly and abruptly."[27]

In such face-to-face interactions an actor does not have to
wait for indices to arise naturally, but can engage in probes
designed to bring them out. For example, in labor negotiations a management negotiator said that he makes a practice of launching strong attacks and watching the reaction
of the union leaders in order to find out what points they
feel strongly about and what they are willing to give
up. When they get mad he infers that he has touched on an
issue important to them. "When asked what cues he utilized
to distinguish bonafide from synthetic emotional reaction
on the union side, he replied: 'I don't think it is anything

[26] For a critical discussion of this aspect of summit diplomacy,
see Alexander Groth, "On the Intelligence Aspects of Personal Diplomacy," *Orbis* 7 (Winter 1964), 833-48.

[27] John Albert White, *The Diplomacy of the Russo-Japanese War*
(Princeton: Princeton University Press, 1964), 243.

that is said, but I notice flushing of the face, and mainly watch the neck muscles in the other fellows.' "[28]

Domestic Events

A state's domestic political system and policies may be used as indices. Indeed, to the degree decision-makers believe internal developments provide the well-springs for foreign policy, the indices from domestic policies set the general framework within which specific predictions about the other are made. For example, Woodrow Wilson felt there was a link between democracy and peaceful policies and dictatorships and aggressiveness.[29] American decision-makers today argue more narrowly that Communist regimes are apt to follow expansionist foreign policies. Perhaps less widely held is the belief that governments that come to power on the crest of newly emerging nationalism will tend to be aggressive. An older belief is that when decision-makers are faced with internal discontent they will tend to look for foreign adventures to divert the attention and energies of their people and to create a unifying spirit.

More specific domestic events can also be used as indices. For example, the fact that in Finland in 1939 huge crowds spontaneously gathered at the railroad station to see off the Finnish negotiators who were on their way to the USSR could have provided the Soviet Union with a hint of the strength with which Finland would resist in wartime.[30] Of course elections in democracies are often used as indices, both because they determine the identity of the top decision-makers and because they presumably reveal information about the distribution and intensity of mass opinion about foreign policy.

[28] Ann Douglas, *Industrial Peace-Making* (New York: Columbia University Press, 1962), 24.

[29] For a discussion of this and other theories linking general characteristics of states' domestic systems with foreign policy outputs see Waltz, *Man the State and War*, chapters 4 and 5.

[30] Max Jakobson, *The Diplomacy of the Winter War* (Cambridge, Mass.: Harvard University Press, 1961), 113-14.

34

Statements as Indices

Statements are indices rather than signals if the listener feels they were not meant to influence him but instead were aimed at some other audience the speaker was not able, would not want, or could not afford to deceive. States may therefore take some aspects of the internal dialogue within other states as indices, but this depends on the listener's theories about the other's domestic political system. It is hard to determine, for example, the degree to which foreign countries, and especially nondemocratic ones, think that American officials can manipulate their testimony to Congressional committees in order to make a desired impression on foreign audiences. Statements and documents that were certainly not meant to project misleading images, e.g. many of those procured by espionage, are indices.

Statements will also be indices on those rare occasions when the perceiver believes the actor is influenced by alcohol or emotion and is expressing his true feelings without control. The French Ambassador to England in the late 18th century who was instructed to ascertain whether Britain was planning war found the Prime Minister, in the Ambassador's words, "drunk as a cabman."[31] When he received the same protestations of innocence he had been given when the Prime Minister was sober, the Ambassador concluded that the statements were sincere. More frequently, although still rarely, a diplomat will be overcome by his emotions. It was crucial for Czechoslovakia in September 1938 to predict what France would do in case of war. After the French Ambassador, M. de Lacroix, had told the Czech Foreign Minister that France would not support Czechoslovakia if she rejected the Anglo-French proposal, the Czech Prime Minister called the Ambassador in for a more complete explanation. The Prime Minister "now put the question bluntly to the [Ambassador]: could Czechoslovakia count on French help or could she not? M. de

[31] James Thompson and Saul Padover, *Secret Diplomacy* (New York: Frederick Unger, 2nd edn., 1963), 175.

Lacroix, a good friend of Czechoslovakia, was deeply moved. He wept. It was some time before he could reply, but when he did speak it was to say that, although he had received no definite instructions, he was convinced that French support would not be forthcoming."[32] There was little question in the Prime Minister's mind that this reflected the Ambassador's honest estimate of the situation. And when the French Ambassador to Russia told the Vice-Commissar for Foreign Affairs of the Munich agreement the Ambassador reported that the official's "emotions gained the upper hand and, although a Slav and a diplomat, he spoke his thoughts freely to me: 'My poor fellow, what have you done? For us, I see no other consequence but a fourth partition of Poland.'"[33] To the degree the listeners believed the speaker was an accurate observer of his own government or a representative, in the literal sense of the word, of it, these spontaneous outbursts could be taken as reliable indices.

Statements the observer believes may be calculated to make a given impression will also be taken as indices if the cost involved in their utterance seems so high as to outweigh any possible gains of having a false but desired image accepted. The person who purposely uses foul language in mixed company reveals himself as a person willing to pay high social costs in certain circumstances (although of course his motives may not be clear). A decision-maker who goes out of his way to insult others is similarly using words that, because of their cost, carry some inherently credible evidence about the speaker.

Finally, there are two kinds of communications that are indices because they are self-validating. One is what Malinowski called "'phatic communication . . . a type of speech in which ties of union are created by a mere ex-

[32] Wheeler-Bennett, *Munich*, 121.

[33] Franklin Ford and Carl Schorske, "The Voice in the Wilderness: Robert Coulondre," in Gordon Craig and Felix Gilbert, *The Diplomats, 1919-1939* (Princeton: Princeton University Press, 1953), 568.

change. . . .' [These] messages . . . serve primarily to establish, prolong, or discontinue communication [or] to check whether the channel works in good order."[34] Schelling points out that "if we want to know whether a man speaks Japanese, we can ask him to speak a little Japanese. And when somebody says, 'Nobody here but just us chickens, boss,' we get information from the evidence of a verbal message, even though the information is not contained in, and actually contradicts, the conventionally encoded message."[35] Furthermore, in tacit bargaining situations such communications can automatically serve other functions. Saying anything about a possible settlement of a dispute or a limit to a conflict—even attacking it—increases its obviousness or "prominence"[36] and thus may increase the chances it will be agreed upon.

Second, there are what J. L. Austin has called "performative utterances."[37] These are cases in which "in saying what I do, I actually perform that action"[38]—e.g. naming a ship in the christening ceremony, saying "I do" in a marriage ceremony. While examples of this are rare, especially in international relations, declarations of war and of diplomatic recognition fit into this category.

It should be noted that unlike other examples of indices, the messages discussed in the previous two paragraphs do not merely carry inherent evidence about a characteristic of the actor but prove that he has the characteristic.

[34] Thomas Sebeok, "Coding in the Evolution of Signaling Behavior," *Behavioral Science* VII (October 1962), 434. For a similar argument, see Michael Polanyi, *Personal Knowledge* (London: Routledge & Kegan Paul, 1958), 93, 253.

[35] Private communication. Also see the discussion of the ways in which messages give information about the sender in Theodore Newcomb, Ralph Turner, and Philip Converse, *Social Psychology* (New York: Holt, Rinehart, and Winston, 1965), 187-88.

[36] Schelling, *The Strategy of Conflict*, 53-80, and *Arms and Influence*, 137-41.

[37] *Philosophical Papers* (London: Oxford University Press, 1961), 220-39. I am indebted to Maury Feld for calling this essay to my attention.

[38] *Ibid.*, 222.

Capability Indices

The final category of indices is composed of statements and actions the perceiver believes alter the distribution of power among the actors. These capability indices lend credence to an image because the actor is now seen as being in a better position to undertake certain policies. The most obvious examples of this category are measures to increase armed forces. Diplomatic activity aimed at securing allies are capability indices. So are efforts by decision-makers to mobilize their own people to more fully support and even make personal sacrifices for the sake of foreign policies. Similarly, aspects of diplomacy, such as state visits surrounded by great publicity, designed to gain public backing in other countries fit in this category. These indices usually involve a change in capabilities but can also be the result of the revelation of capability that has been there all along. Building a new battleship and displaying one previously hidden are, from this perspective, both messages that carry with them some inherent credibility.

Capability indices can also provide convincing evidence of peaceful intentions by revealing that the state does not have the capability to perform aggressive actions. Thus a country that wanted to prove it was no menace could, if this were technically possible, develop only defensive weapons. In the nuclear era, as in the past, it is difficult but often possible to distinguish between predominantly offensive and predominantly defensive weapons systems. Those that could be of use only in a first strike (e.g. soft, liquid-fuel missiles) or would be of especially great value in an attack on the other side's retaliatory force (e.g. very accurate or very large warheads) can be taken as indices of aggressive intentions. Measures designed to protect one's own population against retaliation may be interpreted similarly.[39] However, these indices are far more ambiguous

[39] A United States Air Force General declared that "It will be particularly important for us to know . . . whether the Soviet Union is building civilian shelters for its own people. This can be one of the most significant indicators of its intentions if and when it gets

when the state building such an offensive force has vital
interests it feels it can protect only by threatening to launch
a first strike. Thus if the United States fears a Soviet attack
on Western Europe and believes it cannot be resisted on
the battlefield, it might develop a force posture similar to
that desired by a United States contemplating an unprovoked attack on the Soviet Union.[40]
Put this way it can be seen that capability indices often
provide the necessary but not sufficient conditions for a
policy to be carried out. Lacking the capability to do X is
thus of course persuasive evidence that you will not do X,
but you may have the capability and still not intend to use
it. Thus one cannot put much faith in Secretary McNamara's claim that the fact that the United States has spent a
great deal of money to place nuclear weapons in Europe
and create a strategic striking force should convince Congress, and the Russians, that the United States would use
nuclear weapons if necessary in the event of an attack on
Europe.[41] However, his argument that the Russians would
not maintain a large army with the capability to fight a conventional war in Europe if they did not, contrary to their
official pronouncements, believe that a war in Europe
could under some circumstances be kept limited is more

ready to launch a surprise attack." [Quoted in J. David Singer,
Deterrence, Arms Control and Disarmament (Columbus: Ohio State
University Press, 1962), 10.] Many domestic critics of an American
shelter program make similar claims, arguing that such a move would
be interpreted by the Soviets as an index of aggressiveness.

[40] Herman Kahn shows that the balance of forces can be such
that a state is able to deter its adversary from engaging in a major
provocation without leading the adversary to think the state believes
it in its own interest to launch an unprovoked attack. In Kahn's
terminology, one side can have Type II Deterrence without exclud-
ing the possibility that the other side has Type I Deterrence. Indeed
both sides could have Type II Deterrence simultaneously. [*On
Thermonuclear War* (Princeton: Princeton University Press, 1960),
217-18.] However the forces the United States considers necessary
for Type II Deterrence could well be seen by the Soviets as threatening their Type I Deterrence.

[41] William W. Kaufmann, *The McNamara Strategy* (New York:
Harper & Row, 1964), 68-69. For a further discussion of the impact
of spending money, see below pp. 92-94, 250-53.

convincing.[42] For the purpose of deterrence an actor may wish to procure weapons he does not intend to use, but there is no point in having weapons that do not have deterrent value unless one intends to use them.

[42] Cited in Jeremy J. Stone, *Strategic Persuasion* (New York: Columbia University Press, 1967), 145. I am assuming for the purposes of this discussion that the Soviet force posture represents an explicit choice made by the same centralized decision-makers who will decide the crucial issues of how a war will be fought. This of course may not be true. Furthermore, the recent invasion of Czechoslovakia shows that Russia may desire a large standing army for reasons having nothing to do with their beliefs about whether an East-West war could be kept limited.

CHAPTER THREE The Manipulation
of Indices

ERVING GOFFMAN notes that:

Knowing that the individual is likely to present himself
in a light that is favorable to him, the others may divide
what they witness into two parts; a part that is relatively
easy for the individual to manipulate at will, being chiefly
his verbal assertions, and a part in regard to which he
seems to have little concern or control, being chiefly derived from the expressions he gives off. The others may
then use what are considered to be the ungovernable
aspects of his expressive behavior as a check upon the
validity of what is conveyed by the governable aspects.[1]

In our terms, actors will try to use indices to verify or dis-
confirm what others are trying to communicate through signals. Two problems may arise in these attempts. The more
obvious one, which is implicit in much discussion of decision-making errors, is that the beliefs about the links between indices and the behavior they are thought to predict
can be wrong.

We shall only sketch several dimensions of this huge
subject here since it is secondary to the main concerns of
this book. Excessive use of introspection can lead to faulty
predictions if an actor assumes that because certain of his
actions are linked to certain of his characteristics and intentions there must be identical linkages in others' behavior.[2]
A related error is traceable to actors failing to appreciate
the variation in the identity and meanings of indices from
actor to actor and from time period to time period.
Changes can occur in two general categories. First, the attributes which states wish to judge are not constant. Resolve, though never completely unimportant, is now more

[1] Goffman, *Presentation of Self in Everyday Life*, 7.
[2] See the discussion in Edwin Schwien, *Combat Intelligence*
(Washington: The Infantry Journal, 1936), 12-23.

41

crucial for the great powers than it was in the past. Similarly, with the increase in the number of prolonged low-level conflicts states may now find it more valuable than previously to judge others' patience. Since states have ceased fighting to impose their religions on others, decision-makers no longer need estimate others' religious fervor, although they must still be concerned with the degree to which others' behavior is influenced by secular ideologies. Second, the means of judging these characteristics change because of alterations in the way important attributes are manifested. For example, the indices usually used to judge intention may be absent in new kinds of political systems. Thus Felix Gilbert points out that the common problems the British ambassadors in Rome and Berlin in the 1930s had in predicting the policies of the states to which they were accredited

> clearly derived from the difficulties of the situation in which democratic ambassadors found themselves in totalitarian countries. . . . [The] methods in which diplomats had been trained to evaluate political trends in the country where they were stationed were of little use to them in totalitarian countries. Diplomats are not schooled to base their opinions and recommendations on an intensive study and expert knowledge of economic developments and military budgets; they gauge the trend of future policy from an analysis of public opinion as it is expressed in newspapers, in political meetings, and in conversations with the various political personalities with whom they must keep in contact.[3]

In totalitarian states, however, the control of these cues prevents diplomats from using them to draw valid inferences.

Even in periods of relative constancy the basis for the predictive power of many indices may be uncertain at best. Not only is knowledge about the linkages between indices

[3] "Two British Ambassadors: Perth and Henderson," in Craig and Gilbert, *The Diplomats*, 546-47.

42

and behavior they are thought to predict severely limited, but, since predictions involve a host of assumptions about other variables, even good theories will not yield correct predictions in every instance. Both these factors, for example, reduce the ability of statesmen to draw useful inferences about national behavior from the personal behavior of their opposite numbers at summit conferences. Furthermore, the interpretations of many indices (e.g. those provided by others' domestic systems) are often not supported by well-developed theories and carefully weighed evidence. And even those major international moves that may seem at first glance to show so much about a state are usually susceptible to several interpretations on closer examination. For example, did the fact that Russia tried to place strategic missiles in Cuba mean that she was willing to run much higher risks than the United States had thought? Or did it mean she had greatly underestimated United States resolve and the risks which the Soviet move entailed? Was this a Soviet attempt to stabilize the strategic balance and to gain enough security so that she could feel safe in negotiating tension-reducing settlements? Or was it designed as a prelude to pressure on the West in Berlin and other places? And even in those cases when one general interpretation is felt to be obviously correct, problems of important details often remain.

VARIETIES OF MANIPULATION

The second problem in drawing inferences from indices is that they can sometimes be manipulated, allowing actors to influence others' images of them without paying the high price of altering their valued patterns of behavior and sacrificing other goals. Manipulation can be defined as the use of indices to project desired images by undermining the observers' assumption that the behavior which is the index either cannot be or is not being consciously controlled by the actor to give an impression the actor wants the observer to have.[4]

[4] For an alternative treatment of this subject, see Goffman, *Strategic Interaction*, 20-22.

An actor who can manipulate an index can have a great influence on the other's image since the observer believes he is getting information untainted by deception. Whereas signals must be cynically examined with the knowledge that the actor is trying to get a given image accepted, indices are thought not to be controlled and thus to shed more light on the actor. This means, of course, that an actor has great incentives to manipulate indices.

In most cases the actor will wish to employ manipulation in order to project an inaccurate image, but the possibility should not be overlooked that an actor may use this method to convey an accurate impression that would not otherwise be believed. Thus accurate warnings (i.e. messages indicating that the actor believes he must oppose another if the other does certain things regardless of whether the actor is seen as committed to react in that way)[5] and true statements that the actor has no designs on its suspicious neighbor (as well as misleading statements to these effects) may be discounted if seen as signals but believed if taken as indices. For example, this may be so because they are thought to be aimed only at some audience the actor has no interest in deceiving. Thus Schelling argues that messages in a strategic dialogue are often best conveyed not by speaking directly to the adversary, but rather by speaking "seriously to some serious audience and let[ting] him overhear."[6] This applies, of course, irrespective of the accuracy of the image the actor is trying to project.

Indices are relied on because the perceiver believes the actor is not using the behavior to project a misleading image. More specifically, it may be believed that the actor is incapable of controlling his behavior in this way, that the behavior could be controlled only at a price higher than the value that would be gained by so doing, or that while the behavior could be controlled, the actor is not doing

[5] Schelling, *Strategy of Conflict*, 123-24; Fred Iklé, *How Nations Negotiate* (New York: Harper and Row, 1964), 62-63.
[6] "Signals and Feedback in the Arms Dialogue," *Bulletin of the Atomic Scientists* 21 (January 1965), 10.

so because he does not realize it would be in his interest to engage in manipulation—the usual reason for this being that the actor does not know exactly what controllable aspects of his behavior others are taking as indices. Thus Alexander George has pointed out that content analysis which draws inferences directly from the adversary's propaganda "is on firm ground only when it employs as content indicators those features of content over which the propagandist does not exercise control or of whose correlation with a type of elite intention he remains unaware."[7] The first American attempts to analyze Nazi propaganda during World War II incorrectly believed this to be the case and thus were largely unsuccessful. Only when the analysts employed "indirect" content analysis, which could take account of German manipulations, were they able to make relatively accurate predictions.

If any of the observer's three assumptions about the uncontrolled nature of the index are incorrect the actor can engage in manipulation. Thus a negotiator may be incorrect in his belief that his opposite number has an uncontrollable temper and, even if the latter knows he gives away valuable information by so doing, cannot help but show his anger when presented with a telling argument. By concealing his anger when it is present, or feigning it when it is absent, the negotiator being observed will be able to manipulate the index.

Hitler was a master of manipulating indices of personal characteristics, such as anger and even mental instability. For example, during the negotiations with the Austrian Chancellor, Kurt von Schuschnigg, Hitler said he would invade unless the Chancellor signed an agreement and implemented part of it within three days.

When Schuschnigg explained that, although willing to sign, he could not, by the Austrian Constitution, guarantee ratification, or the observance of the time limit, . . .

[7] George, *Propaganda Analysis*, 39.

Hitler lost his temper, flung open the door, and, turning Schuschnigg out, shouted for General Keitel.

According to [the German Ambassador to Austria], when Keitel hurried up and asked for Hitler's orders, "Hitler grinned and said, 'There are no orders. I just wanted you here.' "[8]

Similarly, in a stormy interview with the British Ambassador a week before the start of World War II, Hitler seemed,

a man whom anger had driven beyond the reach of rational argument, yet [a German official] who was present, records: "Hardly had the door shut behind the Ambassador than Hitler slapped himself on the thigh, laughed and said: 'Chamberlain won't survive that conversation; his Cabinet will fall this evening.' "[9]

These displays were especially effective because those who observed them generally held the correct view that Hitler alone determined German foreign policy.

Second, the assumption that the manipulation of an index would involve costs out of proportion to the gains may be wrong. When the actor is involved in a continuing conflict he may be willing to incur high short-run costs in the expectation of receiving even larger long-run advantages. A state that wants to appear as having great resolve may provoke a crisis over small issues or fight a costly war for a relatively minor stake in the expectation of getting a "free ride" on its resulting reputation.

Not only may the observer be mistaken in his beliefs about the costs and risks the actor is willing to take, but he may also overestimate the costs of manipulation or underestimate the utility to the actor of a desired image. Indeed,

[8] Alan Bullock, *Hitler* (New York: Harper and Row, 1964), revised edition, 424.

[9] *Ibid.*, 528. Throughout the late 1930s there was a difference of opinion among English decision-makers as to whether Hitler's emotional outbursts were spontaneous or put on to impress visitors. Henderson and Chamberlain held the former position. [See Ian Colvin, *Vansittart in Office* (London: Gollancz, 1965), 240, 251.]

manipulation will be more likely to succeed if the actor can convince the observers that taking the actions would involve prohibitive costs for a deceiver. Thus a state that engages in a war for a small issue may want to exaggerate the objective costs it has paid, while stressing its willingness to pay them again in the future for similar goals.

Similarly, if an actor wants to convince others of his moderation and reasonableness (whether this is an accurate image or not) it may be important for him to forgo significant temporary gains. For example, in 1920 the Soviets "wished to impress the world, and more particularly England, with their conciliatory purposes." So in negotiating a peace treaty with Estonia, Russia made more concessions than it otherwise would have. This cost was outweighed by the fact that the Soviet conduct "strengthened the moderates in Britain who urged a more friendly strategy towards Russia."[10] Finally, to take an example from a slightly different context, one reason why Kim Philby's colleagues doubted that he could be a double-agent was that he drank a great deal in their presence. They reasoned that no Soviet agent would do anything that would increase the chance of a disastrous slip.[11]

The assumption that allows an actor to treat certain aspects of the other's behavior as indices even though he believes that controlling this behavior is not beyond the other actor's capabilities—i.e. the belief that the other is unaware that important inferences are being drawn—is the assumption most easily undermined. These indices can easily be manipulated once the actor realizes others are drawing conclusions from them.

The most common illustrations of this kind of manipulation are supplied by the ways states use others' human and mechanical spies. Allen Dulles explains that eavesdropping devices "can be turned against those who installed them.

---

[10] Louis Fischer, *The Soviets in World Affairs* (New York: Vintage, 1960), 180.

[11] Bruce Page, David Leitch, and Philip Knightly, *The Philby Conspiracy* (Garden City, N.Y.: Doubleday, 1968), 155.

47

Once they have been detected, it is often profitable to leave them in place in order to feed the other side with false or misleading information."[12] Similarly, to help convince the Germans that the Allied invasion was coming at Calais rather than Normandy, the Allies created a "phantom army" in southeast England made up of rubber equipment camouflaged just badly enough to permit detection by German reconnaissance planes (which were allowed over the area for this purpose), but not so badly disguised that the Germans could guess that the Allies wanted the "army" seen.[13]

The same process of manipulation is involved when an actor discovers that an individual is a spy for the other side and gives him false information to be reported to the enemy. Better yet, the agent can be "turned"—i.e. made into an agent of the side he was sent to spy upon—and so be more easily employed to transmit a wide variety of misleading information.[14] Even when the nation's intelligence service has not detected or "turned" any enemy agents, national leaders can guess that once a "secret" begins to circulate at all widely within the government, it will get to the enemy. Thus during the second Moroccan crisis the French Prime Minister "had the Army and Navy prepare mobilization orders, calculating that the German government had enough spies about 'to learn these secret orders which may open their eyes to the fact that France cannot be pushed further.' "[15]

If a state discovers that one of its own spies has been

---

[12] *The Craft of Intelligence* (New York: Signet, 1965), 69-70.

[13] Gilles Perrault, *The Secrets of D-Day* (London: Arthur Barker Ltd., 1965), 192-93.

[14] Of course if the agent's acting ability, or, more likely, his loyalty, is suspect it will be wiser not to "turn" him but only to use him without his being aware of it, thus removing the possibility that his behavior will lead the other side to realize he is being used.

[15] Samuel Williamson, *Anglo-French Military and Naval Relations, 1904-1914* (Unpublished Ph.D. Dissertation, Harvard University, 1966), 314. A revised version of this study, under the title *The Politics of Grand Strategy: Britain and France Prepare for War, 1904-14,* will be published by the Harvard University Press.

turned it can accomplish similar manipulations by giving the agent requests for information which will mislead the enemy about its true intentions. One of the more macabre incidents of World War II involved this technique. The Allies knew that the Germans had turned the main spy network in Holland. Shortly before D-Day they selected some reliable agents in England, told them it was vital that they get certain information about the German forces in the Calais region, and dropped them into the network which the Allied authorities, but not the Allied agents, knew was controlled by the Germans. That the agents knew how important it was that they not reveal their mission if captured ensured that they would only do so under circumstances in which their sincerity would seem least open to question.[16]

Less painful methods can sometimes be used to accomplish this kind of manipulation. For example, in the First World War the British let the Turks capture a false set of documents and made several seemingly sincere attempts to recapture them. These measures convinced the Turks that the documents were authentic and they acted on them by reinforcing the defenses of the city marked for attack. The British assault on another area was therefore only lightly opposed.[17] The most famous—and most successful—ruse in recent history was carried out by the British in World War II. To convince the Germans that the Allies were not going to invade Sicily—the most obvious target after North Africa had been conquered—the British planted misleading papers on a dead body dressed as a British officer and floated it ashore in Spain. Furthermore, the documents stated that the Allies were trying to fool the Germans into thinking that Sicily was to be atacked next. Thus if the Nazis believed those documents, which they did, they could explain Allied activities which seemed to indicate that Sicily was the next target as moves designed to trick them.

[16] Perrault, *The Secrets . . .* , 199-211.

[17] Robert Glass and Philip Davidson, *Intelligence Is For Commanders* (Harrisburg, Pa.: Military Service Publishing Co., 1948), 108.

It should be noted that whereas the credibility of the manipulation discussed earlier involving the painful death of Allied agents dropped into German hands was enhanced by the sacrifice, the false messages discussed in the preceding paragraph were accepted only because of the great skill exercised by the British in getting the information into the enemy's hands in a convincing way and in designing the information so that the enemy would think it valid. The British were well aware of the crucial element in manipulation—the information must look authentic to the adversary, rather than being an accurate representation of what would be authentic if the actor had the intentions the message implies he has. As one of the designers of this ruse put it:

> What you, a Briton with a British background, think can be deduced from a document does not matter. It is what your opposite number, with his German knowledge and background, will think that matters—what construction he will put on the document. Therefore, if you want him to think such-and-such a thing, you must give him something which will make him (and not you) think it. But he may be suspicious and want confirmation; you must think out what enquiries will he make (not what enquiries would you make) and give him answers to those enquiries so as to satisfy him. . . . The German operational staff does not know all the Allied difficulties—for example, how short you are of, say, landing-craft—and they may be prepared to believe that an operation is possible which your own Operational Staff know is not on the cards at all.[18]

While espionage and counter-espionage provide the most dramatic examples of actors' engaging in manipulation once they discover that something is being used as an index, the phenomenon is not limited to this setting. If a statesman at a summit conference knows others are judging him from

[18] Montagu, *The Man Who Never Was*, 45, emphasis omitted.

his tone of voice or the speed with which he makes decisions, he may change these patterns in order to project a desired image. Or he may be willing to make concessions on an issue if he thinks others are taking it as an index to a desired characteristic or intention. So if one state considers a particular action of another as a "test of good faith," it should not inform the other of this.[19] Publicly calling it a test increases the chances for a favorable settlement when the other wants to appear as a friend, but reduces its value as an index. For example, Lord Rosebery, an important figure in the British Liberal Party, made either a dangerous slip or a calculated gamble when in reply to a friend who said there was strong and widespread desire that Rosebery return to the party leadership, which he had voluntarily relinquished, Rosebery said, "It is all very well for you to talk of my many friends, but as far as I can see they don't come tumbling over one another. There is no proof of their longing to support me. If they do, why don't they join the Liberal League [a group sponsored by Rosebery]?"[20] If word of this remark spread to those who, whether they were really willing to support Rosebery or not, wanted him to become active in party affairs again, they could join the League. If Rosebery either wanted to induce certain behavior that he could make an excuse for his return, or if he wanted to increase the membership of the Liberal League as a means to other ends, then his remark was shrewd. But if, as seems more likely, he really meant this as a test, then he should have kept silent and the number of people joining the League would have been a more valid index of how many people not only wanted his return to politics, but also supported his policies and presumably would have aided him were he in power.

While it is usually the actor being observed who discovers that a controllable aspect of his behavior is being used as an index, observers sometimes aid him, perhaps inadvertently. Behavior and the interpretations made of it by

[19] I am grateful to Kathleen Archibald for discussion on this point.
[20] Robert James, *Rosebery* (New York: Macmillan, 1964), 442.

the actors may be altered by observers' discussions of them. If a sportswriter reports that certain mannerisms of a pitcher supply clues to what pitch he will throw next, the pitcher will be able to change his behavior. In their discussion of labor negotiations, two scholars point out that in order to test the willingness of the other side to make further concessions, one side "will suggest calling in a mediator. If [the other side's representative] accepts the suggestion, this is taken as an indication that he sees the problem as one of exploring a way by which the positions of the parties can be brought together; he would presumably have some 'give' left himself."[21] But any labor negotiator who has read the book may try to lead the other side to think he will stand firm by refusing to agree to a mediator.

In all cases of manipulation of behavior the actor can easily control, once the actor has discovered what behavior is being used for an index manipulation is usually easy. Perceivers are aware of this and therefore subject information derived from these indices to especially careful examination. Three consequences follow from this. First, since the screening process used to separate manipulated from unmanipulated behavior can never be expected to be perfect, some valid information will be discarded and some misleading information will be accepted. Second, the perceiver of course is aware of the possibility that information of this kind is partly "contaminated," and has to decrease the weight he allots to it in influencing his image. The possibility of manipulation thus prevents the perceiver from receiving full value from unmanipulated indices. Further implications of this will be discussed later. Third, the actor knows behavior of this kind will be thoroughly scrutinized and therefore has to exercise consummate skill in disguising his manipulations. This explains the painstaking care involved in the attempts at using "turned" agents and similar manipulations discussed above.

Finally, frequent manipulation increases the chances of

[21] Richard Walton and Robert McKersie, *A Behavioral Theory of Labor Negotiations* (New York: McGraw-Hill, 1965), 65.

detection. Each manipulation entails a finite probability that something will go wrong and provide evidence that manipulation is occurring, and these probabilities cumulate. Furthermore, if the manipulation involves projecting incorrect images, the perceiver is apt to suspect deception if many of the inferences drawn from the index prove to be incorrect. Thus, an actor is often faced with the choice of being able to occasionally use a powerful tool of deception or manipulating the index more frequently, but with decreasing effect and with the expectation that his activities will soon be discovered.

Necessary Conditions as Indices

Something may be taken as an index of a given intention because it is a necessary condition for the action. Many diplomatic and military moves require preparations that cannot be hidden. In most of these cases the acting state will thus be forced to partially show its hand. But it sometimes can turn this to its advantage. While the main action cannot be taken without the necessary index, the latter does not have to be followed by the former and so can be used for deception. These manipulations generally involve some cost in terms of capability wasted in return for gaining the advantage of deception and surprise. For example, an American division in Italy in the Second World War was greatly weakened by an unsuccessful attempt to cross a river and was vulnerable to a counterattack.

> For [the next] ten days a series of "demonstrations" were carried out, complete with full fire support, to give the impression to the enemy that a new crossing was to be effected. These measures were sufficient to keep the enemy on the defensive and allow the . . . Division to regroup and build up its strength.[22]

Another World War II incident illustrates a slightly different variant of this kind of manipulation. The Allies needed information about the beaches on which the D-Day

[22] Glass and Davidson, *Intelligence* . . . , 107.

53

forces were to land, but it was vital that the Germans not learn which beaches these were. To this end the Allies ordered their agents to explore and retrieve sand samples from *all* the beaches along the French coast. Rather than concentrating their bombing on the Normandy area, they dropped only half as many bombs there as they did on the coast near Calais, the other obvious possible invasion site.[23] From 1902 to 1909 the French sought to keep valuable information from their German adversaries by a similar manipulation. In 1902 Italy signed a secret treaty with France promising to stay neutral in a Franco-German war. The French wanted to keep this information from the Germans (partly because the agreement contradicted Italy's prior obligations to Germany), and therefore maintained two valuable army corps along the Alps.[24]

If a state frequently gave the necessary index without following it with the major action it would soon rob the index of much of its usefulness. Although the other side could still be sure the action would not be taken without the index, there could be so many false alarms that it probably could not afford to constantly implement the measures it would take if it were sure the action was coming. (This assumes that the deceiving state can better afford the cost of frequently taking the action which constitutes the "necessary" index than the perceiving side can afford to take the required precautions.) Of course decreasing the value of the index to the other side also means that the actor cannot use it as effectively when he wants to make the other

[23] Perrault, *The Secrets* . . . , 219. The deception involved in procuring sand samples from all the beaches at best would make it impossible for the Germans to draw any inferences about where the landings would occur, whereas the heavy bombing of the Calais coast was designed to positively mislead the Germans.

[24] Williamson, *Anglo-French* . . . , 420. It may be noted that the French Army did not believe this trade-off between deceiving Germany and sacrificing French military potential was in France's interest—Italy, after all, suffered most from having others learn of her duplicity—and in 1909 when they learned of the agreement they insisted on redeploying the troops.

side believe that the major action is planned, as the American division did in the example above.

The Discovery That an Index Can Be Manipulated

An actor's reaction to the discovery that a kind of controllable behavior is being used as an index will depend on several factors. If the index is a capability index the costs to the actor of manipulating that behavior may be counterbalanced by advantages gained. For example, "In the [First] World War it was observed that certain corps staffs [and individuals] specialized in particular classes of operations . . . [One] general seemed to possess a genius for successful defensive fighting and whenever he was found in command it could always be anticipated that no attack was in prospect. Another general was a specialist in . . . surprise . . . attack and was always used for that purpose. Another was an expert in counter-attacks and when he was in command that form of attack had always to be guarded against. . . ."[25] In this case the state seemed unaware it was divulging valuable information, but even if it knew it might have continued the practice. The advantage of using experts for chosen operations may be worth the cost of warning the other side. Similarly, in the movie *The Enemy Below*, the captain of a destroyer is willing to use a certain tactic which reduces the capability of the submarine he is tracking at the cost of revealing to the enemy that he is a daring and astute captain, and enabling the submarine commander to adjust his behavior accordingly.

States planning to launch an attack against another unless certain concessions are made may be faced with a related tradeoff. By ostentatiously preparing their forces and creating minor incidents they can manipulate indices and thus make their message more credible. However, this alerts the other side and sacrifices the advantages of a surprise attack if the other does not comply. For example, the Chinese may have decided in the Fall of 1950 that the

[25] Walter Sweeney, *Military Intelligence* (New York: Frederick Stokes, 1924), 178.

increased chance of convincing the United Nations forces to withdraw from North Korea, which might have been attained by manipulating indices of their intention of intervening (e.g. by not disguising their presence in North Korea), was outweighed by the military advantages of surprise.[26]

In all these cases the actor knew his behavior was or would be used by his adversary as an index, but decided that manipulation was not advantageous. Under these circumstances, the perceiver can still place some faith in the behavior even if he knows the actor is aware that it is being used as an index.

On the other hand, if an index gives away a great deal of valuable information, is easy to manipulate, and provides few advantages to the actor who forgoes manipulation, manipulation will almost always follow the actor's discovery of what is being watched. The knowledge that this is the case sometimes creates dilemmas in interpersonal relations that are rare in international politics. This is illustrated by an account of a recently married couple who go out for dinner. As they rise to leave the table after the meal the wife bursts into tears and refuses to tell her husband what is wrong. Her unhappiness is caused by the fact that for the first time in their marriage her husband forgot to help her on with her coat, and she takes this as an index of his decreasing love.

> The wife is right; her husband's attention is not so strong as it was before . . . and she cannot tell him of her misery and its cause. If she does, he will be *intentionally* careful and attentive . . . and she will never know for the rest of their lives whether the attention is genuine and spontaneous or a defense against being scolded, nagged at, and punished.[27]

[26] Thomas Schelling, personal communication.

[27] Sandor Feldman, *Mannerisms of Speech and Gesture in Everyday Life* (New York: International Universities Press, 1959), 104. This perspective shows the disadvantage of the following recommendation for alleviating tensions in a marriage in which the wife

56

When a large number of people are available as potential producers or observers of an index, the developments following its being uncovered depend in part upon uncoordinated decisions beyond the reach of an individual. If people believed that the way to make others believe that you are not afraid is to "whistle a happy tune," this tactic might not lose all usefulness. For as long as people thought that many happy people spontaneously whistled, those who were afraid could take advantage of this. Counterfeit money can only circulate because most of the currency is legitimate. The index will lose all utility only if, as in Gresham's law, the bad drives out the good. That is, if when anyone whistles others think, "Is he trying to fool us?" people who previously whistled out of happiness may change their behavior. This, of course, would also destroy the value of whistling for deception.

Multiple Cycles of Manipulation

Of course the cycle of deceiving and drawing inferences does not have to end with discovery of an actor's manipulating an index. If actor A is manipulating an index and B finds this out but conceals this from A, he can derive valuable information from A's manipulations since it is helpful to know what your adversary wants you to believe, especially in high conflict situations. For example, crows are often able to learn that scarecrows are man's method of trying to deceive them into thinking it is dangerous to go near a field (i.e. are attempts at manipulation). Knowing this, "Scarecrows rarely frighten crows. For many, the ap-

---

"looks for . . . the little niceties which she feels indicate true considerateness, kindness and love. For [the husband] these niceties are irrelevant; they are minor details. . . . But once the husband learns how his wife feels he can say: 'Well, if it is really that important to you that I remember your birthday, I'll do my darndest to try.' " [R. D. Laing, H. Phillipson, A. R. Lee, *Interpersonal Perception* (New York: Springer Publications Co., 1966), 31-32.] However if the wife cares about the "little niceties" not because of their intrinsic value but because they are indices to other characteristics, if the husband tells her that he is paying special attention to them to please her, this will not give her a better image of him.

pearance of a scarecrow is simply a tip-off that a free lunch is available."[28] Similarly, an impostor who does not know his adversary knows he is an impostor is in a vulnerable position. His adversary is able to feed him false information against which he has few defenses. For example, a person who knows nothing about cars may have heard that the experts always kick the tires of any used car they are considering purchasing. He may then do this to make the salesman think he is dealing with someone it is not wise to try to fool. However, if experts never kicked tires, or have stopped doing so because pretenders have learned of the index, anyone who does so will be revealed to the salesman as a deceiver. The salesman will then be in an especially advantageous position because not only does he know the customer is ignorant, but the customer does not realize this. The salesman can then convincingly tell the customer that since he is dealing with an expert he knows he has to be completely honest. He can then get the customer to accept misleading information. For the customer to ask further questions about the car would reveal his ignorance, and for him to bargain over the price would imply he believes the salesman has not accepted him as an expert.

This, of course, is not necessarily the last round of the cycle. If A finds out that B knows that A is manipulating an index—and if B does not know that A knows this—A will be able to manipulate the index by transmitting accurate information, which B can be expected to treat as false. This familiar he-thinks-that-I-think-that-he-thinks-etc. cycle is theoretically infinite. However all multiple cycles of manipulation and discovery are analytically identical to the basic cycle discussed previously. Furthermore, I have not discovered cases which go further than the second cycle of manipulation, perhaps in part for the reason given in the following example. In World War II the Allies discovered that a French colonel in Algiers was a German agent. They converted him to their side and used him to feed

[28] "Behavior of Birds Guided by Instinct, Not Intelligence," New York Times, April 2, 1968, p. 12.

false information to the Germans (manipulating an index). After the Germans had been deceived a number of times they guessed what had happened. "But they kept in contact, for it is always useful to know what the enemy wants you to believe," (discovering manipulation and benefiting from it). The Allies, however, knew that the Germans had made this discovery and "with great boldness and truly remarkable perversity, had the colonel announce that the invasion [of France] would take place on the coast of Normandy on the 5th, 6th, or 7th [of] June. For the Germans, his message was absolute proof that the invasion was to be any day except the 5th, 6th, or 7th [of] June, and on any part of the coast except Normandy," (manipulating an index by providing accurate information). "The colonel's stock with the Germans shot up after D-Day, so that the Allies were able to use him in good account for the rest of the war."[29]

An actor who knows his opponent has discovered he is using a controllable aspect of the latter's behavior as an index may try to eliminate the risks involved in this cycle of manipulation and countermanipulation by showing he is no longer drawing inferences from this behavior. This is similar to Schelling's point that an actor who wishes to make it more difficult for his adversary to become committed, and thus to make a credible threat, may destroy or impair his own capacity to receive the message the other side is trying to send.[30] A state that learns the other side has discovered the first state has been drawing important inferences from manipulatable behavior may similarly cut the channel of communication. For example, the United States might want to prevent the Chinese from taking advantage of the fact that a leading American student of China, Alan Whiting, has written an excellent book on the Chinese intervention in the Korean War in which he discusses a series of indices in Chinese internal behavior which should have led analysts to place a high probability on China's entering

[29] Perrault, The Secrets . . . , 211, emphasis omitted.
[30] The Strategy of Conflict, 18.

the war.[31] If China wanted to make the United States think she might behave similarly in Vietnam she could duplicate her previous domestic preparations, hoping the United States would draw the desired conclusions. To ensure that the Chinese would not take a strong stand in the belief that they could credibly communicate a readiness to go to war by such a manipulation, the United States could announce that it realized China could easily manipulate these indices and thus would either ignore them or, as we shall discuss further in the next section, treat them as signals.

Transformation of Indices Into Signals

Instead of, or after, becoming part of a cycle of manipulation and countermanipulation or merely dropping out of use, easy to manipulate indices may become signals. That is to say, actors may find it convenient to add these behaviors to the stockpile of those cheap measures whose purpose is understood by all to be the influencing of images. This transformation occurred for example in the exchanging of naval visits in the late-nineteenth century. The first such exchange, between France and Russia, was at least as much an index as a signal. But as states saw that these visits had great international impact and could be manipulated, they gradually became less tightly linked to political ties and instead were used as signals. Some emotional behavior in labor-management negotiations may have been similarly transformed.

The transformation of behavior from indices to signals can occur without the actors being totally aware of the change and with the existence of an interim period of manipulation, as seems to have been the case with the exchange of naval visits. On the other hand, if it is quickly obvious that a behavior is too vulnerable to remain an index and yet too valuable to be neutralized completely, the actors may immediately see that while long-run manipulation is impossible, they have a common interest in

[31] *China Crosses the Yalu* (New York: Macmillan, 1960).

explicitly using the behavior as a signal. For example, in the fifteenth century it was common for ambassadors to receive official instructions for their guidance.

It was not long before ambassadors began to be asked [by the state to which they were sent] to produce their instructions. The tenor of their instructions, after all, would show more quickly than anything else whether agreement was possible. . . . The point was a ticklish one, for, of course, the instructions would also show the extreme concessions that the ambassadors could make.

Soon a "common dodge" developed: "the issuance of two sets of instructions, one to be exhibited or even handed over as a token of confidence, the other to be closely guarded . . . [and] to furnish real guidance."[32] When each side's instructions were known to the other they served as reliable and detailed indices which gave away too much information for effective negotiations. So it was in the interests of all states to change the status of the open instructions to signals.

Getting Caught Manipulating Indices

Getting caught manipulating indices has both advantages and disadvantages for the actor. The main advantage is that after others make such a discovery they will not rely nearly as heavily on similar channels since they will not be sure the information obtained has not been similarly tampered with. Thus if it is revealed that nation X has known for years that its embassy in state Y is filled with microphones and has been staging misleading conversations in the building to deceive the listeners,[33] Y will place less confidence in information received from similar sources. This may also aid other states whose embassies in state Y have been bugged but do not know it. The expectation of deception can thus lead an actor to discount evidence de-

[32] Garrett Mattingly, *Renaissance Diplomacy* (London: Jonathan Cape, 1955), 41.
[33] The United States probably did this in its Moscow Embassy.

rived from unmanipulated indices. A few days before the invasion of the Continent, German

> night reconnaissance flights . . . reports a great deal of road traffic in the south-west [where the Allied troops were massing], apparently because the drivers were careless about lights. Von Rundstedt is suspicious of this so-called carelessness; [he believes] they are trying to hoodwink him into thinking that the landings are to be in Normandy and not in the Pas-de-Calais.[34]

In other words, indices and information channels may be significantly degraded by the discovery or suspicion of manipulation. This advantage may be greater than the manipulation itself, especially in the case of a state that discovers another is getting valuable information from an index difficult to frequently manipulate, such as domestic propaganda. In such circumstances, the state could sporadically engage in manipulation not for the short-run advantage of deceiving others on a specific issue, but for the long-run advantage of reducing the reliance others can place on this index. Thus the state would want to be sure that the matter selected for manipulation was one about which the truth could not be indefinitely disguised.

The disadvantages of being caught include, as I have noted previously, providing clues to how one will act by revealing what impression one is trying to make. For example, if the Germans knew the papers saying the Allies would not invade Sicily were designed to fool them, they could be quite sure Sicily was the target of the invasion. Another disadvantage is having others place less reliance on indices similar to the one manipulated, which may not be in the state's interest. The state may wish to use these indices to convey desired impressions and thus will want information conveyed in this manner to be credible. Also, the state may not want a reputation for manipulating indices. Such behavior may itself be taken as an index of undesired characteristics. This is apt to be true only for

[34] Perrault, *The Secrets* . . . , 216.

relations among close allies, for such behavior is expected among adversaries. But if it were discovered that, say, the British were manipulating their behavior to deceive the United States, the American image of Britain would be unfavorably affected and the level of American trust of the British would fall. For these reasons actors may often want others to believe not that they manipulated indices, but rather that the indices were naturally unreliable. Much of the information degradation effect would remain, but the actor would not have divulged valuable information or be seen as one who is trying to give false impressions. If others believe an actor did not intend to deceive his behavior will not be particularly suspect in the future.

The exposure of one kind of manipulation apt to cause great discomfort in interpersonal affairs is not a major problem in international relations or interorganization relations in general. In personal relations much behavior is taken as an index because it is thought to be essentially unplanned and uncalculated. The display of anger, grief, joy, etc. is often thought to be spontaneous. When we discover the actor thinks about the impression he wants to create and consciously tries to seem spontaneous, we are apt to feel he is acting inappropriately, even if there is no deception (i.e. if he is consciously trying to display the emotion he actually feels). Thus there is something upsetting about realizing that mourners at Senator Robert Kennedy's funeral were aware that they should be careful lest they were caught smiling by the television cameras.[35] Similarly, people at the railroad station in Baltimore were quietly singing "The Battle Hymn of the Republic" before and during the passage of the funeral train. Television commentators remarked that this spontaneous display was the most moving tribute which had occurred along the train's route. Observers would feel they had been tricked and played false were it to be learned that the people in Baltimore started singing because they thought this would seem mov-

[35] John Coan, Jr., "A Telegram and a Train Ride," *Boston Globe*, evening edition, June 11, 1968, p. 39.

ing or continued to sing because they heard the praise being given them by the television announcers. With the exception of certain behavior discussed earlier, nations and national leaders are not expected to act spontaneously. Calculation and planning are the norm (in sense of what is thought proper, if not in the sense of what usually occurs). Furthermore, when the observer learns that national officials have been manipulating behavior thought to be uncontrolled (e.g. when one state finds out that the other knew there was a microphone in its embassy) there is no indignation or feeling of betrayal because this kind of deception is an accepted part of international politics.

NONMANIPULATABLE INDICES

An index which is a necessary and sufficient cause cannot be manipulated. At most, the actor may be able to prevent others from obtaining information about the index. Evidence of internal discontent with a given policy that observers may believe will lead the state to change its position can sometimes be disguised, or news about economic hardship others would believe would make a revolution more likely can be limited by press censorship. But since these causes involve large-scale phenomena, they are difficult to keep completely hidden.[36]

Other kinds of indices, although not causes, cannot be manipulated even if it is known they are being used to make inferences. Some involve phenomena too deeply rooted in the individual or political systems to be controlled. A person being given a lie-detector test may not be able to control his physiological responses even though he knows they are revealing information he would like to conceal. A negotiator may be unable to control his emotional reactions even if he knows it is in his interest to do so.

[36] The prediction of the future of underdeveloped countries, on the other hand, is made more difficult by the absence of accurate statistics of certain gross characteristics (e.g., rates of economic growth and social mobilization) which seem to be causally related to domestic political outcomes. This lack, however, is not the result of attempts to thwart other actors' desires for prediction.

Sometimes these indices can be concealed when they cannot be manipulated. Thus when jade dealers learned that the dilation of the pupils of a customer's eyes involuntarily revealed his interest in what he was being shown, knowledgeable customers began wearing dark glasses.[37] With some indices the person observed will be unable to either manipulate or totally conceal his behavior because he does not know the theories that guide the inferences of the observer. This is true, for example, with Rorshach tests.[38]

In other cases manipulation may be impractical because it would require control of too many disparate pieces of information. For example, in World War II a Swiss journalist was able to give "amazingly accurate" reports of the movement of German troops by keeping track of all mention in the German papers of the location of military personnel and units.[39] While once the Germans discovered this they might have been able to withhold information (at a considerable cost to home morale), it would not be worth the huge expenditure of resources needed to manipulate this minutiae. Similarly, it seems unlikely that it would be worthwhile for Communist China to systematically alter all the complex and interrelated statistics dealing with her internal economic progress in order to deceive Western experts.[40]

To keep the discussion in this chapter in perspective, it should be noted that the bulk of major international actions are nonmanipulatable indices since they involve actions inextricably linked to the pursuit of important goals. This is one of the main reasons, as I tried to make clear in the introduction, why actors have only limited leeway to project images on the cheap.

[37] R. Gump, *Jade* (New York: Doubleday, 1962). Cited in Eugene Webb *et al.*, *Unobtrusive Measures* (Chicago: Rand McNally, 1966), 148.

[38] Goffman, *Strategic Interaction*, 30.

[39] Irving Heymont, *Combat Intelligence in Modern Warfare* (Harrisburg, Pa.: Stackpole, 1960), 39-40.

[40] Dwight Perkins, *Market Controls and Planning in Communist China* (Cambridge, Mass.: Harvard University Press, 1966), 215-25.

CHAPTER FOUR   Signals and Lies

INDICES can be used to project desired impressions only when actors are able to control them without the knowledge of the perceiver. It follows from the definition of signals that the problems of issuing and detecting misleading signals are different. Since signals derive their meanings from tacit or explicit agreement among the actors, an actor can lie as easily as he can tell the truth.[1] A signal used to convey an accurate message can also convey a misleading one. It is logically impossible to design a signaling system that does not have this attribute. In this chapter I will trace the ramifications of this fact, discuss the restraints on issuing misleading signals, examine special problems of signaling when these restraints are loosened, and discuss the consequences of the excessive use of any individual signal. These topics are designed to reveal why faith is placed in signals and the costs and benefits of deception. The implications of the approach developed here seem to correspond fairly well to observations of reality, although one important discrepancy will be discussed.

A deceiving state will try to give exactly the same signals it would give were it honest, since these are most apt to convince the listeners. To put it more exactly, whether the state is lying or honest it will try to issue those signals which it thinks will get its desired image accepted. For example, in the summer of 1939 when the Russians were negotiating with Britain and France as well as Germany, Stalin wanted it believed that he might sign a treaty with the democracies. So when military conversations began, the Soviet Union took pains to demonstrate the sincerity of its intentions.

The Kremlin had appointed its highest military authority, General . . . Voroshilov, . . . to conduct the discussions on

[1] I will generally not deal with problems created by the fact that actors may not know how they will act in a given situation. I will thus assume that when an actor is honest he is giving accurate signals. As Erving Goffman points out, signals can be simultaneously self-

the Soviet side. Voroshilov received the foreign missions with much pomp and circumstance and the meetings opened . . . in an atmosphere of warm cordiality which left the French convinced that the Russians meant business.[2]

The Soviets would have selected those signals to convey the impression of a desire to come to an agreement whether this image was accurate or not.

Being aware that such convincing signals are the type a deceiver will want and be able to issue will not tell us when not to believe them, but at least it shows that we should not be too quickly convinced. Urie Bronfenbrenner and Hans Bethe make such an error when the latter argues, in a paragraph approvingly quoted by the former, that the United States was too suspicious of the USSR in the test ban negotiations.

The Russians seemed stunned by the theory of the big hole. In private, they took Americans to task for having spent the last year inventing methods to cheat on a nuclear test cessation agreement. Officially, they spent considerable efforts in trying to disprove the theory of the big hole. This is not the reaction of a country that is bent on cheating.[3]

One wonders how these gentlemen would expect a country bent on cheating to act, for that is obviously the kind of behavior such a country should avoid. Whether the Russians were going to cheat or not they would try to create the impression of honesty.[4] Both an honest man and a liar will

---

believed (i.e. believed by the actor to be correct) and incorrect (*Strategic Interaction*, 6-7).

[2] William Langer and S. Everett Gleason, *The Challenge to Isolation* (New York: Harper and Brothers, 1952), 176.

[3] Quoted in Urie Bronfenbrenner, "The Mirror Image in Soviet-American Relations," *Journal of Social Issues*, xvii (1961), 52.

[4] It has been pointed out to me that Bethe had other information that supported his conclusion and so was not as naïve as this discussion suggests. Also one could believe the Soviet scientists were sincere and still deny that much faith could be placed in their words

answer affirmatively if asked whether they will tell the truth.

Bethe's remark implies that thorough-going deceptions are so rare in international relations that decision-makers can ignore the possibility that they will occur. However such instances are quite common. The examples of Russian policy in the summer of 1939 and Hitler's efforts throughout the 1930s have been mentioned. From 1957 to 1961 the USSR seems to have engaged in a concerted bluff to get the United States to believe it had a great many more strategic missiles than it had.[5] In the years preceding the First World War Russia sent Britain a long series of misleading signals to make Britain believe she was limiting her penetration of Persia.[6] In 1800-1801 France tried to convince America that she wanted peace and good relations. But she sent these signals of friendship (and also manipulated several indices) in order to lull the United States and thereby enable France to take actions she knew America would otherwise vigorously oppose. Napoleon "wanted to play down words or actions that might arouse suspicions and jeopardize the regaining of Louisiana."[7] "Secrecy and American goodwill were important, for if the Americans found out about the [Spanish] cession [of Louisiana to France] and were angered, they might take over Louisiana before Bonaparte could send troops to defend it."[8]

The knowledge of the existence of cases like these and the awareness of the possibilities and potentialities of lying lead actors to treat signals skeptically when they feel it would be in the interest of the other to have the signals

---

on the grounds that (1) Soviet politicians, not scientists, would make the relevant decisions and (2) the lack of present intention to cheat is no protection against future cheating, especially since the Soviets had been told by the United States of a relatively riskless way of doing so.

[5] Arnold Horelick and Myron Rush, *Strategic Power and Soviet Foreign Policy* (Chicago: University of Chicago Press, 1966), passim.

[6] Grenville, *Lord Salisbury* . . . , 292-303 and 423-27.

[7] Alexander DeConde, *The Quasi-War* (New York: Scribner's, 1966), 295.

[8] *Ibid.*, 296.

believed whether they are correct or not.[9] This problem is brought out clearly by the dialogue in a Ray Bradbury short story in which a small military expedition is lost in the rain forests of Venus:

> How much farther Lieutenant?
> I don't know. A mile, ten miles, 1,000.
> Aren't you sure?
> How can I be sure?
> I don't like this rain. If we only knew how far it is to the base, I'd feel better.
> Another hour or two from here.
> You really think so, Lieutenant?
> Of course.
> Or are you lying to keep us happy?
> I'm lying to keep you happy. Shut up![10]

This also reveals an initial reaction to the dilemma common in interpersonal relations: to ask the other if he is really telling the truth does not solve the problem. The equivalent to the dialogue in the Bradbury story occurs in politics or society when a rumor spreads that is contrary to the image an actor is trying to project. Whether the rumor is true or not, it will be denied in exactly the same manner. Since the denial will always be made, it conveys no information. That is, the denial does not alter in the minds of the receivers the probabilities attached to the range of possible realities and meanings.

It can be claimed that the possibilities and incentives for lying are so great that an actor will always use signals for deception. Thus Stalin argues: "a diplomat's words must have no relation to actions—otherwise what kind of diplomacy is it? . . . Good words are a concealment of bad deeds. Sincere diplomacy is no more possible than dry

[9] It should be noted that those relatively rare signals which convey an image which an actor would not want believed were it not true are at least partially self-validating. The discussion in this chapter thus does not apply to them.

[10] Ray Bradbury, "The Long Rain," in Ray Bradbury, *The Illustrated Man* (New York: Bantam Books, 1952), 53.

water or iron wood."[11] A less extreme view would be that actors believe signals when, and only when, the information derived from them is in accord with conclusions drawn from indices. This position, like the one taken by Stalin, implies that signals are useless, since their interpretation would rest solely on other inferences. Thus they would convey no information and could therefore be ignored by statesmen and scholars. But if this view were correct, or if actors followed Stalin's injunction, the issuing of signals would be futile. For if the recipients ignored all signals, there would be no reason for actors to send them.

RESTRAINTS ON LYING

The fact that states send and pay attention to signals indicates that statesmen feel they are more apt to give true than false information. If an actor signals an intention to do X this generally increases the probability that others attach to his doing X. Signals then must be providing some evidence as to how the actor will behave. In other words, there must be some restraints on lying, some pressures that tend to make actors issue accurate signals.

Moral Restraints

Decision-makers may feel that lies, or at least certain types of lies, should not be undertaken regardless of the advantages because of moral restraints. This is most likely to have force when the stakes in international conflict are relatively low and when decision-makers feel bonds of loyalty to their counterparts in other states.[12] Thus, morality may have been a more important restraint on lying in

---

[11] Quoted in Vernon Aspaturian, "Dialetics and Duplicity in Soviet Diplomacy," *Journal of International Affairs*, Vol. XVII, 1963, 49. Similarly, Lenin claimed that "Promises are like pie crust made to be broken. . . ." [Quoted in Nathan Leites, *A Study of Bolshevism*, 532.]

[12] It should be noted that the effectiveness of such solidarity will partly depend on the extent to which the general ethos and outlook of the decision-makers values honesty, since if it does not, one could practice unrelieved lying and still retain one's membership in good standing in the group of international statesmen.

the late-seventeenth and eighteenth centuries than it has been since. Hans Morgenthau has made this argument for the more general question of the importance of morality in all aspects of international politics.[13]

Stake in the International System

The second restraint on lying is less direct. It involves the stake a country has in the international system. When a state deceives, it affects the general international system. One can make rough statements about the amount or relative proportions of honesty and deception in the signals used in a particular system. For example, Karl Deutsch has noted that there is less relation between initial signals and later actions in an economic system based on individual bargaining than there is in the modern system of public, established prices.[14] It may be very hard for a complex system to survive if the level of deception is too high. Stability depends in part on the ability to predict other's actions. In international relations, of course, signals are only one basis of prediction, and therefore a complete lack of faith in them would not mean complete unpredictability. Nevertheless, signals are significant contributors to predictability because states often find it important to convince others that they will act in a given way and lacking—or being unwilling to use—means of proving to others what their policy is they must rely on signals. This is true for all nations at some time or other. Thus they all have a stake in the collective honesty of the signaling system. None of them—with the possible exception of those desiring the complete and immediate overthrow of the international system—wishes to see the signaling system degenerate to uselessness. But, on the other hand, it is obviously frequently in a state's interest to lie.

States have an inevitable conflict between three aims. They want to be able to convince others that they intend to

[13] *Politics Among Nations*, 3rd edn. (New York: Knopf, 1961), 245-48.
[14] Personal communication.

act in a given way when they do intend to act in that way; they want to be able to convey the same impression when that impression is misleading; and they want to be able to tell when others, who are using the same tools and techniques, are signaling true intentions or engaging in deception. They want to get a "free ride" by lying, but not be deceived by others. So just as states have common and conflicting interests in almost any specific international situation, they have common and conflicting interests in the maintenance of the signaling system. If too many states cheat too often the system will be degraded (i.e. it will carry less information) or destroyed, but states will often be under pressure to make gains through bluff in any given situation.

The desire to maintain the system will be a fairly direct restraint when the number of actors in international society is small enough so that if any one engages in deception frequently the general credibility of signals will be endangered. When there are more actors present the restraint is less direct. This is an instance of what Herman Kahn calls "systems bargaining," which occurs in

> situations in which all or almost all members of a system would be better off if every individual abided by certain rules. It is a characteristic of such situations that while all members would be worse off if the rules were generally broken, individual members of the system could gain great individual advantages by breaking them, provided that this were not done by too many other members of the system.[15]

This paradox is not limited to international interaction, but occurs whenever the benefits of a good are indivisible, yet the costs of obtaining the good are born individually and where the chances of its being obtained will not be significantly affected by the behavior of any one actor. For example, Anthony Downs points out the

15 Herman Kahn, *On Escalation* (New York: Praeger, 1965), 19.

simultaneous truth of two seemingly contradictory propositions [about the rationality of citizens in a democracy being informed]: (1) rational citizens want democracy to work well so as to gain its benefits, and it works best when the citizenry is well-informed; and (2) it is individually irrational to be well-informed [because whether he himself is well-informed has no perceptible impact on the benefits he gets]. Here . . . the goals men seek as individuals contradict those they seek in coalition as members of society.[16]

Thus the payoffs are in one way akin to those of game theory's prisoners' dilemma. No matter what one prisoner does, it is in the other's interest to talk. And if both follow this rule they will be worse off than if they had both kept silent.

The desire to preserve the international system and the signals that lend it greater predictability will be more important when the actors value the system, prefer long-run over short-run gains, and have more common than conflicting interests. These conditions hold in most labor-management negotiations. Edward Peters, a professional conciliator, stresses the costs to both sides of defaulting on a pledge, which he labels "bad faith."[17] Entering a severe judgment on the use of this tactic, he says that "the one basic criterion of good faith, recognized and accepted by the parties, is contained in the iron rule: Preserve the sanctity of your lines of communication. . . . Misusing [signals] is the unforgivable crime."[18]

Changing the International Environment

A third restraint is created by the fact that a state's signals, although meant to be deceptive, may be an accurate

[16] Anthony Downs, *An Economic Theory of Democracy* (New York: Harper & Row, 1957), 246. For a thorough discussion of this problem see Mancur Olson, *The Logic of Collective Action* (Cambridge, Mass.: Harvard University Press, 1965).

[17] *Strategy and Tactics in Labor Negotiations* (New London, Conn.: National Foremen's Institute, 1955), 208-23.

[18] *Ibid.*, 222.

indication of the way the state will act because they change the international environment. If others believe the signals they may act in such a way as to alter the distribution of power in the system and make it in the state's interest to act in accord with its signals. For example, state A may openly profess friendship toward B and hostility toward C, while it really hopes to privately convince C to ally with it against B. However if C believes the public signals, A may then find that it is in its interests to actually ally with B. Or if A's statements that it would protect B against C, although designed to be a bluff, caused a large number of allies to rally to A, A may then be able to defend B. These are somewhat odd self-fulfilling prophecies, since the signaling state itself does not originally believe the prophecy. Of course, prophecies may be self-denying as well as self-fulfilling,[19] and the reaction to a state's signals may change the international environment so as to make it even less likely that it will act in accord with its signals.

Internal Restraints

A fourth restraint is placed on states by domestic factors. If a nation publicly makes claims or commitments and then does not act accordingly, domestic public opinion may be offended, or at least the decision-makers may fear this reaction. This will be especially true when the policy announced is popular and the people expect their government to be honest with other governments and with them. The last point may be particularly important in democratic states. For although the people in those countries may not object to their governments deceiving other states, they do object to the deception of domestic audiences. And in the modern era it is hard if not impossible to do the former without also doing the latter. Similarly, one part of the government may object to another part deceiving it, as has been demonstrated by the Congressional reaction to the revelation that the Export-Import Bank was financing the sale of arms

[19] Herman Kahn, *Thinking About the Unthinkable* (New York: Horizon Press, 1962), 29.

to underdeveloped countries without the knowledge of Congress as a whole or even of the relevant Congressional committees.

However, it is usually hard to separate the opposition created by the substance of a policy from disappointment of an expectation or the reneging on a commitment. A policy may be unpopular regardless of its relationship to previous signals. For example, those in the United States who feel the government should vigorously protect and support Israel criticize decision-makers who do not implement such a policy. If these decision-makers not only failed to support Israel in a conflict, but did so in violation of their previous signals, the increase in the attacks on them would probably be slight compared to the total opposition. The failure to distinguish between opposition caused by the substance of what the government is doing and opposition rooted in the belief that this action contravenes previous assurances mars Theodore Lowi's argument that many Congressmen vigorously fought Truman's decision to send troops to Europe because they felt the Administration had previously misrepresented its intentions to Congress. Lowi does not take into account the possibility that this opposition would not have been any less had the executive admitted from the start that it would probably send troops abroad.[20]

Fear of domestic opposition to deception is reduced when it is difficult for even attentive publics to determine whether a government has in fact acted in harmony with its signals. When the situation is confusing and the signals a bit ambiguous, domestic audiences cannot easily tell either what the state is pledged to do and what it has actually done. Under these circumstances, the bulk of the people are apt to take their cues as to whether their state has lied from the definition of the situation provided by the state's leaders.[21]

[20] "Making the World Safe for Democracy," in James Rosenau, ed., *Domestic Sources of Foreign Policy* (New York: Free Press, 1967), 317-18.

[21] Kenneth Waltz, *Foreign Policy and Democratic Politics* (Boston: Little, Brown, 1967), 296.

A second aspect of domestic restraints may be brought into play if an announced policy, even though not immediately popular, gradually attracts a great deal of political support, perhaps partly because of official encouragement. This position could gain enough backing, in the government as well as in the general public, that the decision-makers might feel compelled to act in accord with the announced policy instead of acting out their planned deceit.

A related mechanism can be brought into play by decision-maker's signals that lead the public to believe a certain settlement will probably be attained. If these expectations are not met the public may turn the leaders out of office. If both the decision-makers and the other side know this the former are more apt to live up to their signals and the latter more apt to believe them. By promising the union members a certain settlement, labor negotiators strengthen their bargaining position by invoking this process.

Third, if only a small group within the government is aware of the planned deception the uninitiated parts of the state's foreign policy-making organization might be so zealous in carrying out the announced policy that it might become hard to reverse. A great many officials, like the public at large, learn the general outlines of their government's policies from the mass media. They usually have to assume that what is said by the decision-makers in public represents or approximates true preferences and they act accordingly. Thus, too many interconnected commitments may have been made or the damage to the morale of the bureaucracy may be too great to allow the deception to be carried out. In extreme cases, as Selznick shows, the policy goals of an organization get infused with affect and tasks become bound to organizational identity, thus limiting the top decision-makers' flexibility.[22]

This phenomenon is most important when the leading decision-makers are themselves unsure if they will act in accord with their signals. Here the bureaucracy may make

[22] Philip Selznick, *Leadership in Administration* (Evanston, Ill.: Row, Peterson, 1957).

myriad small decisions and provide day-to-day information that over time shape the leadership's definition of the situation. Without fully realizing what is happening, the decision-makers may find themselves believing in the wisdom of a policy they doubted they would fulfill when they first announced it. This restraint is not unlike the force which Anselm Strauss has noted operating in interpersonal relations. "When you act without much conviction of strong identification, [you may] . . . find that others assume that you really meant what you had done, that this act was really 'you'."[23] The mechanism of cognitive dissonance may add slightly to this pressure.[24] That is, the decision-makers' voluntary and repeated enunciation of a certain policy would be dissonant with their knowledge that they did not intend to carry it out, and they might reduce the dissonance by becoming more favorable toward the policy.

A fourth domestic restraint, related to the one just discussed, is created by the tendency of subordinates to give their superiors information they believe to be consistent with the latter's policies and desires. Thus if the bureaucracy believes a signal is honest the information it transmits to the decision-makers on this subject is more apt to be supportive of the policy implied by the signal. This effect will be compounded if the signaling state is powerful, since other nations may choose to mute any disagreements they may have in the hope that others will carry the burden of opposition. Thus the decision-maker is likely to receive information that indicates his signal has received a more favorable reaction than it in fact has. This process creates most problems when signals were intended as

[23] *Mirrors and Masks* (Glencoe, Ill.: Free Press, 1959), 40.
[24] Leon Festinger, *A Theory of Cognitive Dissonance* (Stanford: Stanford University Press, 1957), sets forth the basic approach. Also see Jack Brehm and Arthur Cohen, *Explorations in Cognitive Dissonance* (New York: Wiley, 1962); Arthur Cohen, *Attitude Change and Social Influence* (New York: Basic Books, 1964); Leon Festinger, *Conflict, Decision and Dissonance* (Stanford: Stanford University Press, 1964); and L. Festinger, H. Riecken, and S. Schachter, *When Prophecy Fails* (Minneapolis: University of Minnesota Press, 1956).

probes and feelers to help estimate the costs and benefits
of a policy the decision-maker considers only conditional
and tentative. A good example is provided by the development of American policy on the Multilateral Force. President Johnson wanted to ascertain the degree of European
interest in the project, but his subordinates, and through
them the European decision-makers, took his initiative to
mean that the United States was committed to the policy.
As a result, they overstated their approval of the MLF.[25]

Signaling Reputation

The fifth and most important restraint is imposed by the
costs of unsuccessful lying. If an actor is caught he is less
likely to be believed next time. It is in a state's interest to
be believed, and an important determinant of whether it
will be believed in any given situation is its reputation for
telling the truth and doing what it says it will do.[26] It is
partly for this reason that states often avoid explicit statements of their intentions. They not only may not wish to
reveal their plans and goals, but they also want to be able
to change their policies without running the risk of being

[25] The last two categories of restraints differ from the first two and
the next one in that they make it more probable that signals originally
meant to be misleading will accurately indicate a state's future behavior. The signals were intended to be deceptive, but changed the
world so that they were accurate. These two restraints then do not
make it less likely that an actor will issue signals that he thinks
are lies.

[26] An actor's reputation for issuing accurate signals is only part of
his general reputation and image. An actor may be thought to be
unwilling to run high risks and also believed to almost always act
in accord with his signals. Or he may be thought to be both a liar
and a high-risk taker. Or, to take another characteristic, he may be
thought to issue accurate signals yet be aggressive. However, decision-
makers may take lying as an index to other characteristics, and other
characteristics may be taken as an index of whether the state will lie.
Thus the state's reputation for issuing accurate signals may not be
totally independent of the rest of its image. This question requires
further investigation and cannot be considered here. For the sake of
brevity we will use the word reputation to mean only reputation for
issuing accurate signals. Furthermore, while individual decision-
makers have signaling reputations somewhat independent of the
reputation of the state, we shall not consider them as separate here.

known as liars with the consequent cost of not being believed in the future. Because the other restraints on lying do not seem to be, and are not believed to be, very effective, perceivers' judgments about the accuracy of signals have to depend to a large extent on their beliefs about the actor's honesty, thus increasing the value to the actor of a reputation for truthfulness.

The importance to an actor of his reputation depends partly on the system within which he is operating. Being caught lying generally has lower costs in international relations than in the domestic politics of most states. In the latter outright lies of any sort are not expected and their occurrence therefore immediately casts grave doubts on all of the actor's other signals.[27] In labor-management relations, a reputation for honesty is often of the utmost importance. As one union negotiator said after an incident which cast doubt on his honesty: "All a guy like me has is his reputation for keeping his word, for honest dealings. If you ever lose that in this circuit, you're washed up!"[28] While this statement could not be applied to the international arena where trust is low and deception is expected, a state must still carefully protect its reputation.

A reputation for issuing accurate signals plays a major role in the process of commitment whose importance has been so clearly demonstrated by Schelling.[29] It is often in an actor's interest to convince others that he will act in a given way. When special efforts are needed to accomplish this, it can sometimes be done through the manipulation of

[27] See Burl Noggle, *Teapot Dome* (New York: Norton, 1965), 75, for an incident showing the impact of the discovery that a political actor has lied on the subsequent interpretations of his behavior. President Johnson paid a high price for the small number of instances in which it was believed he was misleading the mass media and the American public. Not only was doubt cast on many of his other signals, but his general reputation as a national leader was seriously damaged.

[28] Quoted in Walton and McKersie, *A Behavioral Theory of Labor Negotiations*, 102.

[29] *The Strategy of Conflict*, 24-30, 36-38, and 121-31, and *Arms and Influence*, 35-91.

indices, as discussed in a previous chapter. Where manipulation is impossible, the actor may want to show that it is difficult or impossible for him to fail to act in a given way. The most obvious method of commitment is to demonstrate that the decision to carry out a policy has already been made and is irrevocable. Thus the United States or USSR could build a "doomsday machine" that would automatically destroy the world if the other country launched a nuclear attack. Furthermore, the machine would set off the nuclear explosions if any attempt were made to change its instructions. But as Kahn points out, no government would be willing to totally relinquish its freedom to make these vital decisions.[30]

There is an inherent conflict between the desire to be able to convince others that you will act in a given way and the desire to preserve freedom of action, and an actor unwilling to completely sacrifice the latter value needs to be able to do things that will make it difficult, but not impossible, for him to fail to act in a given way. He must be able to increase the costs to himself of not acting this way. This is the value of an actor's signaling reputation. Issuing signals ties the actor's reputation to acting according to them. Although the actor can still behave differently, doing so entails the cost that others will be less apt to believe the actor in the future. The others' knowledge that the actor's reputation is at stake gives them grounds for placing faith in his signals. An actor whose reputation is so tarnished that it can hardly be damaged any further (i.e. a chronic liar) cannot employ this valuable method of commitment. One cannot pledge one's word, or one's honor, to a course of action if one does not have any word or honor to place in jeopardy.[31]

---

[30] Kahn, *On Thermonuclear War*, 147-48.

[31] Analogously, one cannot pledge one's reputation for having a skill or being able to predict correctly unless that reputation has been acquired. During the Second World War, an officer was briefing General Marshall on the merits of a proposed operation. At the end of his exposition he said "I'll stake my military reputation on this plan." Marshall's reply was to the point: "You don't have a reputation to stake."

The problem of maintaining a reputation for carrying out one's threats is the best known aspect of restraint on lying resulting from the importance of an actor's signaling reputation, but it has wider applications. For example, a country having designs on territories A and B may be tempted, in its efforts to first gain A, to quiet the fears of others by telling them that its aims are limited to A. But if it later moves to take B, its assurances that this is its last demand, although this time true, may not be believed and others may oppose it out of fear that it has much wider ambitions.

We can thus make a distinction parallel to the one Schelling and Iklé make between a warning (a signal that your interest would lead you to act in an unfriendly way in given circumstances whether or not you had issued the signal) and a threat (a signal that you will act in an unfriendly way in given circumstances partly because you have now staked your reputation on doing so).[32] We can distinguish between a *reassurance,* a descriptive statement that you believe it is in your interest to leave another actor alone, and a *promise* which, because it has been given, makes it in your interest to do so. It should be noted that whereas false threats are exposed only if they do not have their intended effect, usually because others do not believe the actor will carry out the threat, misleading promises will be shown to have been deceptive if the actor carries out his policy, since the policy involves acting in ways that contradict his signals. Thus one might expect to find more unsuccessful threats not carried out than misleading promises. But this does not seem to be true, largely because statements of peaceful intent are so common as to be ritualistic and the cost of defaulting on them are therefore less. This acts as a self-reinforcing cycle. Because states frequently do not live up to their peaceful statements, such behavior comes to be expected. The cost of breaking these promises

[32] *The Strategy of Conflict,* 123-24. Iklé, *How Nations Negotiate,* 62-63.

is therefore lowered, and this in turn reduces the restraint on this form of deception and makes it more common.

The more explicit a threat or promise, the greater the cost to the actor's reputation if he defaults. This explains why states declaim their peaceful intentions in the clearest and most emphatic terms, and why concerned states ask for such unambiguous assurances from nations they fear. Obviously getting ringing promises from another state does not diminish its capacity to act. And it can be argued that a state with aggressive intentions will gladly supply such assurances in the hope of lulling its victims. However, if an ironclad commitment to nonaggression is broken, others will be less likely to believe future pledges of peaceful intention from that country.

This same process works with threats, but leads states to take opposite positions. That is, the more explicit the threat the greater the incentive to carry it out. Therefore the target state will try to discourage the other from stating a threat clearly. Or, as Schelling has pointed out, it may indicate it has not heard or understood such statements of commitment.[33] So whether a state wants another to put forth its intentions explicitly or not depends on its perception of what the other's stated intention is apt to be. If the state expects the other's signals to be friendly it will want them explicit. If it thinks they will be hostile it will want them implicit.[34]

A state's reputation is so important that others may try to lure it into a situation where it will have to break its word. For example, nation A may indicate it is not willing or able to use military force against territory C, hoping that state

[33] *The Strategy of Conflict*, 18.

[34] This line between friendly and hostile intentions is not the same as that between aggressive and nonaggressive intentions, since the former distinction is made entirely from the vantage point of a particular state. Thus Russia does not want the United States pledges to defend Europe to be clear and the United States does not want Russian pledges to end the "abnormal" situation in Berlin to be clear. While both these intentions are hostile to the interests of the other side, only the second is aggressive.

B will take the seemingly low-cost step of promising to defend C. If it does, A may then move or threaten to move against C with overwhelming force. Since B was not prepared for such a major effort as would now be required to defend C, it may default on its pledge. The pay off for A is that in future conflicts with B it can indicate that it believes that B is a bluffer (as shown by the incident with C) and therefore will back down rather than fight over the issue in question. If B believes that A really believes this it is more apt to make concessions since it will feel that A is likely to stand firm.

Alternatively, the fact that commitments and reputations are not objective but have their impact only through images can permit an actor to affect another by convincing him that his signaling reputation is at stake. State A can try to make B think it believes B had agreed to act in a certain way. B's claims that it made no such commitments will be met with the accusations that it is trying to renege and that no excuses or contradicting interpretations will cover this up. If A is successful in giving B the impression that it believes the commitment was made, B may be willing to act as though it had made the commitment because the costs of not doing so will be the same as those incurred if it had actually issued the signals. This is the intuitive strategy of children who try to convince their parents that their casual and conditional statements were taken as firm promises.[35]

The other side of this coin is that in other situations actor A can persuade B to abstain from actions harmful to A by indicating that it does not perceive B is committed to take these actions. If successful, this makes it easier for B to retreat, because doing so does not damage its signaling reputation in A's eyes.

AVOIDING THE REPUTATION OF LIAR

When a state issues a signal and then does not act accordingly, it can avoid the reputation of liar if it can convince

[35] For a further discussion of this tactic see below pp. 165-73.

the others that its original statement of intent was not a conscious lie, but rather, for various reasons, failed to predict how it would react when the situation arose. In fact, this seems to be the explanation for many apparently explicit bluffs.[36]

But a reputation for misanalyzing situations in such a way as to lead the actor to believe that he will act in a given way when in fact he will not may be almost as bad as a reputation for lying, since others will still doubt the actor's signals. Thus in explaining his belief that the Russian government would not keep agreements reached demarking their boundary with Afghanistan, Lord Salisbury said: "I do not attribute to the Russian Government an intention to deceive. . . . [When they broke past treaties] it is very possible that they were not acting with any intention to mislead the English Government, but that circumstances were stronger than men. But it really does not matter. If a man does not keep his promise in commercial matters, if he does it intentionally you say he is a swindler; if he fails to keep his promise because he cannot keep it you say he is a bankrupt. But whether swindler or bankrupt you are very careful about trusting him the next time. . . ."[37]

So the actor also has to convince others that his error in calculation was caused by unique factors and that he is not prone to be unable to fulfill his pledges. Other actors are apt to be suspicious of such explanations since they know that it is in the first actor's interest to have them believed.

ADVANTAGES OF BEING KNOWN TO LIE

We should note an exception to the rule that actors always want a reputation for issuing accurate signals. The opinion that it is always in an actor's interest to maximize his reputation for honesty is widespread but incorrect.

[36] This was the case, for example, with the unfilled British promise to aid Denmark against Prussia in 1864. Iklé points out that one finds few cases when states clearly say they will carry out a threat when they know they will not do so. (*How Nations Negotiate*, 64.)

[37] Rose Louise Greaves, *Persia and the Defence of India, 1884-1892* (London: Athlone, 1959), 105.

Being known to sometimes issue misleading signals can help an actor deter adversaries and restrain allies.

Illustrations of this are two possible interpretations of the American decision to enter the Korean War after signaling that Korea would not be defended by American troops. First, the Communists could believe that American policy was a large-scale deception designed to lure them into launching an attack that could be turned to America's advantage by rallying the United Nations against Russia, building up Western alliances, and inciting the American people to support much higher defense budgets.[38] Therefore the Soviets might be suspicious in the future if the United States renounced its interest in a particular area. They might think it was another trick designed to use their actions for American purposes. The Soviets are especially susceptible to such suspicions because of their fear of being used by their enemies.[39] Thus, ironically, America might deter Russia from attacking a country by claiming to be uninterested in it.[40]

The more common interpretation of American Korean policy is that America did not try to deceive anyone. Rather, her prewar signals were based on incorrect beliefs about how she would react in the event of an attack on South Korea.[41] Up to a point, this reputation too may be useful. For the Soviets could fear that in similar situations the United States would again react more strongly than she had thought and said she would and thus they might

[38] Alexander George, "American Policy-Making and the North Korean Aggression," World Politics, 7 (January 1955), 229. Shulman, Stalin's Foreign Policy Reappraised, 144.

[39] Leites, A Study of Bolshevism, 46-47.

[40] This is similar to the fact noted by Morton Kaplan that "in poker it is sometimes desirable to get caught in the bluff. If the opponent then persists in believing that one is bluffing in future games where one is not bluffing, his belief will cost him money and be worth money to the player who bluffed originally." [System and Processes in International politics (New York: Wiley, 1957), 237.] However this analogy holds only so long as being "called" when one is not lying in international relations does not involve a major war.

[41] See, for example, Ernest May, "The Nature of Foreign Policy: The Calculated Vs. The Axiomatic," Daedalus (Fall 1962), 653-67.

be deterred in cases where the United States gave no deterring signals.[42] But this reputation may have drawbacks, for the other side may infer that you are also unable to predict your reactions in situations where you claim you will act strongly. However if a state never defaulted on a pledge to defend an area and occasionally, and with no discernible pattern, acted much more strongly than its previous signals indicated, it might gain a very effective deterrence posture. The opponent would know that for every hostile action he took there was a small but significant chance that the state would react very strongly and this knowledge might increase his expected costs enough so that he would undertake fewer aggressive actions. Furthermore, if the adversary did take such actions and the state did not react, its reputation for keeping commitments would not be damaged. Thus the state could buy a significant amount of extra deterrence at moderate initial cost with relatively low maintenance costs.[43]

Acting differently from the way your signals indicate can also be used to project a general image of recklessness and/or lack of internal control. If others cannot rely on a state's signals they are apt to find it more difficult to predict its behavior. Unpredictability can be an asset since others may seek to appease the state as soon as any conflict arises, fearing that it will be impossible to tell what will happen if the dispute continues.[44] Of course this image entails risks since

[42] If the cost of taking the unexpected action was very high, however, observers may believe the state would not behave similarly in the future. They might even draw the conclusion that now that the state is fully aware of the costs involved in even a small war it would rather have its reputation damaged than pay the price of defending states to which it had given commitments.

[43] For a related argument see Schelling, *The Strategy of Conflict*, 181.

[44] For a general discussion of the advantages of seeming reckless, see *ibid.*, passim. A slightly different example is shown by the benefits that accrued to Spain from her apparently " 'irrational' and quixotic behavior" during negotiations with Allied and Axis powers during World War II. [Annette Baker Fox, *The Power of Small States* (Chicago: University of Chicago Press, 1959), 177-78.]

the other states may decide that the first state is an intolerable menace and must be conquered.

Similarly, to restrain yet not alienate its allies, a state may want to prevent them from being confident that it will fulfill its obligations. Bismarck realized this, and one of his successors' cardinal errors was forgetting it. They allowed Austria-Hungary to be sure that Germany would support them in the event of war, thereby decreasing Austria's willingness to compromise. While nations generally want to be known as trustworthy, and deserting an alliance undermines credibility, a nation will lose bargaining leverage if their allies are sure they can count on it to live up to its original commitments to enter and stay in a war. As George Liska notes, "too great a facility in separate-peace making lowers one's value as an ally," but the ability to make a separate peace and the reputation for doing so occasionally (treaty obligations notwithstanding) increases one's power over allies.[45] An American withdrawal from Vietnam in the face of South Vietnamese opposition might

[45] George Liska, *Nations in Alliance* (Baltimore: Johns Hopkins Press, 1962), 47-48. For example, during the First World War there was widespread fear that Japan might break her treaties with the Allies and aid the Central Powers. "Japan was not displeased by the universal suspicion of her intentions. The greater the doubt of her loyalty, the higher the price the Allies would pay to keep her loyal." [Barbara Tuchman, *The Zimmermann Telegram* (New York: Viking Press, 1958), 62.] This phenomenon is further illustrated by the consequences of Russia's discovering in 1889 that Bismarck had offered England a defensive alliance. "Word of [the negotiations] trickled through to St. Petersburg, and a mistrustful inquiry came from the Russian capital: why was Bismarck's son Herbert in London? Bismarck replied that he has been negotiating the Samoa question. Furious, the Czar wrote on the margin of Bismarck's letter: 'This knave has something up his sleeve again and is trying to throw dust in our eyes.' Had the chancellor learned of this comment he would only have smiled; anxiety and respect were just the feelings he wished the Czar to have toward him. It only secured his hold on Russia" because the Czar had to fear that Bismarck would desert him if he did not cooperate with Germany. (Reiners, *The Lamps Went Out in Europe*, 10.) Iklé misses this point when he argues: "Like a businessman's credit rating, the reputation of fulfilling the treaty obligations toward one's allies is too important to be sacrificed for a one-time gains except in cases of dire emergency." (Iklé, *How Nations Negotiate*, 7.)

87

then increase America's influence over its clients in other parts of the world.

INCENTIVES FOR LYING

We have seen that in most instances there are significant restraints on lying. Statesmen have to weigh the expected costs of issuing false signals (the probability of being caught multiplied by the disutility that would be incurred in that event) with the expected gains (the probability of successful deception multiplied by the advantage that would thereby be won). The state is apt to deceive if either the probability or disutility of being caught is low or if the probability or utility of successful deception is high. The likelihood of getting away with a lie depends partly on a state's signaling reputation. If others think the state is generally unlikely to lie, it is more apt to be believed in any given situation. This increases the incentives for it to lie, since it knows it is less likely to be challenged. Similarly, if a state has a reputation for lying, it will have to be careful when issuing signals it is unwilling or unable to carry out, since the chances are greater that others will act on the belief that it will back down. It will not have much of a reputation at stake and therefore, while it will still be able to issue warnings, it will only rarely be able to make threats. Of course if all states thought and acted completely in this way states with reputations for lying would suddenly acquire a reputation for acting according to their signals since others would realize that they know that their signals are apt to be challenged. If all states realized this, the states with a bad reputation could lie, and so on through the infinite regression now familiar in the national security literature.

Although there is little data on this point, it seems plausible that there is a cycle in the reputation of actors. If they are known to act in accord with their signals they will be tempted to lie with increasing frequency. As they are caught more often their reputation will fall and they will have to lie less. As others then test them and find their signals to be less misleading, the actors' reputation will rise again, and so on. For example, the fact that Britain's reputation in Europe decreased markedly following her failure to aid Denmark in 1864 after she strongly implied she would seems to have made her more cautious in the use of such statements of commitment.[46] But this self-regulating mechanism can operate only when there are multiple opportunities to test, and these may no longer exist.

The other factor to be considered is the gains from lying. As the stakes of the conflict increase, the pressure for deception is apt to increase. This is especially true when successful deception can change the basic power relationships in the international system. For if the use of a lie can help a state gain a dominant position in the world it may not matter a great deal that it has a reputation for lying.

This possibility is greater in the nuclear era than it was in the past. Until recently there were usually several actors of comparable power, none of which could hope to gain ascendancy over all the others by an instance of deception. This has not been the case in certain periods since World War II. If it is believed that if either side struck first it would destroy the other at the cost of bearable damage to itself, the pressures for trying to lull the other into believing one is peaceful and then launching an attack would be very great.[47] A similar, but less extreme, type of instability was a major factor in the start of World War I. This configuration may have existed in the mid-1950s, but neither the United States nor the USSR was aware of it because the distinction between a first and a second strike was not fully understood.

[46] In this case domestic audiences reacted sharply to the events by an increased desire for isolation from Continental affairs. This was a more important factor in later British policy than the changes this incident produced in other states' images of Britain. Although one cannot make a blanket prediction as to the direction of the reaction of domestic elites and public opinion it should be realized that these reactions may be very important in determining the country's future policies.

[47] For a full discussion of the instability of this situation, see Schelling, *The Strategy of Conflict*, 207-29.

Even if technological developments do not now permit the development of such extreme instability,[48] if a state feels a situation is developing in which nuclear weapons may be used, the pressures to lie are still considerable for three reasons: 1) once a crisis reaches this stage there is a significant chance it will develop into a major war, 2) the psychological and political impact of the use of nuclear weapons is apt to overshadow that of the use of deception, and 3) the stakes are apt to be very high. Thus the expected costs to a state's reputation are likely to be outweighed by the possible gains. Furthermore, under these circumstances all the actors are apt to realize there are high incentives for others to lie and thus are apt to be especially suspicious of others' signals.

But it is in these very cases, when tensions are highest, that states most want to show either their firmness—if they are making a threat—or their peaceful intent—if others mistakenly fear an attack by them. But if they cannot physically commit themselves to their announced policies they cannot prove their intentions to others. The alternative means of commitment usually employed—staking one's reputation on one's signals—loses its compelling nature. In the face of this it would take special efforts to convince others of one's honesty, and yet the situation that creates this need has made such efforts terribly difficult.

Signaling in Crises

Statesmen are placed in a dilemma, then, when they want to signal their intent during a major crisis. To illustrate this let us assume a crisis in which state A's intentions are peaceful, but B has good reasons to believe otherwise. If B's suspicions were correct, it would be in its interest to deepen the crisis or even start hostilities. In all probability A would be unwilling or unable to change its capabilities

[48] For a statement of the view that technological changes may again give one side or the other a first strike capability, see J. S. Butz, "The Myth of Technological Stalemate," *Air Force and Space Digest* 50 (March 1967), 46-58, and Butz, "Under the Spaceborn Eye: No Place to Hide," *Air Force and Space Digest* 50 (May 1967), 93-98.

so that it would be obvious to even the least trusting states that it could not be aggressive. Excepting the rare occasions when A can manipulate indices, it must rely on signals to show its intent, but for the reasons discussed above it cannot effectively use many of the commitment methods of the past. Alternatively, especially if it has little reason to fear a pre-emptive strike, A may want to signal its intent to stand firm.

In these situations, several other signaling techniques can be used. First, special channels or methods can be employed. The fact that they would be used only in the most dire emergency will increase the salience and might increase the credibility—perhaps for irrational reasons—of the message. Direct personal messages between national leaders who do not usually communicate in this way might be substituted for traditional methods of international communication. As we mentioned when dealing with morality as a constraint on lying, this would be more potent when the leaders were bound by some ties of mutual loyalty. Direct messages should not be ignored today, however. The Washington-Moscow "hot line," for example, is important not only because it allows authenticated messages to be transmitted instantaneously but also because it permits an unprecedented method of signaling during crises. This effect might be produced by the employment of more dramatic signaling techniques, such as exploding a nuclear weapon harmlessly over an opponent's desert to communicate one's resolve. Traditional diplomatic language can be dropped and states can express their intentions bluntly. This is the equivalent of saying "I really mean this," in interpersonal communication. This only needs to be done when there is special reason to think that the other will not believe you are being honest.

Second, instead of using unusual means to communicate, states can use channels that have been especially trustworthy in the past. If they exist, channels never used to transmit misleading signals can lend the messages greater credibility. For example, particular individuals may have been sent from one country to another in difficult situations in the past and the messages they transmitted may have always turned out to be correct indications of future actions.

Third, because of the norms of interpersonal relations, reliance may be placed on messages delivered personally by a high official of one country to the leaders of another. It is one thing to lie in a written document; it is another to lie to a person's face. Indeed, President Kennedy apparently was especially disturbed that Foreign Minister Gromyko could look him in the eye and claim that Russia had no intention of placing offensive missiles in Cuba.

Fourth, when a crisis makes an actor's signals suspect, he can try to prove he will follow a given policy by spending money on it. Thus when the critics of Secretary McNamara charged that his stress on conventional forces undercut the credibility of the nuclear deterrent he replied: "We have spent $2 billion to strengthen our nuclear deterrent. . . . It is absurd to think that we would have unbalanced the budget simply to strengthen a weapon that we had decided never to use."[49] Herman Kahn argues that a decent sized civil defense program "would clearly announce to the Soviets . . . that the U.S. takes controlled response seriously."[50]

[49] Quoted in Kaufmann, *The McNamara Strategy*, 68-69. With greater reason, Secretary McNamara has also claimed that the fact that the Russians support a large standing army shows that they do not really believe, as they claim, that any fighting in Europe would automatically escalate into an all-out war. "You would not think," he told a Congressional committee, "they would maintain a military force structure of 3,200,000 men if they planned to use large numbers of nuclear weapons in any military action." (Quoted in Jeremy J. Stone, *Strategic Persuasion*, 145.) There would be no reason for the Russians to want the United States to believe they were willing to fight a conventional war in Europe if that were not the case. However, the Soviets may feel they need a large army to control East Europe.

[50] Kahn, *On Escalation*, 181. Less attention has been paid to the occasions when an actor does not want others to believe he will act to protect or utilize the money he has spent. One reason many countries do not believe American statements that it does not want military bases in South Vietnam is that the United States is spending hundreds of millions of dollars to construct permanent installations such as the facilities at Cam Ram Bay.

Expenditures like these usually put the state in a better position to carry out its policy, and thus to some extent are capability indices.[51] But three factors indicate that this does not seem to be their major significance. First, quick improvements can rarely be sufficient to make major changes in the balance of power. In the nuclear age it seems impossible to bring casualties in an all-out war below the level usually considered unacceptable. McNamara implicitly admitted that the expenditure mentioned above was more a signal than a capability index since he did not say: "This additional money will enable us to carry out many military measures which would have been irrational before." Rather he argued it was the very spending of the money, not the results which were produced, that showed we would fight. The Russians have carried this tactic a step further and have announced they were spending money in a way that would not purchase maximum military advantage. In the midst of the Berlin crisis of 1961 "Khrushchev announced a decision to increase defense spending 'in the current year' by almost one-third. Since such a major increase could not be spent on a rational program within a year, a major purpose of the announcement must have been to demonstrate the seriousness of Soviet intentions."[52]

Second, once the money is spent it does not increase the incentive to follow the policy it was spent on since the money is a "sunk cost" and thus irrelevant to the calculation of gains and losses that alternative policies entail. Third, even if the amount of money spent is large in absolute terms, it will usually be small in comparison to the political issues at stake. If the United States could ensure the credibility of its nuclear deterrent by spending $2 billion, this would be a great bargain. Indeed, the money would be worth spending if it purchased even a slight increase in the Russian estimate of the probability that we would use nuclear weapons.

[51] Spending money or wasting resources in other ways can also be an index of a different kind. This is discussed in Chapter 8.

[52] Horelick and Rush, *Strategic Power* . . . , 124.

For these reasons, as long as the country spending the money is relatively rich, observers may feel an attempt is being made to fool them. Thus at one point in World War II the controversy between the United States and Britain over the priority to be given to a landing on the Continent grew so heated that "American military leaders discounted the repeated pledges of loyalty by the British to the cross-Channel strategy." When they considered "the immense investment Britain already had in the cross-channel operation . . . [the Americans] could only conclude that the great Anglo-American invasion army amassing in the United Kingdom was intended by the British to be 'a gigantic deception plan. . . .' "[53] In many cases, then, spending even large sums of money does not provide inherent evidence of the way the state will act nor does it make it less rational for the state to leave the facilities purchased unused. Rather, the spending often gains its impact as a signal by staking the state's reputation on a policy.

Statesmen may realize the danger of not being believed in a crisis and may utilize a fifth method and try to agree to set aside certain channels or methods to be used only in special situations. In his discussion of honesty in labor-management negotiations, Paul Diesing notes that "bargaining parties may reserve some special form of words for honest statements."[54] In other words, actors may reach an understanding that when a message is delivered in a given way it indicates their true intention and should be believed.

Putting the point as bluntly as this is helpful since the four mechanisms discussed previously can be reduced to this formulation. This shows that the techniques do not avoid the basic dilemma. Indeed they accentuate it. The fact that a channel or method of delivering a signal might,

[53] Richard Leighton, "Overlord vs. the Mediterranean at the Cairo-Tehran Conferences," in Kent Roberts Greenfield, *Command Decisions* (Washington, D.C.: Office of the Chief of Military History, Department of the Army, 1960), 262-63.

[54] Paul Diesing, "Bargaining Strategy in Union-Management Relations," *Journal of Conflict Resolution* 5 (December 1961), 376.

at first glance, make it especially credible is all the more reason to suspect it. For if the sending state wanted to deceive it would use that very method. Actors often realize this and are especially mistrustful of signals that plead to be believed. A psychiatrist says that "on the basis of the analysis of persons who were addressed by 'to be perfectly frank' and similar phrases, I can claim that . . . the listener *feels* that the first person did *not* tell the truth. The mannerism of speech was a giveaway."[55] As we observed before, without the five restraints on lying a state would issue the same signal whether it intended to act as its signals indicated or not. The very fact that a "good" signal is one that the receiving state is apt to believe provides the pressure for the state to use that signal to mislead in crises.

This perspective leads us to expect that in a crisis actors will be skeptical of signals if the adversary would want the actor to believe those signals whether they were honest or not. At the brink of war there is apt to be little reason for telling the truth or believing the other side. Thus we need not look to the psychological effects of tension or the irrational influence of emotion on decision-makers to account for the fact that they discount or ignore many messages from their opponents. In July 1914, for example, when each side felt there were great advantages in mobilizing and attacking first and knew that the other side shared this incentive, it is not surprising that actors did not place much faith in their adversary's denials of mobilizations. And with the stakes terribly high, calm and calculating actors may not be impressed by their opponents' deterring signals.

This analysis also applies to noncrises situations where the stakes are believed to be greater than the possible losses of signaling reputation. Under these conditions actors may not believe anything the other says and so cannot be satisfied with mere "paper agreements." For example, in the negotiations with the Boers in 1899, first Milner, the British High Commissioner at the Cape, then Chamberlain,

[55] Feldman, *Mannerisms* . . . , 30, emphasis his.

the Colonial Secretary, and finally Salisbury, the Prime Minister, reached the point where no conceivable agreement could suffice. In the words of one historian, Milner believed that "once the excitement passed away, the Boers would be back at their old tricks and the Imperial Government and the Uitlanders [Britons in the Transvaal] would then be cheated and left empty handed."[56] Chamberlain grew to believe that one of the greatest dangers was "that the Transvaal may yield in the present controversy and then continue to strengthen their military position with the intention of taking advantage of it on the first occasion when we are occupied elsewhere. . . . The only remedy [other than war] is some agreement to mutual disarmament."[57] Lord Salisbury answered that even disarmament was not a solution. "The Boers will hate us for another half century: and, therefore, *would never adhere to any promise of the kind they might make. . . .*"[58] There are no signals, and almost no indices, the Boers could have used to modify this image. War thus seemed to the British the only course available. The Arab-Israeli conflict may be a contemporary parallel. Neither side is apt to place much faith in the other's signals and will feel that the adversary will break any agreements to gain military or political advantages.[59]

Unexpected Belief in Signals

From this analysis the question that arises is not "Why do states fail to believe others' signals in a crisis?" but "Why do they ever believe signals in a crisis?"[60] Part of the reason is that in the past, few situations had the potential for completely changing the international system, thus the

[56] Grenville, *Lord Salisbury . . .* , 251.

[57] Quoted in *ibid.*, 254.

[58] *Ibid.*, emphasis added.

[59] This discussion does not apply to the possible utility of signals and guarantees given to the mid-Eastern states by the major powers, although in light of the diplomacy surrounding the June 1967 war it is not clear how much reliance either side is apt to place in such signals.

[60] For another analysis of this question, see Goffman, *Strategic Interaction*, 128-32.

restraints discussed earlier were still operating. But from the theory outlined above one would still be surprised at the number of times during crises when states asked others their intentions and placed considerable weight on the answers.[61] It may be that statesmen do not like to think of the possibility of basic changes in the system or the possibility that others are expecting such changes. Or they may operate on the assumption that others believe their state's reputation in the new system will be affected by their present conduct. Or they may never have thought through the logic of signaling which leads to increased pressures to deceive in a crisis. Or there may be very little else available to help predict others' behavior. The last two considerations may be the most important, although there is no strong evidence on this point.

Thus it is worth noting a few of the cases where none of the restraints on lying were operative and yet the receiver carefully studied the signals and paid little attention to the possibility that the actor would not behave in accord with them. This was true in the Japanese decision to surrender in 1945. Although the military was much less willing to surrender than the civilians, both factions believed a necessary condition for Japan's surrender was the retention of the Emperor after the war.[62] The Japanese decision-makers generally did not base their analyses of whether the Allies would change the Imperial system on the political philosophy and attitude of the Allies and the objective challenges they could be expected to face in the postwar situation, but rather on signals such as the Potsdam declaration and Secretary of State Byrnes' answer to the Japanese offer to accept the declaration if the status of the Emperor was not affected.

The messages the Allies sent were the object of the closest

[61] See, for example, the incidents discussed in Raymond Sontag, *European Diplomatic History, 1871-1932* (New York: Appleton-Century-Crofts, 1933), 108, and Franklin Ford, "Three Observers in Berlin," in Craig and Gilbert, *The Diplomats*, 457.

[62] Much of the military favored additional conditions but this is not crucial to the discussion here.

97

scrutiny, and interpretation of these signals occasioned great debate. When the American reply to the Japanese offer of conditional surrender was received, the officials of "the Foreign Office . . . wrack[ed] their brains to come up with a Japanese translation of the English text that would reflect not just the meaning of the original but, more particularly, *their* interpretation of the meaning." They assumed "that the military would do everything in their power to garble the meaning of the Allied note and would probably also prepare their own slanted translation."[63] Much attention was paid to the question of whether the letter "g" in the word "government" in the Byrnes note was capitalized (and thus referred to the Imperial system).[64] In explaining why he had changed his mind and now wished to surrender, the Prime Minister said that "When he had first seen the Byrnes note . . . he had considered it unsatisfactory. . . . Upon reading the note over and over again, however, he had come to the conclusion that the Allies had not drafted their reply with any malicious purpose in mind."[65]

Although these views were partially used to cover conclusions reached on other grounds, much of the concern was sincere. While there was dispute as to what the Allies were saying, no one seems to have argued that no matter what the Allies said, once Japan surrendered they would have the power to impose any solution they desired. The decision on the future of the Imperial system would depend on the Allies' analysis of whether that system contributed to their goals. Paper commitments, especially when vague, would not be a reliable predictor of what the Allies would do.

Interestingly enough, the Americans also ignored the possibility of lying.[66] No one in Washington seems to have

[63] Robert Butow, *Japan's Decision to Surrender* (Stanford: Stanford University Press, 1954), 193. Emphasis in the original.

[64] *Ibid.*, 198.

[65] *Ibid.*, 202.

[66] However, Harry Hopkins reported to President Truman that Stalin suggested that the Allies might "agree to milder peace terms but once we get into Japan to give them the works." [Quoted in

argued that we send the Japanese messages designed to get them to surrender and not worry about later having to break our word. Yet it is clear that the United States could have done so at only a slight cost—a cost much less than prolonging the war. If it were later decided that the Imperial system had to be destroyed, the United States could, for the benefit of Japanese and American audiences, point to an ambiguity in its pledge and claim conditions were different from those envisioned when the surrender was accepted. It could have been argued that thorough historical analysis indicated that the institution of the Emperor was incompatible with the development of a peaceful and democratic Japan and any instances of noncooperation with the occupation forces, which could have been exaggerated, could have been cited.[67]

The fact that the United States never considered using misleading signals is attributable to its general belief in the virtues of honesty in international relations, disagreements within the government, and the lack of understanding as to what assurances would satisfy the Japanese. The Japanese faith in Allied signals seems to have been caused by the difficulties in arriving at predictions by other means, the desperation of the situation, and the structure of the internal debate. Still, the lack of cynicism is unexpected.

Instances of great reliance on signals when the signaling actor can break his word at relatively low cost are not limited to situations at the end of a war in which one can expect to find the need for a quick decision coupled with intellectual and emotional exhaustion. For example, the United States studied with some care the signals of Hanoi and the NLF about how South Vietnam would be ruled

Robert Sherwood, *Roosevelt and Hopkins*, revised edn. (New York: Grosset and Dunlap, 1950), 904.]

[67] Even had the Japanese known the United States was not lying, it is questionable how much faith they could have reasonably placed in the signals. For if events during the occupation had changed the Americans' views on the advisability of deposing the Emperor, the cost to the United States' reputation would not have been enough to deter a change in policy.

and how quickly reunification would come about if the Communists gained control of the South.[68] Yet once the NLF was in power it would be difficult to hold it to any previous commitments since the substantive issues are likely to be much more important to the NLF than its signaling reputation with the West.

The perceiver has to take account not only of the possibility that the actor is consciously lying, but also of the chance that the actor does not himself know how he will act in a future situation when the stakes are high and, when the situation arises, will not feel that damage to his signaling reputation is particularly important. Yet in many of these cases in which the actors' promises seem to have a relatively minor influence on how they will behave, signals seem to be carefully studied. For example, a major issue between the central government and Eastern Region of Nigeria was whether the former would be granted the authority in an emergency to make certain decisions that otherwise would be made only with the consent of the regions. Given the lack of a democratic political tradition in Nigeria and the feeble hold of constitutional authority, it would seem the behavior of the central government in a crisis would be determined more by its analysis of the distribution of power and interests than by previous agreements.

Often a state's decision to go to war fits in this category. The gains and losses from alternative courses of action can be so high as to render relatively insignificant the effect on the state's signaling reputation. Furthermore, in some countries the decision to go to war rests heavily on mass opinion, opinion which is influenced by the details of the crisis. This, British leaders after 1905 kept telling the French, was the case in England. The British Government therefore could not promise to aid France in a war with Germany because it could not predict the parliamentary and public reaction to a situation whose details could not be foreseen. The

[68] See, for example, Hedrick Smith, "Liberation Unit Bars Vote in Vietnam Till U.S. Goes," *New York Times*, July 10, 1968, p. 1.

French generally accepted this view of the British decision-making process, but nevertheless continually devoted significant resources to trying to get the British Government to commit itself to join with France in the event of war. The French do not seem to have clearly thought through how the pledges would aid them, although they may have hoped the commitments would weigh heavily if war came, that they would influence public opinion, or that they would influence the British leaders' general outlook and conduct in favor of stronger ties to France.[69] In fact, the commitments Britain did give to France seem to have been a relatively unimportant factor in the decision to go to war.

Interpersonal situations analogous to these cases also present interesting dilemmas for scholars and actors. A spy captured by the enemy may be promised his freedom in return for information and cooperation. But unless some mechanism can be arranged whereby this signal is transmitted to others who may find themselves in the same position, there is no cost to those who are holding him in breaking their word. This makes it harder for the prisoner to predict his captor's behavior and for the same reasons makes it hard for the signaler to convince his captive that he will carry out his pledge. Thus this situation does not automatically benefit the actor who possesses overwhelming power. The interrogator who has a monopoly on the use of force but who cannot convince the spy that his life will be spared if he cooperates may lose valuable information. To return to the example of the Japanese surrender, if the Japanese had felt that the United States would remove the Emperor once it gained control of the country, the United States would not have been able to convince Japan to surrender.

In other, probably less frequent cases, the actor with little power in the immediate situation may want, but find it difficult, to get others to accept his word because the stakes are much greater than the impact on his reputation. Thus

[69] See the end of this chapter for a discussion of the reasons states place faith in treaties.

101

the victim of kidnapping may be faced with essentially the same problem as the person who is interrogating the spy. The kidnappers will fear that if they release the victim he will, regardless of any promises he has given, identify them to the police; and the victim, like the interrogator, will be unable to stake his reputation on his signals and thus may be unable to save his life. But in many cases the kidnappers do place at least some faith in their victim's pledge.

The reasons for the surprising reliance on signals in these cases are not clear. Undoubtedly there are special considerations at work in many of them, but one factor generally present is the lack of alternative means of predicting the actor's behavior.

DEBASING

While the ability to issue completely credible signals would be of great benefit to an actor in some situations, it would also present him with grave problems. Schelling points out the advantages to a bargainer who could, by saying "cross my heart" before a statement, convince others of the correct proposition that the statement is true.[70] But if the actor had this ability, others would demand that he always say "cross my heart," thus robbing him of the ability to ever mislead them. If he refused to say "cross my heart" in any situation he probably would not be believed. Similarly, if a state had a method of definitely establishing that it was not about to start a war, or, in another case, that it would defend a given area, others would get nervous whenever it attempted to show its commitment by any lesser measures.[71]

Certain policy proposals and historical incidents should

[70] Schelling, *Strategy of Conflict*, 24-28.

[71] In theory, there is a way to ameliorate this dilemma. Several times the actor could refuse to say "cross my heart" but still stand by his signals. Others would then learn that failure to invoke the special formula does not automatically mean that the actor is lying. However this tactic requires that there be multiple opportunities for testing bluffs and that the cost to the actor of having others believe he is lying when in fact he is not be fairly low.

102

be seen in this light. It has been noted that there may be times, especially during acute crises, when a state would wish to prove to others that it is not about to launch an attack. Nations might want to see standing groups organized that could be called upon by the host country to observe and report on the condition of the nation's military preparations, thus producing "positive evidence" of the country's peaceful intent.[72] This is not unlike the problem facing management when it wants to influence a union's perceptions by showing it confidential cost figures that reveal its difficulties in meeting the union's demands. Having done this once, if it later refuses to divulge similar information the union "will assume that [management's] position is weak and his arguments are designed to mislead."[73] Similarly, an American political figure who disclaims interest in running for President but refuses to employ a "Sherman-like" statement will usually be thought to be at least open to a draft, if not planning an active candidacy.

A diplomatic example of the impact of refusing to make a stylized disclaimer occurred in 1888 when the British government was subjected to questions in Parliament about the existence of agreements with Italy and Austria to maintain the *status quo* in the Mediterranean. The government spokesman's denial may have satisfied Parliament, but to

[72] Thomas Schelling, "Surprise Attack and Disarmament," in Klaus Knorr, *NATO and American Security* (Princeton: Princeton University Press, 1959), 195-205. Such an inspection force was proposed by President Eisenhower in a speech to the UN in September 1960 [Robert Osgood, NATO, *The Entangling Alliance* (Chicago: University of Chicago Press, 1962), 206.] Versions of this plan have at times been carried out, with results not entirely reassuring. During the "May crisis" of 1938 Hitler allowed the representatives of Britain and France to travel around certain areas to ascertain that the Czech charges (which had been believed by Britain and France) that Germany had mobilize were false (as indeed they were). This episode further weakened the Allied trust in the motives and judgment of the Czechs. Shortly before the Arab-Israeli war of June 1967, Premier Eshkol invited the Soviet Ambassador to inspect the Syrian border to see that Israel was not massing her armies there as Russia had charged. The Ambassador declined the offer.

[73] Walton and McKersie, *A Behavioral Theory of Labor Negotiations*, 72.

diplomats trained in the nuances of what statesmen say when they want to completely deny that understandings have been reached with other states, the statement clearly implied that England had, in fact, entered into at least consultations with Italy and Austria.[74]

These are illustrations of the principle that the existence of a method of showing that one is not deceiving will cause suspicions to be higher when this way of proving honesty is not used.

This is related to the dilemma of an actor who wants to have two threats believed, but also is especially concerned that one of the threats be heeded. To stress one is to implicitly downgrade the other. In the negotiations that ended the War of 1812, the British did this, perhaps without realizing it. Early in the negotiations the British made two major demands. When asked whether they were *sine qua non*'s for agreement, they replied that one was, but "one *sine qua non* at a time is enough. It will be time enough to answer your question when you have disposed of what we have given you."[75]

Similarly, when states give special guarantees to protect some areas this may downgrade the credibility of the promise to defend other places. Thus the Locarno Pact may have cast doubt on the general commitments contained in the League of Nations' charter. For what was the former if not an admission that the League could not be relied on? And the United States may not wish to stress the "tripwire" function of its troops in Europe and Korea for fear of leading the Communists—and America's allies—to doubt pledges to defend areas where troops are not stationed.[76] Finally, the Laotians can hardly have been reassured to learn that at the Vienna summit meeting President Kennedy tried to make the American commitment to Berlin clear to

[74] C. J. Lowe, *Salisbury and the Mediterranean, 1886-1896* (London: Routledge and Kegan Paul, 1965), 38-39.

[75] Quoted in Bradford Perkins, *Castlereagh and Adams* (Berkeley and Los Angeles: University of California Press, 1964), 77.

[76] I wish to thank Glenn Snyder for these two examples.

Khrushchev by telling him, in Sorensen's words, that "Berlin was no Laos. It was a matter of the highest concern to the United States."[77]

This illustrates the general tendency for the currency to be debased. That is, if any general pledges are given there will always be pressures to make additional commitments for certain areas or issues because of their vulnerability or special importance. Thus Israel and West Germany have indicated that before they sign the non-proliferation treaty they strongly desire, if not insist on, a special American guarantee against aggression over and above the commitment made by the three main nuclear powers through the United Nations.[78] But such additional pledges would undercut the general one and lead to pressures for a stronger general pledge or perhaps to special language or commitments being employed in all cases. But this merely returns to the original problem. Because others tend to see the strength of commitments as at least somewhat relative, they may well discount all commitments to some degree. Thus the actor will have to use stronger language to serve the same function that was served by more gentle language before.

Actors aware of this process sometimes refuse to give special signals. Queen Victoria had the words on the proposed Victoria Cross changed from "For the Brave" to "For Valour" because she felt the former "would lead to the inference that only those are deemed brave who have got the Victoria Cross."[79] The Mayor of San Francisco vetoed a resolution establishing a "Decency Week" on the grounds that this would imply that indecency was occurring during the other weeks.[80]

Debasing operates whenever a signal is used so much

[77] *Kennedy* (New York: Harper and Row, 1965), 584.

[78] *San Francisco Chronicle*, July 6, 1968, p. 8. John Finney, "Israelis Reported to be Reluctant at this Time to Sign Treaty Barring Spread of Nuclear Arms," *New York Times*, November 20, 1968, p. 11.

[79] Gamini Seneviratne, "Gathering of the Valiant," *San Francisco Chronicle Sunday Punch*, June 30, 1968, p. 8.

[80] *Boston Globe*, evening edition, April 28, 1968.

that it loses its impact. For example, with the growth of the importance of domestic public opinion in the foreign policy of democracies and the emergence of a vitriolic style of discourse from totalitarian states, messages that at one time would have presaged active hostility if not war are now accepted as indicating mild protest. Although this process had been underway for some time, it was greatly accelerated in the 1930s by fascist diplomacy. Thus under Ciano "The reports [that the Italian diplomats] sent home sounded frequently more like the descriptions of military encounters than the résumés of polite diplomatic interviews."[81] The other states soon adjusted to this style and the violent language had little impact. The increased use of vituperation altered not only the perception of German and Italian messages, but also affected the entire signaling system. Thus when the Japanese foreign minister made a very blunt and hostile statement to the American ambassador in May 1941, "in Washington no one made much ado about his words. Hitler had hardened statesmen to the whole vocabulary of abuse."[82]

In the same way, Communist China's prolific use of street demonstrations against foreign countries decreased the impact of these unorthodox signals. A British official was asked whether there was uneasiness in the Foreign Office over the protests made by China in conjunction with the rioting in Hong Kong. He replied, "There might have been if the Chinese had not staged demonstrations in front of nine embassies in Peking in three months and fired off protests to four different countries in a single day."[83] Since China does not have the resources to enter into a serious conflict with all of the states she had protested to in the same manner, the signals cannot predict her actions and thus carry little weight. Similarly, in the years before World

[81] Felix Gilbert, "Ciano and his Ambassadors," in Craig and Gilbert, *The Diplomats*, 523.

[82] Herbert Feis, *The Road to Pearl Harbor* (Princeton: Princeton University Press, 1950), 202.

[83] Quoted in "China's Quarrels Cheer Hong Kong," *New York Times*, July 10, 1967, p. 3.

War I, naval visits and demonstrations, having been transformed from indices to signals, were employed with increasing frequency without being followed by any significant action and so lost their value.[84] Indeed by 1914 "shock treatment by way of armed demonstration had become so thoroughly ineffective and discredited that there was no thought of such a display during the July crisis."[85]

A parallel can be found at the other end of the friendship-hostility continuum. As a nineteenth-century book on etiquette put it, "if you paid a compliment to one man, or have used toward him any expression of particular civility, you should not show the same conduct to any other person in his presence. For example, if a gentleman comes to your house and you tell him with warmth and interest that you 'are glad to see him,' he will be pleased with the attention . . . ; but if he hears you say the same thing to twenty other people, he will . . . perceive that your courtesy was worth nothing."[86] Indeed, many courtesies have become meaningless through constant use and create impact only when they are omitted.

Debasing occurs not only when a signal is given to a large number of actors, but also when a pledge has been repeatedly given to one actor. If in a tense situation a promise of aid is given in a slightly ambiguous form, the recipient state

[84] For example, the Anglo-German exchange of naval visits in 1904 —which seemed to provide as many opportunities for the gathering of military intelligence as it did for showing friendship—set off the following chain of events. "In order to reassure the French, with their almost morbid impressionability about these things, that such an Anglo-German exchange of visits meant no threat to the Entente, a British fleet visited Brest in July 1905. This was followed by the meeting of Kaiser and Tsar in Bjoerkoe, which in turn was followed by a stay of French ships in British ports in August. The British-French exchange took on greater meaning as a joint demonstration against the German-Moroccan policy. . . . In fact, the exchange was arranged as an answer to the Kaiser's visit to Tangiers . . . which had already been given a counter-demonstrative answer before the event." Alfred Vagts, *Defense and Diplomacy* (New York: King's Crown Press, 1956), 247.

[85] *Ibid.*, 255.

[86] Quoted in Goffman, *Presentation of Self in Everyday Life*, 50-51.

107

will be more frightened than assured. For example, no alliance has ever been more frequently and clearly reaffirmed than NATO. When the Soviet Union threatened Britain and France during the Suez crisis

> the façade of political steadiness [in London] was supported by the conviction that in the last analysis the United States would throw a protective umbrella of nuclear authority over its allies. Wisely, however, [Britain and France] asked Washington to confirm that this would be the case. A brief message from the State Department, however, shattered the façade and let disintegration set in.
>
> "The Government of the United States," said the message, "will respect its obligations under the North Atlantic Treaty arrangements. . . ."[87]

But Britain and France feared that Russia would attack not their homelands but their forces in Suez, a contingency not explicitly covered by the Treaty or by the American message. Had the United States not given these two countries so many promises in the past, the impact of this omission would not have been so great. But contrasting as it did with the degree of protection implied earlier, it led Britain to feel quite exposed. Similarly, the effect of a given threat depends partly on a comparison with other signals. If an actor has repeatedly threatened another with destruction, signals of merely great hostility are apt to be taken to mean that peace can be expected, at least in the short-run, and tensions may be eased.

An actor who wants third parties to believe a signal of his is not as significant as the receiver is claiming can take advantage of the phenomenon of debasing. When the Soviet Union wanted to conclude a non-aggression pact with Poland in 1932, she had to be careful lest this destroy her relationship with Germany, since Germany valued good relations with Russia largely for the pressure this allowed

[87] Terrence Robertson, *Crisis* (New York: Atheneum, 1965), 253.

her to put on Poland. The less certain Poland was about Soviet intentions, the greater the chances of territorial adjustments favorable to Germany. So while Germany had been reconciled to the idea of a Soviet-Polish non-aggression treaty, she strongly objected to any clause that might be interpreted as guaranteeing Poland's borders. To placate her, Russia tried to minimize the increase in security Poland had gained. "As a final gesture to rob the 'integrity clause' of its sting and to demonstrate that it did not recognize frontiers, as the Poles pretended, [Soviet] negotiators included an *explicit* frontier guarantee in their separate nonaggression treaties with Estonia and Finland,"[88] which were concluded at about the same time as the Polish Treaty. Chile was able to similarly partially solve a problem in the 1901-1902 Inter-American Conference. She favored a resolution calling for the voluntary arbitration of disputes while her rivals pressed for compulsory arbitration. As a compromise, the two plans were to be signed by those who agreed with them and incorporated into the final act of the Conference without being officially adopted by the meeting. But at the last minute Chile was able to have the Conference officially endorse voluntary arbitration, thus by comparison lowering the status of the other proposal.[89]

When an actor wants to convince his adversary that he is not taking the latter's signal seriously he can sometimes claim it has been used so often as to have become debased. For example, when the Soviets "declined to guarantee the safety" of Western flights to Berlin, an Allied official replied that this was "not the first time" the Soviets had sent such a signal. "In fact, it is routine for them to say this every day about our flights to London, Paris, and New York."[90]

[88] Harvey Dyck, *Weimar Germany and Soviet Russia* (New York: Columbia University Press, 1966), 247. Emphasis in the original.

[89] Robert Burr, *By Reason or Force* (Berkeley and Los Angeles: University of California Press, 1967), 243.

[90] David Binder, "Soviet Cautions West Travel by Air to Berlin," *New York Times*, March 3, 1969. In fact, the Soviet threat did differ from earlier ones and it seems clear the Allies were misrepresenting their perceptions to try to gain a bargaining advantage.

109

Conversely, signals rarely used have greater impact. This is especially true when no such signals are expected. For example, if the world went through a long period without wars, and without threats and demonstrations, minor signals like an unpleasant speech or the display of a new weapon, which under the present circumstances would be heavily discounted, would take on a great significance. The same process operates in interpersonal relations. In Hindu customs "Women wear long veils, and are expected to look demurely at the ground on the approach of a man. A corollary of the fierce restraint on meetings between young men and girls is that every slightest encounter is interpreted as leading inevitably to sexual intercourse."[91]

TREATIES OF ALLIANCE

Treaties of alliance are signals and the restraints discussed above are usually present. But the decision to go to war in fulfillment of a treaty will be made on the basis of an overall evaluation of the probable gains and costs of various courses of action. Damage to a state's signaling reputation is apt to be of slight importance when compared with all the other factors. However, two processes, related to the third and fourth restraints discussed above, are often significant. First, decisions to go to war and the specification of the national interest that such decisions involve are often difficult to reach. In this context, a treaty can be an important factor by constituting a tentative decision of the national interest. Except in cases of outright bluff, this tentative definition is apt to contribute to the intellectual framework in which the decision-maker analyzes the world and alternative policies. If major events do not undermine this framework—and sometimes if they do—tentative decisions and definitions of interest tend not to be re-examined and to harden into firm premises for action. Second, the carrying out of some provisions of the treaty may change the international environment so as to pull the treaty partners

[91] Quoted in Erving Goffman, *Behavior in Public Places* (New York: Free Press, 1963), 117.

110

together. This effect may be unintended, undesired, and even unnoticed. In other words, the "spill-over" effect detected by Ernst Haas in regional integration has a counterpart in the implementation of other forms of cooperative agreements.[92] The best example of this is provided by the Anglo-French Entente. Originating in 1904 as a colonial agreement, it developed into a much closer bond partly because of the positive feedback created by implementing that limited understanding. The agreement initially was designed merely to clear up a constant source of friction between Britain and France—i.e. disputes about British control of Egypt and French control of Morocco. Britain did not wish this agreement to affect its policies toward Continental conflicts and did not think it would do so. However, as France moved to consolidate her control of Morocco, Germany protested vigorously, partly to destroy the Entente. Britain felt obliged to support France in the resulting crisis (although the Entente did not actually commit her to do so), thus incurring German hostility. This hostility, which Britain could not perceive to be largely traceable to her own actions, was an important factor contributing to the development of a more pro-French British policy. This greater cooperation with France created further German hostility, which in turn increased the British willingness to enter into new conversations with France.[93]

Thus Britain made an agreement to reach a very limited goal, but found that implementing the agreement changed the environment in a way which increased pressures for further cooperation. A comparison with Anglo-German negotiations brings out two additional similarities with the "spill-over" concept. First, an impediment to Anglo-German

[92] Ernest Haas, *The Uniting of Europe* (Stanford: Stanford University Press, 1958), 283-317.

[93] This brief account of course should not be taken as a statement of the "basic cause" of World War I. I only want to single out for attention one element that contributed to the hardening of alliances in this period. I am not claiming that this is the most important factor in the formations of these alliances or that the alliances were the main cause of the war.

111

agreement was the lack of small disputes to provide opportunities for limited settlements. Thus, the choice was either reaching a general military and political understanding or no agreement at all. Neither side was willing to take a large step, and the general absence of the possibility of small steps meant that none would be taken. Second, the one limited agreement that was reached was self-executing and thus did not change the environment the way the Entente did. In 1890 Germany acquired Heligoland from England in return for giving up claims to territory in East Africa. But, unlike the Anglo-French agreement, each country had the power to carry out the agreement without consulting or involving other parties. There was no spill-over causing the agreement to expand because it could be implemented without creating positive feedback in the form of hostile policies undertaken by others. Two points should be noted to resist overgeneralization from this case. First, an agreement or its implementation can create enough third-party hostility to destroy rather than aid the budding alliance. The German policy of trying to break the Entente was not totally without its logic and indeed came close to succeeding. Second, outside hostility is not the only possible force that can produce a spill-over. Benefits of entering into closer ties, as well as costs of not doing so, may be created by fulfilling the initial agreement.

CHAPTER FIVE

Signals and Ambiguity

CODES AND THE PROTECTION OF IMAGES

THE MOST thoroughly discussed international signals are those that form a "diplomatic language." However the attention paid to these signals in the literature on diplomacy has obscured the important function of creating uncertainty served by many other signals. This becomes clear if we examine the nature of diplomatic language and the unconvincing reasons given for its use. In employing this language, statesmen use an established set of phrases to indicate the position their government is taking on an issue. The meanings of these phrases are well understood by all actors and it is easy to make translations between this language and other ones. As Harold Nicolson explains:

> [If] a statesman or diplomatist informs another government that his own government "cannot remain indifferent to" some international controversy, he is clearly understood to imply that the controversy is one in which his government will certainly intervene. If in his communication or speech he uses some such phrases as "His Majesty's Government view with concern" or "view with grave concern," then it is evident to all that the matter is one in which the British Government intend to adopt a strong line. . . . If he says, "In such an event His Majesty's Government would feel bound carefully to reconsider their position," he is implying that friendship is about to turn into hostility. If he says, "His Majesty's Government feel obliged to formulate express reservations regarding . . ." he is, in fact, saying "His Majesty's Government will not allow. . ." The expression "in that event, my Government will be obliged to consider their own interests," or "to claim a free hand," indicates that a rupture of relations is being considered. If he warns a foreign government that certain action on their part will be regarded "as an unfriendly act," that government [will] interpret his

words as implying a threat of war. If he says that "he must decline to be responsible for the consequences," it means that he is about to provoke an incident which will lead to war. And if he demands, even in terms of exquisite politeness, a reply before "six o'clock on the evening of the 25th," then his communication is rightly regarded as an ultimatum.[1]

In the same way, many of the actions surrounding diplomacy have meanings clear to all participants. Thus protests delivered by identic notes (similar notes by a number of powers to another state) are considered less strong than collective notes (notes with identical texts sent by several nations to a target state). And the protest will be stronger still if the collective notes "are presented simultaneously by the ambassadors concerned."[2] The target nation also has well understood means available to indicate its reaction. If the state wishes to show extreme disdain the foreign minister may refuse to meet personally with the ambassadors and may force them to "leave their notes in his anteroom."[3]

Similarly, in labor-management negotiations there are signals that, although not quite as well established as diplomatic language, form a language that can easily be translated into English. Edward Peters, a professional conciliator, gives the hypothetical case of a union demanding a fifteen cent an hour wage increase. The union negotiator may say: "Unless we get a fair and reasonable settlement, your plant will be shut down tomorrow," but not mention any specific sum. To check that this is a signal and not a slip, management may reply: "You insist that 15¢ is fair and reasonable." If the union representative interrupts to affirm management's statement, then his previous speech will be taken as a slip and ignored. If he says nothing it is

---

[1] Harold Nicolson, *Diplomacy*, 3rd edn. (New York: Oxford University Press, 1964), 123.

[2] *Ibid.*, 133.

[3] For an example of this see Jakobson, *The Diplomacy of the Winter War*, 112.

clear to both sides that the union is no longer insisting on a fifteen cent raise and is willing to settle for a smaller sum.[4]

Actors may even agree that the same words will have vastly different meanings depending on the state of an artificial variable that can be altered at the actors' convenience. This can facilitate negotiations when the parties wish at times to speak freely without having the other side interpret their position as fixed and at other times want the same statements to be considered as binding. The distinction between "official" and "unofficial" contacts may be created to do this. In one labor-management negotiation the mediator "was most emphatic that a party should never *reach* a decision in one of [the official] meetings, only *announce* a decision arrived at earlier in an 'unofficial' context. . . . [The] mediator encouraged everyone in the belief that sundry speculations which had stretched out interminably over the caucuses, when thrown out on the table in 'official' exchange could safely be read as, if not firm offers, certainly ones to be worked out with some degree of confidence."[5] The meeting could be changed from official to unofficial and back again by a mere announcement.

While the development of these special devices and language shows ingenuity, the functions they serve are not clear. In cases like those cited above, the phrases and actions are clearly understood by the diplomats and negotiators who are using a standard system of coding and decoding messages. But unless they are used for amusement, codes are only valuable if they transmit information to some actors while concealing it from others. Signals completely understood by the main actors can partly meet this func-

[4] Peters, *Strategy and Tactics* . . . , 38. Similarly, the first hint that the Russians might lift the Berlin blockade was given when, in reply to a newsman's question, Stalin failed to mention the currency reform dispute. When the United States noticed this fact, it asked the Soviets whether the omission was accidental. A month later the Soviets replied that it was not and negotiations that led to the lifting of the blockade then proceeded quickly. See W. Phillips Davison, *The Berlin Blockade* (Princeton: Princeton University Press, 1958), 254-55.

[5] Douglas, *Industrial Peacemaking*, 85-86.

tion if they keep information from the general public, which lacks the keys to the code. Of course, sometimes statesmen may use language and actions the public can understand to increase support for their policies and/or make it harder for them to retreat. However, if they feel no need to use this tactic to increase their capability and commitment, they can use the code to gain the advantages of semiprivate discussions while avoiding the charge of secret diplomacy.

This may be of considerable value, especially when one wishes to convey differing impressions to one's citizens and to foreign nations. A state may want to dampen a crisis and may be willing to sacrifice its image of resolve in the eyes of other states, but it may need to preserve this image among its own populace. Thus it will want to indicate to the other state that it is not pressing the issue, but simultaneously show domestic audiences that it has upheld the national interest and honor. One interesting way to terminate a dispute in this way is to withdraw from the field while announcing you are satisfied with the outcome.[6] For example, "the tension that followed news of the fighting [on the Israel-Jordan border in November 1966] eased considerably when Jordan reported that she had won a major victory. This indicated to Israelis that the Jordanians were not preparing the ground for a counter-retaliation."[7] Senator Aiken's proposal that the United States couple a withdrawal to enclaves in Vietnam with an announcement that we had militarily won the war may have been motivated by a similar intent. Similarly, union and management negotiators may think they have a more realistic view of what the other side will accept than do their constituents. They may therefore need to develop signals that their opposite numbers correctly understand to mean a willingness to make concessions if the negotiations become deadlocked,

[6] For another function of such claims see below, pp. 201-4, 270-71.
[7] James Feron, "Doubt Over Raid Stirred In Israel," *New York Times*, Nov. 15, 1966, p. 19.

but that those they are representing think mean they will stand firm.[8]

One problem with this strategy is that public explanations of it, like the one quoted above, limit its utility. Since elites pay closer attention to foreign affairs than does the general public, they are more apt to note such explanations and thus to be unmoved by this tactic. Furthermore, even if state A's original announcement of victory to its public has the desired effect, a problem will be created if state B's public hears this claim, for then B's leaders may feel the need to make a public rebuttal, thus making understandings between the states' leaders more difficult to reach.[9]

The second advantage of a code is that even if it does not conceal anything from anybody, it can be preferable to "plain language" because it is so different that it cannot be confused with a casual expression of a general position. Thus, the very stilted nature of diplomatic language ensures that it is unlikely to be used when the actor does not wish to convey the standard message.[10]

The common explanation of the functions of diplomatic language and similar codes, however, makes a different and less qualified claim for their utilty. Harold Nicolson argues that diplomatic language "maintains an atmosphere of calm, while enabling statesmen to convey serious warnings to each other which will not be misunderstood."[11] It "enables diplomatists and ministers to say sharp things to each other without becoming provocative or impolite."[12] Robert Mowat makes a similar claim: "The language of diplomacy may often have simply covered a mailed fist with a velvet glove; but so long as forms of courtesy were preserved and naked force was not openly threatened, pas-

[8] See the discussion in Walton and McKersie, *A Behavioral Theory* . . . , 336-38.

[9] For an example of this see Jacques Freymond, *The Saar Conflict* (London: Stevens & Sons, Ltd., 1960), 178.

[10] I would like to thank Erving Goffman for pointing this out to me.

[11] Nicolson, *Diplomacy*, 123.

[12] *Ibid.*, 122.

sion was restrained; the *sang-froid* upon which peace depends in critical negotiations was preserved."[13]

In other words, a special code may make it easier for diplomats to separate their professional roles from their personalities and personal feelings and thereby reduce the probability and impact of emotional outbursts. It provides for a degree of impersonalization and insulation. But most decision-makers are quite self-controlled. Those who have risen through the ranks of domestic or intra-organizational politics are apt to be used to personal abuse. More importantly, it is not clear how the code contributes to calm and detachment. A person who speaks two languages is not apt to have his mood and self-control influenced by which one is used. The decision-maker who receives a diplomatic note which he knows means, say, "make concessions or else," is not apt to react any differently than if a "plain language" code was generally used and he were openly told "make concessions or else."

An alternative explanation that at first seems more satisfactory is offered by Peters in his discussion of the importance of "sign language" in labor-management negotiations. (Sign languages are those signals that do not involve a straightforward statement of intent understandable to the uninitiated, and yet are clearly comprehensible to anyone who knows the code.) According to Peters, sign language is used as "a protective device. You want to offer a concession, but you want to protect yourself against rejection. You want to protect your strength even as you indicate a concession. . . . Sign language enables you to offer a concession without having your actions interpreted as weakness. It gives you the flexibility to move in the direction of peace—or to *move back* to a position of strength. . . . Through symbols you convey a new position without making explicit your concessions until you have received reasonable assurance of their acceptance."[14] Thus Peters sees

[13] *Diplomacy and Peace* (New York: Robert McBride and Co., 1936), 49-50.

[14] Peters, *Strategy and Tactics* . . . , 153-54.

118

these signals as providing flexibility. Both sides gain the freedom to explore regions of possible agreement without being forced to make unilateral concessions.

The inadequacy of this formulation can be seen clearly by referring to the distinction made earlier between the two levels on which a receiver has to make inferences about a signal.[15] First, the receiver has to decide what the actor is trying to say. Then he has to decide whether this message accurately indicates how the actor will behave in the future. By not making this distinction Peters fails to see that he has not explained how "sign language" allows an actor "to protect his strength" and to make concessions "without having these actions interpreted as weaknesses." Whether an actor can successfully reach these goals depends almost entirely on the other side's perceptions. Peters does not discuss the crucial elements that prevent the other side from developing undesired images. Since the other side can read the sign language, it can see the first side has made a concession. The concession of course can later be retracted, and in this sense sign language provides for flexibility (although this flexibility could be built into almost any other signaling system), but if making a concession damages the actor's image, sign language will not have afforded a protection that enables actors to explore possible compromises.

There are two requirements for protecting an actor's image, and neither of them is met by diplomatic or sign language. First, if an actor sends a signal that could be seen as contradicting a desired image (e.g. making a concession and not wanting others to believe he is weak or lacking in resolve), this image will be protected if the others do not draw undesired inferences (e.g. do not think that the actor will retreat much further). Once a signal has been understood on the semantic level, the protection of this type is a function of variables unrelated to the intrinsic nature of the signals used. While actors may have learned

[15] For a more detailed treatment of the subject see above, pp. 24-25.

that a concession signaled by sign language can be trans- lated to mean "I will retreat this far but won't quickly re- treat further," and may have learned that a statement to that effect in plain English can be translated to mean "I will make additional concessions if pressed," there is nothing in the nature of sign language or plain English that requires that these translations be made. Rather these inferences depend on tacit or explicit agreements the actors have made about the signaling system.

This is of course not to deny that misleading impressions will be created if one actor thinks straightforward signals should be used because they will save time, eliminate mis- understandings, or contribute to honesty, while his adver- sary believes he is abiding by the established and less straightforward convention. Thus sometimes an inexperi- enced management negotiator will know what the union is willing to settle for but make the mistake of making his offer too soon. The union is apt to infer from this that fur- ther concessions will be forthcoming. Similarly, if a girl on a date bestows too early in the evening the only favors she is willing to give, she is apt to find her partner acting on the expectation that more will follow if he persists. The Kaiser's failure to observe the rules of diplomatic etiquette when he decided not to renew the Reinsurance Treaty with Russia led Russia to overestimate the degree of hostility involved in the new German policy. But these dangerous misunderstandings are caused by each side using a different signaling system. The degree of protection would be the same once the actors reached agreement on the signals and would not depend on whether a diplomatic language or a more straightforward one was adopted. The protec- tion here depends on the actors' believing that a given sig- nal should not lead them to draw inferences undesired by the other side.

Second, an actor can protect his image by issuing sig- nals that are ambiguous at the first, or semantic, level. Then the receiver cannot be sure of exactly what the actor is trying to say. This will be the subject of the remainder of this chapter. Here it should be noted that sign and diplomatic languages cannot provide this type of protection because the receivers can confidently translate the signals and be sure of what message the actor wants to communicate.

The difference between this conception of protecting one's image and the more common view can be brought out by an examination of the following quotation:

> The sounding out process can be illustrated by the problem of the boss with amorous designs on his secretary. . . . He must find some means of determining her willingness to alter the relationship, but he must do so without risking rebuff, for a showdown might come at the cost of his dignity or his office reputation, at the cost of losing her secretarial services, or in the extreme case at the cost of losing his own position. The "sophisticated" procedure is to create an ambiguous situation in which the secretary is forced to respond in one of two ways: (1) to ignore or tactfully counter . . . (2) to respond in a similarly ambiguous vein (if not in a positive one) indicating a receptiveness to further advances. It is important in the sounding out process that the situation be ambiguous for two reasons: (1) the secretary must not be able to "pin down" the boss with evidence if she rejects the idea, and (2) the situation must be far enough removed from normal to be noticeable to the secretary. . . .

> The situation described above illustrates a process that seems to explain many organizational as well as personal interaction situations. . . . In interaction over goal-setting problems, sounding out sometimes is done through a form of double-talk, wherein the parties refer to "hypothetical" enterprises and "hypothetical" situations, or in "diplomatic" language, which often serves the same purpose.[16]

[16] James Thompson and William McEwen, "Organizational Goals and Environment: Goal Setting as an Interaction Process," in J. David Singer, ed., *Human Behavior and International Politics* (Chicago: Rand McNally, 1965), 151-52.

121

This view misses the point. What is crucial is that if the perceiver intends to rebuff the offer, most of the loss is incurred as soon as he perceives that the offer has been tendered. For this will alter his image of the actor making the initiative. If the perceiver is relatively certain that he knows what message the actor is trying to convey, the special language used provides no protection. The secretary will know, or think she knows, her boss's desires; the state will know, or believe, that the other side, which has made an offer in this "sophisticated" way, is weakening, is aggressive, or has some other characteristics the state does not want others to think it has. Thus, to protect the actor's image, the other side must be uncertain the offer was indeed an offer.[17]

While much attention is given to diplomatic language and similar signals, this analysis leads to the conclusion that they are relatively unimportant. They cannot provide the protection of images, nor the flexibility so important for negotiations. Merton has explained that patterns of behavior can continue without being eufunctional,[18] and this may be the case for the phenomena discussed by Nicolson, Mowat, and Peters. This view is supported by the fact that the decreasing use of code-like signals in international relations, while a symptom of the decline of traditional diplomacy, does not seem to have had much independent impact.

[17] This analysis only applies to losses from unfavorably changing the perceiver's image. In the example cited, as in many international cases, the effect on third audiences is important. But here ambiguity has no function. The secretary who has received a blunt, but private, offer has no more proof than one who received a "sophisticated" approach. Similarly it would be just as easy, and just as difficult, for the Russians to exploit an explicit American offer to join in destroying the nuclear capacity of France and China as it would be for her to exploit an ambiguous one, since the bluntness of the offer does not affect the ease with which others can be convinced to accept the Soviet version of the situation rather than the American counterversion.

[18] Robert Merton, *Social Theory and Social Structure*, rev. edn. (New York: Free Press, 1957), 30-32.

THE UTILITY OF AMBIGUITY

Discussions of diplomatic language and sign language have diverted attention from the larger and more important category of signals that are ambiguous on both the first and second levels. The receiver often cannot be sure what message the sender is trying to convey because the signals are ambiguous and the communications system noisy. Noise consists of all the statements and actions not designed to provide the listener with information. Examples are many messages designed for domestic audiences, actions taken by low-level officials without central sanction, and behavior unmotivated by considerations of concern to the receiver.[19] Even a casual reading of diplomatic history and the newspapers indicates the large amount of noise in the international communications system. Ambiguity partly arises from accidents, but often is consciously created by actors who, for reasons discussed in greater detail below, intend to be ambiguous. It is the noise and ambiguity in the signaling system that provide flexibility and protection by reducing the danger of damage to an actor's reputation when he undertakes probes and initiatives.[20]

Many times, especially at the start of negotiations or informal soundings, an actor will wish to put out feelers that can be denied if the response is not appropriate. If need be, the actor will want to be able to have the other later believe that it had not issued feelers. To take a hypothetical case: state A may wish to start negotiations with B to ease tensions between them. However it may be afraid that B might take this to mean that A was losing its will to resist B's demands.[21] A may therefore send an ambiguous

[19] Cf. Roberta Wohlstetter, *Pearl Harbor* (Stanford: Stanford University Press, 1962), 3.

[20] Much of the analysis in the rest of this chapter can also be applied to the interpretations of indices. For a related discussion, see Chapter 7 below.

[21] Russia did interpret a general British offer in 1903 to negotiate the whole range of problems separating the two powers as an indication of British weakness. She therefore responded with renewed

signal to B, perhaps through a noisy channel. If B's response indicates negotiations might yield fruitful results, A can issue more open signals. But if B's reaction implies that it takes the signal as evidence that A is weak and will retreat further, A can indicate the feeler was not a signal at all (e.g. claim that the message was unauthorized, that it had been misinterpreted by state B, or that it was meant as propaganda). Because the communications system is noisy and the original signal was designed to be ambiguous, this claim may well be believed. At a minimum, B will not be sure the feeler was a signal and not noise. In this way A is able to send a signal that contradicts an image it wants to maintain if B reacts in an undesired way and, if B does react that way, protect that image by convincing B that such signals were in fact never sent. This allows an actor to move back to his old position if he has to, not in the sense of retracting an old offer (which would not restore the damage done to his image), but in the sense of retaining his previous image. This explains, for example, why the United States, when considering de-escalation of the war in Vietnam in the spring of 1967, tried to judge Hanoi's response by sending feelers through what one diplomat called a "quasi-disavowable channel."[22]

Erving Goffman has noted that "When individuals are unfamiliar with each other's opinions and statuses" each seeks to protect himself by admitting "his views or status to another a little at a time. . . . By phrasing each step in the admission in an ambiguous way, the individual is in a position to halt the procedure by dropping his front at the point where he gets no confirmation from the other, *and at this point he can act as if his last disclosure were not an overture at all.*"[23] Similarly, the signaling system is more

---

aggressiveness. Raymond Sontag, *European Diplomatic History 1871-1932* (New York: Appleton-Century-Crofts, 1933), 89.

[22] Hedrick Smith et al., "The Vietnam Policy Reversal of 68-II," *New York Times*, March 7, 1969, p. 14. For a further discussion of the methods of creating ambiguity, see below, pp. 135-38.

[23] Goffman, *The Presentation of Self in Everyday Life*, 192-93. (Emphasis added.) For a similar analysis of the development of

valuable to the actors because states can usually take very small and ambiguous steps, the meaning of which the other cannot be certain until it has taken similar steps. Schelling has shown that cooperation is made easier in many situations by the ability to break up one large transaction into a number of smaller ones, each one dependent on the successful completion of the preceding ones.[24] In signaling, as opposed to other transactions, it is often difficult for the actors to be sure the first steps have actually been taken.[25]

I am not talking about cases in which the actor merely tries to "save face" by enunciating a favorable definition of the situation the other actor does not openly reject even though both sides realize it is false. Rather, the sending of ambiguous signals in a noisy environment enables the actor to leave the other in doubt, to influence the final impact of the signals after the initial reactions to them have been observed, and thereby to gain greater control over the images others have of him.

This ability allows an actor to keep several paths open simultaneously and to initiate conversations without seriously endangering an image contradictory to the message sent and which the actor will want preserved if the other side's reaction is not favorable. A communications system with less noise would make it harder to send signals that could later convincingly be claimed not to have been signals at all. Peace feelers or initiatives designed to increase cooperation are the most obvious examples of signals actors want to be able to disguise if the reaction is inauspicious, but the argument here is a general one. It applies when-

interpersonal trust, see Warren Bennis, et al., *Interpersonal Dynamics* (Homewood, Ill.: Dorsey Press, 1964), 217.

[24] Schelling, *The Strategy of Conflict*, 44-46.

[25] Carl Stevens argues that the use of sign language as discussed by Peters facilitates the protection of images by allowing major issues to be broken down into smaller ones, thereby permitting each side to make its own concessions contingent upon those of the other side. [*Strategy and Collective Bargaining Negotiation* (New York: McGraw Hill, 1963), 106.] But he does not show that sign language has this characteristic to any greater degree than a straightforward one.

ever an actor wants to send a signal that could lead to an undesired image. This will be the case, for example, if an actor wants to entice another to ally against a third party, test the reaction of others to aggressive moves, or see what costs and gains are involved in offers to protect others. And it is important to actors irrespective of the accuracy either of the images they want to preserve or the signals they want to send. Thus, while the flexibility ambiguous signals introduce into the international system makes it easier to open negotiations and make concessions, it can also facilitate aggressive and destabilizing initiatives.

The ambiguity in the signaling system is significant even when the messages are clear enough so they cannot later be claimed to have been only noise. In these cases the actor often can allege that his signals were misunderstood. Thus a state that signaled its desire to take over some territory in a manner too clear to be completely denied may be able to avoid the undesired image of dangerously aggressive intentions by explaining to others that it had, of course, intended to see that other states received compensation. In other circumstances a state could admit its signals indicated that it would, say, defend area X when in fact it later did not do so, but can claim that it also implied that it would do so only if conditions A and B were fulfilled, and they were not. Thus, it could say, other states should not believe it is a bluffer. It would be hard, if not impossible, for the state to make these plausible claims if the signals formed a code completely understood by all and if the channels were noiseless.

Since the existence of ambiguity facilitates the sending of feelers and the sounding-out process, an actor opposed to such an exchange will try to cut off the most ambiguous ranges of signaling, thus raising the price the other will have to pay to start an exchange and thus making communication less likely. This was Bismarck's tactic in 1876 when he did not want to tell Russia whether Germany would remain neutral should the conflict in the Balkans lead to war between Russia and Austria-Hungary. Bismarck felt this policy should have been obvious to all German officials, including the German military attaché in Russia, von Werder, who had transmitted home an unofficial Russian request for information about Germany's policy. Bismarck angrily noted on von Werder's telegram that "He must be prohibited from lending himself to the posing of questions at the address of his own Government. ... [Werder was] so to speak under the power of Gortchakov [the Russian Foreign Minister] who, through the channel of Werder, under the mask of *bonhommie* can ask us for more than is fair, for something so imprudent that it cannot even be submitted in the official diplomatic way. ... What Werder was moved to transmit was so irresponsible and evasive in its nature that it would be an easy thing to afterwards disavow it as a mere confidential conversation with just the Tsar's own 'aide.'" By forbidding Werder to transmit political questions in an informal manner, Bismarck forced the Russians to pay the price of raising the subject of Germany's intentions officially if they were to raise it at all, thus discouraging the Russians from doing so.[26]

A final function of ambiguity and noise is to make it easier for actors to strike and maintain bargains. At first glance the contrary argument seems more plausible—that the easier it is for each side to make its views understood (at least on the semantic level), the more the bargaining process is facilitated—and this claim is made by a great deal of the superficial literature on understanding and conflict.[27] This position might be correct if the actors could also be convincing on the second level—i.e. if they could make the other side believe they would act the way they said they would. But since this is normally impossible, noiseless bargaining not only would make tentative and probing initiatives harder to undertake, but could make it harder to reach

[26] Alfred Vagts, *The Military Attaché* (Princeton: Princeton University Press, 1967), 287-89.

[27] See, for example, Anatol Rapoport, "Rules for Debate," in Quincy Wright, William Evan, and Morton Deutsch, *Preventing World War III, Some Proposals* (New York: Simon and Schuster, 1962), 252.

127

stable agreements by encouraging the actors to try to make their opponents retreat as far as possible, a process that increases the chances of miscalculation. As Iklé points out with reference to the limits in the Korean War, "the very uncertainties of a tacit understanding may have made these restrictions more stable, because both sides were unwilling to probe and push toward the limits of the 'bargain' lest all be upset."[28] Not only do the states have even less idea than in explicit bargaining of the point at which the other side will refuse to make a deal or will denounce a bargain already struck, but since the communications have been ambiguous, the nations' signaling reputations are not as clearly engaged. This lowers the cost of reneging, and, since both sides know this, paradoxically reduces the chances of either side giving the other any extra reason to reopen the deal.[29]

Many discussions of diplomacy have ignored or denied the functions of noise and ambiguity. Nicolson stresses that "essential for the ideal diplomatist . . . is precision."[30] Kennan argues that "in communication between governments precision is the first requirement of effectiveness."[31] These views are either true by definition or incorrect. It can be argued that there is always an impression the diplomat wants to convey, and it is obvious that he wants to convey it as precisely as possible. But the desired impression may not be one of clarity. It is well known that one actor may want to leave another uncertain, but, as we have seen, to

[28] Iklé, *How Nations Negotiate*, 5. Cf. "The key to any policy of weapon limitations must be a reasonably clear-cut definition of the violations that would invoke massive retaliation." [Malcolm Hoag, "The Place of Limited War in NATO Strategy," in Klaus Knorr, ed., *NATO and American Security*, 124.]

[29] The gentleman who proposed "a system of five-year marriage contracts renewable only on approval by both partners" claimed that this "might dissuade husbands and wives from 'playing around' for fear their partner would not agree to renew the contract." ("5 Year Terms Urged for All Marriages," *New York Times*, July 9, 1968, p. 11.)

[30] Nicolson, *Diplomacy*, 60.

[31] George Kennan, *Russia Leaves the War* (Princeton: Princeton University Press, 1956), 234.

protect the actor's image he may also want the other to be unclear about what message he is trying to deliver. Nicolson does not see this when he approvingly talks of "a notable British diplomatist, who had long experience in the Far and Middle East, [who] was in the habit of providing younger negotiators appointed to Oriental capitals with the following bit of advice: 'Do not waste your time in trying to discover what is at the back of an Oriental's mind; . . . concentrate all your attention upon making quite certain that he is left in no doubt whatsoever in regard to what is at the back of *your* mind.' "[32] This is good advice as long as we remember that what is at the back of your mind may be to keep your listener in doubt as to what, if anything, *is* at the back of your mind.

Many criticisms of the lack of clarity of statements made by the United States before it halted the bombing of North Vietnam concerning the conditions under which it would de-escalate the war have ignored the functions of ambiguity. For example, C. L. Sulzberger argued that the attempts to start negotiations in early 1967 showed "there is evident danger in trying to convey policy attitudes by Delphic public signals instead of through specific secret talks. . . . One may only hope if another prenegotiation phase develops that instead of engaging in public utterances, too easily misunderstood, both sides will engage to meet in absolute secrecy."[33] This ignores the fact that one or both sides may want to preserve a great deal of confusion. While this may seem frustrating to observers, it allows the actors to protect their images. Secret meetings are often useful, especially when the actors are ready to clearly define their positions and make concessions. But if they have not reached this stage they may wish to avoid such encounters where it may be difficult to maintain the degree of ambiguity they require. An actor who agrees to meet his adversary in private may find himself pressed to

[32] Nicolson, *Diplomacy*, 59.
[33] "Foreign Affairs: Blind Man's Buff," *New York Times*, February 24, 1967, p. 32.

129

clarify his values, priorities, and demands. And premature attempts by third parties or one side to get the actors to take clear positions may only make future compromises more difficult.

Costs and Risks of Ambiguity

This is not to imply that ambiguity and noise, even at preliminary stages of negotiation, are always in the interest of either or both parties. The benefits of commitment to an actor who has a great deal of information about his adversary's preferences are well understood. Here we will be concerned with the drawbacks of noise and ambiguity that arise when actors desire to avoid clarity and commitment. First, ambiguity may prevent the signal from leading to an exchange in which both sides can move toward a compromise. If the signal is too ambiguous the other side may not even suspect that a tentative offer is being made. Or the receiving state may take advantage of the fact that the sender knows this is a possibility and, by ignoring the first soundings, try to make the sending state issue clearer signals that cannot later be denied.[34] Or the receiving state may signal back in terms it too can later discredit. Neither side may be able to tell if the other has understood its message at the semantic level and may not be willing to send clearer signals for fear the other is trying to get it to reveal valuable and damaging information. The line between what can and what cannot be later convincingly claimed to have been noise is not sharp. Actors often approach this line gingerly, trying to leave paths open to protect a different image if need be. This understandable hesitancy can make it much less likely that the actors will reveal enough information for them to determine that agreement is possible.

The second and greater problem is that several different kinds of unfortunate misunderstandings can occur. Actors

---

[34] For a discussion of a slightly different aspect of this tactic in labor management negotiations see Peters, *Strategy and Tactics . . .* , 158.

can receive unintended and inaccurate impressions. Furthermore, the signaling actor may not know what inferences the perceiver is drawing. Thus state A may believe B has signaled a fairly firm intent to cooperate. But B may not have meant to send such signals, and, being unaware of A's perceptions, B may act in a way A interprets as a betrayal. Consequently, relations between the two will be embittered and A will be less apt to later respond favorably to genuine signals from B. To take an example from labor-management negotiations, during a strike "Max, the international representative . . . received word that the company might be ready to settle. He called the divisional manager, Foster, who asked, 'What's it going to take to settle this thing?' Max indicated the union's terms. Foster inquired, 'Well, if we do that, can you give us some relief on the equalization of overtime during the rush season?' Max replied, 'I'll talk to the committee.' Foster had received the critical sign; he assumed that the matter was settled. He recalled that whenever he had conferred with Max about pending grievances, and Max had said, 'I'll talk to the committee,' the grievances would disappear." But when Foster agreed to the main union proposals at the formal meeting the union refused to make concessions on the overtime issue. "Max was accused of a double cross; the situation almost produced physical blows. Max stressed that he had only promised to 'talk' to the committee and that Foster's interpretation of his 'sign' was correct for grievances but not for negotiations."[35] And even if Max could have convinced Foster that he had not intended to deceive him, Foster would have been very wary of responding to ambiguous signals from the union representative in the future.

This dangerous problem is compounded by the fact that an actor who wants to discredit a rejected initiative and make the other doubt that he ever took it cannot be sure how much he has to do to accomplish this. To "play it safe" he may take such drastic actions that the other side

[35] Walton and McKersie, A Behavioral Theory . . . , 101-2.

131

may believe that what it initially suspected was an accurate signal was either meant to deceive or was a message to other audiences. This too is apt to make the other side less willing to respond to similarly ambiguous signals in the future, thus making it more difficult for the states to reach solutions in their common interest.

The implication of the analysis of these pitfalls is that the actor will usually be best off if he makes his signals ambiguous enough so he can deny having issued them if he has to, but clear enough so they attract sufficient attention to be studied by the receiver and interpreted as the sending actor intended. Needless to say, this balance often cannot be struck.

Certain perceptual tendencies increase the chances that the receiver will misinterpret ambiguous signals even if he realizes they are signals rather than noise. It is well-known that people interpret incoming information in the light of their pre-existing views.[36] Furthermore, the greater the ambiguity of the information, the greater the impact of the established belief.[37] There are several implications of this. First, since actors tend to perceive what they expect to perceive, a signal in accord with the receiver's expectations can be quite subtle and still have the desired impact. Indeed, such signals may be perceived even if they are not sent.[38] The other side of this coin is that signals that go against the established view of the perceiver will have to be much clearer before they are noticed, let alone understood. Thus the screen that provides protection for an actor's image while he sends ambiguous signals may at times be too strong for everyone's good. Signals of a desire to re-

[36] Jervis, "Hypotheses on Misperception," 455-62.

[37] Floyd Allport, *Theories of Perception and the Concept of Structure* (New York: Wiley, 1955), 382.

[38] For a psychological experiment showing this, see Isreal Goldiamond and William Hawkins, "Vexierversuch: The Log Relationship Between Word-Frequency and Recognition Obtained In the Absence of Stimulus Words," *Journal of Experimental Psychology* 56 (December 1958), 457-63. For political examples of this, see Whiting, *China Crosses the Yalu*, passim, and Charles Burton Marshall, "Eisenhower's Second Term," *New Republic* 153 (March 6, 1965), 25.

lax tension sent by one or both sides in a situation of mutual tension will have difficulty penetrating. The sender will want his signals ambiguous lest he endanger his image, and the receiver will be apt to miss or distort the ambiguous signal since it is at variance with the established image.

Similar problems exist in judging how others are responding to one's signals. Given the varying time lags between when a signal is sent and the reply received, and the large number of possible motives behind any act, it is difficult for states to determine which aspects, if any, of their adversaries' behavior constitute a reply to their signals. It seems probable that actors often interpret as responses to their signals actions the other took autonomously.[39] There are three reasons for this. First, actors tend to underestimate the obstacles that may lead the other state to miss the signal entirely or to misinterpret it even at the semantic level. Second, actors tend to overestimate the coordination of the other side. Actions taken by a local or low-level officials in opposition to, or in ignorance of, the views and wishes of the top decision-makers may be taken for official policy. Third, once an actor has sent an important signal he will be expecting and looking for a reply and because of the influence of expectations on perceptions he may interpret as a response actions taken for other reasons. The first two of these influences, and probably the third, were at work in limiting the American perception of what seemed to China to be the clear signals of her intent to enter the Korean war if the UN forces crossed the 38th parallel. Speeches by the United States in the UN and by General MacArthur were taken by the Chinese to mean the United States had picked up and rejected the Chinese signals. In fact, the United States never fully realized what the Chinese were trying to say and the speeches in question had

[39] For examples of this, see Kennan, *Russia Leaves the War*, 404, 408, 500; Kennan, *The Decision to Intervene* (Princeton: Princeton University Press, 1958), 108-9, 174-78; William Langer, *Our Vichy Gamble* (New York: Norton, 1966), 133, 341, 346; and Arthur Waley, *The Opium War Through Chinese Eyes* (New York: Macmillan, 1958), 23, 186.

nothing to do with the Chinese signals. Those in the UN were directed not at the Chinese but at neutrals and allies and those by MacArthur did not represent government policy.[40]

Similarly, in early 1884 Bismarck thought the British had received and understood his signals that Germany was now interested in African colonies and were rejecting his requests for support in this venture. He saw a number of British actions in West Africa (e.g. the treaty between Britain and Portugal that recognized the mouth of the Congo river as Portuguese) and in other parts of the world (e.g. the rejection of a mixed Anglo-German commission to deal with the conflicting claim on Fiji) as indicating that Britain was responding to the German signals with renewed efforts to deny her any colonial holdings. In fact the British did not understand what Bismarck was trying to say, and when he made his signals clearer the British quickly moved to satisfy him, but not before the misunderstanding had created bad feelings on both sides.[41]

The signaling actor may try to compensate for the fact that ambiguous signals sent in an environment of noise are especially susceptible to distortion. This would be relatively easy if all actors had the same perceptual predispositions. Introspection would then permit the actor to understand the influences present when the signals were received and allow him to correct for them. But these predispositions vary and are determined by complex factors, some of which are beyond the knowledge of even the most careful and intelligent observer. In this category are aspects of political conflicts within the perceiving state, events that have been analyzed shortly before the incoming signal and which set the framework for its interpretation, and any signals the receiving state has recently sent and to which it is expecting a reply. Many distorting influences, however,

[40] Whiting, *China Crosses the Yalu*, 170.

[41] Henry Ashby Turner, "Bismarck's Imperialist Venture: Anti-British in Origin?" in Prosser Gifford and Wm. Roger Louis, eds., *Britain and Germany in Africa* (New Haven: Yale University Press, 1967), 64-65, 78.

will not change so rapidly or be so hidden from outside observers. The most important are apt to be the state's image of the signaling state and its general views of world politics. While these are not easy to determine, signaling actors must at least try to take them into account if they are to communicate effectively. That actors do not do this enough is attributable only partly to the inherent difficulty of the task. In addition, it is hard for actors to realize that signals so clear to them can be interpreted radically differently by others. This difficulty is compounded by the fact that the differences in outlook may involve aspects of the signaling actor's behavior. Actors often cannot believe that others can fail to see them the way they see themselves and that others may interpret their signals against a background of beliefs holding that the signaling state is deceitful and aggressive.[42]

METHODS OF CREATING AMBIGUITY

The disadvantages of ambiguity are often seen to be outweighed by its benefits, and decision-makers frequently select methods of communication with this in mind. For example, Alfred Vagts notes that the popularity of naval demonstrations as signals was due partly to the fact that the movements of naval forces "can . . . readily be changed from a peaceful to a hostile character—by diverse announcements—and back again. . . . Their movements can be stopped on short notice and their meanings can thus be quickly re-interpreted. Their actions can be easily disavowed as due to the initiative of local or subordinate commanders."[43]

Several well-known methods of diplomacy are employed at least partly because they create or take advantage of ambiguity and noise. First, messages may be sent through a third party. The ultimate receiver then cannot be sure the intermediary is not distorting the message for his own purposes or has not made inadvertent errors. The receiver, if

[42] For an instance of this, see Sontag, *European Diplomatic History* . . . , 125.

[43] Vagts, *Defense and Diplomacy*, 235.

he is interested in the signal, must take an initiative in seeking clarification and the actor who sent the signal has
greater opportunities to protect his image. Indirect channels are especially apt to be used when dealing with sensitive questions. For example, one of the initial Soviet feelers
that led to the Nazi-Soviet nonaggression pact was sent
through the Bulgarian minister in Berlin, who told the
German Foreign Office that "the Soviet Russian Chargé,
with whom he had no intimate relations, called on him
yesterday without any apparent reason and stayed with
him for two hours." The Russian said that his country was
interested in an understanding with Germany. "The fear
of a German attack, however, . . . was an obstacle. . . . If
Germany would declare that she would not attack the
Soviet Union or that she would conclude a nonaggression
pact with her, the Soviet Union would probably refrain
from concluding a treaty with England. However, the
Soviet Union did not know what Germany really wanted."[44]
This message was sent through devious enough channels so
that Germany had to indicate her own willingness to consider striking a bargain before she could be sure the offer
was genuine, but the signal was clear enough to gain the
attention of the German policy-makers.

Similarly, in 1917-18 when the Allies wanted to convey
messages to the new Communist government of Russia,
which they did not recognize, they often employed intermediaries whose status was unclear. While these emissaries
frequently did not convey the impressions desired by their
home governments (partly because they did not completely
share their governments' values), their use not only enabled
the Allies to maintain a nonrecognition policy, but also let
them communicate with the Russians in a way that was
ambiguous enough so that their signaling reputations were
only slightly at stake.

Second, to create additional ambiguity actors may select
intermediaries or channels they know the other side be-

[44] Quoted in Feliks Gross, *Foreign Policy Analysis* (New York:
Philosophical Library, 1954), 149-50.

lieves are somewhat unreliable. Thus the emissaries employed by the United States and North Vietnam to convey peace feelers in 1967 were not skilled diplomats with established reputations for transmitting messages accurately. A press conference attended by reporters who were known to be either slightly deaf or not very competent could be used for this purpose. If the editors and typesetters are inexperienced, so much the better. College newspapers might find a significant international role to play by serving as conduits of this sort. In fact some stories "leaked" to the press in a slightly garbled form may represent a less extreme case of this technique.

This consideration leads to a rejection of the universal applicability of the common view of the requirements for an effective go-between. "The intermediary . . . supplies a critical link of communication. He can pierce the boundaries which otherwise constitute barriers to communication. . . . His success is based primarily on the goodwill and confidence that his reputation and his status as one who belongs to neither group creates."[45] But this argument does not take into account the instances when an actor, to cast further doubt on the signals he is sending, may transmit them through an intermediary known to be not completely competent and disinterested.

Third, ambiguity can be purchased by a government's ambassador telling another country that his "personal view" is that a certain settlement or agreement might be accepted by his home government. The state that receives this message would then be more likely to officially broach the subject to the first country, either because it believes the message may be a signal or because it believes the envoy was really speaking on his own, in which case it would treat the statement as an informed judgment about the other state similar in kind to the data produced by its own intelligence service. The UN may provide a specially appropriate setting for such communications. Not only is there a high rate

[45] Robert Blake, "Psychology and the Crisis of Statesmanship," *The American Psychologist* 14 (February 1959), 89.

137

of interaction among the diplomats, but the relative in-
formality lends itself to the issuing of signals that can later
be claimed to have been entirely unofficial. In 1950 the
Indian representative to the UN, Sir Bengal Rau, told the
American representative that "speaking personally" he
thought a UN observation group should be sent to Yugoslavia to determine the validity of the Soviet charges that the
former was preparing aggression. "Sir Bengal could say that
he was speaking personally, not having yet consulted his
government, and it would not be implausible, but rather
quite appropriate in the UN forum. It would have been difficult for Sir Bengal to have called upon the Secretary of
State to discuss 'my own idea'. . . ."[46]

On some occasions, states employ special envoys who
really are uninstructed and who can explore various possible settlements of disputes. Not only can such an envoy
not legally bind his country, but, more importantly, his
statements are not considered to be signals, but rather
only semi-reliable indices (because the agent presumably
was selected partly because his views were in general agreement with those of his government). Such arrangements
can be institutionalized in the form of a "working party" to
which all governments send uninstructed agents. Images
can thereby be protected to a great extent while alterna-
tives are examined.

In summary, the complex signaling system is often useful
because it is not noiseless and unambiguous, and thus signals are often intentionally unclear even at the first, or
semantic, level. This allows actors to issue signals they can
later disown and gives them more flexibility to explore possible policies without changing others' images of themselves
to their detriment. The advantages of this often outweigh
the disadvantages and many techniques of signaling are
adopted to utilize these potentialities.

[46] Arnold Beichman, *The 'Other' State Department* (New York:
Basic Books, 1968), 182. The corridors of the UN also provided the
setting for informal conversations leading to the lifting of the Berlin
blockade.

CHAPTER SIX

Coupling and
Decoupling of Signals

THE CONVENTIONAL NATURE OF SIGNALS

THE IMPORTANCE of ambiguity should not obscure the
point that signals depend for their effectiveness on agreement, usually implicit, as to the meanings of particular behaviors. Signals are not natural; they are conventional.
That is, they consist of statements and actions that the
sender and receiver have endowed with meaning in order
to accomplish certain goals. What Adam Schaff says of
symbols applies as well to signals: "To understand any
symbol, the appropriate convention must be known."[1] And
the conventions are somewhat artificially created by the
users. They are not inextricably linked to the international
system as a whole. This is one of those cases where what
actors believe to be true is true. Or, as C.A.W. Manning
puts it in a more general connection, "conformism is
enough."[2] Just as there is nothing in the nature of a language that demands that particular words be connected
with particular meanings, there is nothing in most situations to compel the adoption of particular pairings of signals and meanings.[3]

Some kinds of signals, for example the diplomatic language discussed by Nicolson, developed slowly over time,

[1] *Introduction to Semantics,* translated by Olgierd Wojtasiewicz
(New York: Pergamon Press, 1962), 188.

[2] *The Nature of International Society* (London: London School of
Economics and Political Science, 1962), 32.

[3] The conventional nature of signals is also clear in some domestic
conflicts. Whether an act or issue is important will sometimes be
determined by whether it is seen as a symbol for larger questions.
And while an act may rally the emotions of one side if it proclaims
it to be a symbol, it will not become a major issue unless the other
side also treats it as such. For example, several people burned their
draft cards in 1965 and 1966 without attracting much publicity. The
head of the Selective Service belittled the importance of this and
said he would send the offenders new cards. But when Congress
passed a law imposing stiff penalties for this act and arrests ensued,
widespread attention was focused on the act.

are quite stable, and can be used in a variety of contexts. Others, for example many of those in labor relations, seem to "flow out of the specific situation and [have] meaning as a symbolic mode of expression in a particular conflict."[4] While in the latter cases the agreement between the parties as to the meaning of signals is apt to be more tentative and less explicit, and the parties are therefore more likely to misunderstand each other on the first level, communication still depends on a shared perception of the meanings of the signals.

The actors have less need and freedom to establish the signals and the meanings to be attached to them if certain signals seem natural and therefore clear to the actors for reasons beyond their immediate control. This can be the case because of the previous experience of the actors, because of commonly accepted analogies, or because of the prominence of certain characteristics of the situation.[5] If common experience, traditions, or prominence determine the signals that will be used and the meanings attached to them, the signaling system will be anchored in elements of the international system and thus cannot be easily and cheaply altered by the actors. Although the signals still get their meanings from conventions among the actors, these conventions can be seen as merely ratifying a long-lasting arrangement. For any single actor the meanings of some signals are determined by on-going agreements and understandings established before he appeared that shape the expectations and behavior of others. An automobile driver will not survive long if he decides a green light should mean stop and a red light go. However the international system has a relatively small number of actors, no central control, relatively few experiences common to all actors, and few lasting traditions. Under these conditions the ac-

---

[4] Peters, *Strategy and Tactics* . . . , 34.

[5] For a discussion of the general importance of prominence—an attribute of a solution of an act that makes people ask, "If not here, where?"—in the coordination of expectations in tactic bargaining see Schelling, *The Strategy of Conflict*, passim.

tors are rarely as unable to establish and change the meanings of the signals as the lone automobile driver is.

Prominence may be especially important in diminishing the control actors have over selecting signals by providing distinctions that seem obvious to all concerned. There has been frequent discussion of this characteristic in connection with the question of the existence of "firebreaks" along the path of escalation. Thus as Kahn notes, while none of the limits are completely "objective and unambiguous . . . the nuclear threshold and the central [i.e. home territory] sanctuary are probably the two most salient and objective of the thresholds."[6] Most Americans would probably agree that the line between conventional and nuclear war is especially clear and although less attention has been paid to the homeland-nonhomeland distinction, it would also probably strike most of us as relatively obvious. However, for these or any other distinctions to be significant for signaling they must be salient for *both* parties. It may be difficult to be sure what is obvious to another, especially when he does not share your history, values, norms, and theories, and may have different plans or have designed his military forces in different ways than you have.

This is probably less of a problem with signals involved in limiting wars than it is with those dealing with political settlements. In the latter case what seems clear and distinct is apt to be influenced by what one thinks is fair and equitable. These beliefs are determined in large part by assumptions and theories, often implicit, about norms and political rights that may not be shared among conflicting states. Thus while prominence may provide "natural" signals in some cases, they do not provide nearly a wide enough range of message to fill states' needs. Furthermore, there is a danger that actions or attributes of a situation that seem to have an obvious meaning to one state may have no meaning, or a quite different meaning, to other nations.

In the course of negotiations procedural questions usu-

[6] Kahn, *On Escalation*, 133.

141

ally become prominent because they cannot be ignored and must somehow be dealt with. However, the meanings attributed to various responses to the issue may not be self-evident or governed by a well-established tradition. For example, in labor-management negotiations long bargaining sessions will often start in the afternoon and have to be continued after dinner. Management may offer to buy the labor team a meal. Some unions will reject the offer as "a mild attempt at bribery," while others will feel that it is only what they deserve after management had made them spend a hard day's work bargaining. Thus "two different unions [take] diametrically opposite approaches to give the same impression of militant independence; one proudly rejecting an invitation that the other demands as a concession."[7]

Thus in situations that may naturally seem to provide the occasion for signaling, the meanings of the signals are still often consciously selected by the actors from a wide variety of possible meanings that could conceivably be attributed to a given bit of behavior.

COUPLING AND DECOUPLING

The freedom to establish the meanings of signals allows actors to influence the relationships that are perceived between some of their actions—i.e. to influence whether others regard things they do as signals and what the meanings of the signals are. They can thus create new signals or destroy linkages previously believed present. The first process I shall call *coupling* and the second *decoupling*.[8]

An actor can exert pressure on another to adopt a given signal by indicating that it will act as though the other had adopted the signal. If state A implies that it attaches a certain meaning to one type of B's acts, B may find it in its

[7] Peters, *Strategy and Tactics* . . . , 31.

[8] For a related use of the terms "coupling" and "decoupling," see Roger Fisher, "Fractionating Conflict," in Roger Fisher, ed., *International Conflict and Behavioral Science* (New York: Basic Books, 1964), 91-109.

interest to use that act only to indicate that meaning. B will be especially apt to do this if it does not think it can convince A at a reasonable cost that it is not using signals in the way A says it is. For example, by indicating that it takes B's behavior as a signal that a concession is forthcoming, A can bring pressure to bear on B to act in accord with the "signal" because B will have reason to believe that A expects B to act in this way. Thus B will be more apt to believe that A will stand firm longer because of the belief that B will live up to its signal and make a concession. In addition, B will fear that not making a concession will damage its signaling reputation. So A can try to act as though B were committed to a given policy, and indeed can commit B to that policy. To take a hypothetical example, if the USSR indicated it would take the signing of a Russo-American trade treaty as a signal that the United States favored a greater détente, the United States would have three choices. It would have to show Russia it intended no such connection between the treaty and a more general understanding, or it would have to govern its attitude toward trade by what it wished to indicate about a détente, or, if it took a stand on the trade issue not consistent with its position on the general question of détente, it would have to pay the price of damaging its signaling reputation, since it will not have acted according to what the other side believes was its signals. The Greek citizens who did not support the military junta but wished to vote for the new Constitution were placed in a difficult position by the statement of a government spokesman that "The vote, in principle, is on the draft Constitution. Since, however, this document is inspired by the principles of the revolution, it follows that this would mean . . . endorsement" of the revolution and of the present government.[9] Lacking an ability to contest this interpretation, the voters had to act within the definition of the situation established by the government.

[9] "Athens Says Vote for Charter Would Imply Approval of Coup," *New York Times*, September 26, 1968, p. 11.

Similarly, by indicating it will take an action of B's (e.g. trading with a third party) as a signal of hostility toward A, A may present B with the choice of having A believe it is hostile or abstaining from the behavior A says it is taking as a signal. If B cannot convince A not to so regard this behavior, B may decide that engaging in it incurs costs out of proportion to the gains. In addition, if the actor undertakes behavior considered by his adversary to be hostile (although the actor does not mean it as such a signal) and later does not take a firm stand in a conflict, the adversary may believe the actor had bluffed earlier. But usually the main cost of allowing the adversary to couple signals of hostility is that the actor will have to abstain from desired behavior if he does not want to lead the other side to believe he is hostile.

Although coupling signals of hostility may lead to the same result as the familiar policy of deterrence, the two processes are quite different. In both cases actor A tries to affect the way B will behave by saying that if B takes certain actions A will react in a way that is against B's interests. But in coupling, A claims it will react as it does not because B's action is itself so undesirable that it must be blocked, but because it is a signal for a general change in relations to which A feels it must respond. State B may try to *persuade* A that A's perception is incorrect and that the behavior is not a signal, but bargaining is not a part of this process.[10] Similarly, coupling signals of friendship and concessions is superficially like compellence[11] in that actor A tries to get B to do something desired by A. But the sanction that lies behind this is not a threat, but rather the implication that if B does not act in the desired way its signaling reputation in A's eyes will be damaged because A believes that B has signaled that it will act in this way.

Coupling should also be distinguished from tie-ins, in which at the end of a long negotiation one actor insists that

[10] Of course, even if B's efforts to prevent the coupling fail, it can still bargain with A over what action each of them will take.

[11] Schelling, *Arms and Influence*, 69-91.

he will not sign the agreement unless
is settled in his favor.[12] The actor car
forwardly employing his bargaining ⊦
ing any of the tactics discussed here, al.
voke these tactics to strengthen his position. .
can try to stake the other's signaling reputa.
complying with the demand by claiming that a ⊦.
had been made earlier.

Impact of Different Signals on Conflicts

It can be argued that it does not matter what specific
signals are used in a conflict. Actors need some way to
communicate intent, and the signals used are unimportant.
However, closer examination shows that the nature of the
signals may have important influence on the outcome of
the conflict.

First, the signals selected may give one side an advantage. For various reasons, one side may find it especially
easy or hard to convey the image it desires by means of a
given signal. For example, the control of internal affairs by
dictatorships presents them with a problem that does not
trouble democracies. In democratic countries the press and
public opinion are not controlled by the government and
perceiving nations usually realize there may be a great gap
between attitudes of the press and public and that of the
government. While public opinion, influenced by and reflected in the mass media, may set limits on official policies
one cannot hope to get specific signals or indices from it.
There may be times, such as when foreign leaders arrive
for visits, when the government will not wish to reveal its
attitudes to other states. The reactions of the press and
public will be of little help to observers in inferring government views. This is not so in countries where all public
reactions are controlled by the government. Thus when the
Tsar agreed to let the French fleet visit Kronstadt in 1891
the French Ambassador knew that if the police "allowed
'the people' to assemble and greet the visitors . . . this would

[12] Iklé, *How Nations Negotiate,* 222-24.

145

practically mean that Russia favored ties with France."[13] In this case Russia could not avoid giving a signal. She could bluff if she wanted, but could not remain silent.

Certain signals work to the disadvantage of an actor who wants to behave in a way normally taken for a signal yet does not wish to convey the associated meaning. Thus the dilemma of the man in a homosexual bar who wants a light for his cigarette: "The legitimate phrase, 'Could you please give me a light?' was, in these circumstances, a recognized approach. . . . I walked up to the counter and bought a box of matches."[14] In the areas of concern in this study, the problem may not be so easily solved. The negotiator who wants to lose his temper because he is in a bad mood, the statesman who cannot attend an important meeting because he really does have other pressing business, and the country that wants to stage military maneuvers near the border with its sensitive neighbor because the terrain there is especially good for practice will have to abstain from the desired action, pay a high cost for taking it, or convince the audience that no signal is intended.

The second way the signals selected can influence the outcome of an interaction is by making a conflict easier or harder to solve without giving either side a bargaining advantage. A minor incident may gain wider and mutually undesired significance if each side fears the other is taking it as a signal on a more important conflict. Thus the conflict may become more heated and drastic than either side intended. A kind of escalation can occur—and, as we shall discuss in Chapter 8, the line between signaling and certain kinds of escalation is often unclear. Since it is important for an actor to use a signal in the way others use and understand it, self-fulfilling prophecies and bandwagon effects are common. This is especially apt to be true for signals of resolve. Uncertainty as to whether the other side has sent a signal and if so what its meaning is will often be resolved by trying to "play it safe." The belief that actor A may re-

[13] Vagts, Defense and Diplomacy, 244.
[14] Quoted in Goffman, Behavior in Public Places, 142.

146

gard an issue as an occasion for such signals can thus lead the actor B to make special efforts to maintain its position on that issue, which in turn can lead A to believe that B has posed a challenge that must be met.

This process has been observed in labor-management negotiations. Peters reports that tests of strength "must of necessity be limited in nature if the parties are to keep control of their strategies and tactics. Otherwise a result will be produced which neither party has desired or intended. A partial test of strength which gets out of hand can develop into a full-fledged test—a premature all-out contest—and usually over a secondary issue."[15] Not only may this procedure enlarge the conflict more than either side desires and draw them to stake their reputations so it is hard for them to retreat, but the signaling issue may be more difficult to resolve than the main issue. Indeed some issues may be selected for signaling purposes because lasting settlements are unlikely and they thus can be used many times.

Multilateral Decoupling

When actors believe certain signals are consistently making disputes more difficult to solve they can take advantage of the conventional nature of signals to agree to change the meanings attached to them. These cases of multilateral decoupling, as I will call them, will only occur when the actors have a preponderant common interest in removing or altering the signaling significance of given behaviors.

An excellent example of multilateral decoupling is provided by a change of protocol concerning the order of precedence of ambassadors. Before 1815 precedence was assessed on "the highly controversial basis of the relative status and importance of the Ambassador's sovereign."[16] The order of the ambassadors was taken to stand for the ranking of the states. This led not only to such humorous incidents as one ambassador leaping over the back of a row

[15] Peters, *Strategy and Tactics* . . . , 117-18.
[16] Nicolson, *Diplomacy*, 14.

147

of seats to sit in what he considered to be his rightful place usurped by an ambassador of a rival power,[17] but also created serious and lasting conflicts. For example, when a new Swedish Ambassador arrived in London in 1661 there was a violent fight between the coachmen and soldiers of the French and Spanish Ambassadors as to whose coach would be in the most honored position. As a result, "Louis XIV . . . severed diplomatic relations with Spain, and threatened to declare war unless a full apology were given and the Spanish Ambassador in London were punished." These conflicts made the transaction of diplomatic business more difficult. "It often happened that a French Ambassador had been instructed by his sovereign in no case to yield precedence to the Spanish Ambassador, whereas the latter had received exactly similar instructions. Undignified scenes took place at court functions; at a court ball in London in 1768, a scuffle took place between the French and Russian Ambassadors which terminated in a duel."[18]

No one gained a bargaining advantage by making precedence a signal. All lost because the system created constant challenges that countries could not ignore even if none of them wanted a conflict. Furthermore these disputes, by damaging lines of communication, made existing conflicts harder to resolve. So at the Congress of Vienna the powers agreed that precedence would be based on the clear and noncontroversial criterion of the date of the appointment of the ambassadors. Thus the states were able to remove the signaling significance from this question by adopting rules similar to those of etiquette in interpersonal relations. As one scholar has pointed out: "Etiquette formalizes the rank order of claims for deference, thus avoiding in most cases the problem of deciding between one individual's right to attention and another's. The very arbitrariness of the ritual takes the problem out of the realm of idiosyn-

[17] Charles Thayer, *Diplomat* (New York: Harper and Brothers, 1959), 255.
[18] Nicolson, *Diplomacy*, 99.

148

cratic judgment: precedence is automatically evaluated according to the institutionalized criteria."[19]

Similarly, multilateral decoupling aided diplomacy by changing the signals whereby the order in which the names of states were given in a treaty signified their relative power. In developing the *alternat* by which the order was changed each time the parties were mentioned, treaties were made easier to conclude by avoiding the charged issue of states' rank.

To facilitate agreement, states may cooperate in removing the signaling significance from other procedural matters. Thus neither the United States nor the Soviet Union wanted the test ban treaty impeded by problems involving the accession to the treaty of states, like East Germany or Communist China, which one side did not recognize. So they made "all three of the Original Parties . . . depository governments, instead of naming just one government as is the normal practice."[20] East Germany would then not sign the treaty in Washington and could not claim she had implicitly been granted diplomatic recognition.

There may be other good candidates for multilateral decoupling—especially those that create barriers to communication without serving a function that could not be filled by other signals—that actors have not yet tried to neutralize. Signaling significance is now often attached to asking for meetings in a dispute, and it might be best for all if there were some system of mandatory periodic meetings. The question of where meetings take place sometimes also becomes a signal, or is so considered by domestic audiences. Thus in German-Soviet negotiations in the late 1920s "the [German] press . . . reproached the Foreign Ministry for being too lenient in agreeing to send a German . . . delega-

[19] Jackson Toby, "Some Variables in Role Conflict Analysis," *Social Forces* 30 (March 1952), 325. For further discussion of this point, see Andrew McFarland, *Power and Leadership in Pluralist Systems* (Stanford: Stanford University Press, 1969), 207-9.
[20] Harold Jacobson and Eric Stein, *Diplomats, Scientists, and Politicians* (Ann Arbor: University of Michigan Press, 1966), 458.

149

tion *to* Moscow instead of vice-versa."[21] Some general formula for determining the site of negotiations might avoid these problems.[22]

While multilateral coupling is also possible if the actors perceive a shared interest in establishing certain signals, this is much less frequent because of the difficulties in predicting the effects of new signals. The existence of an experienced hardship is more of a goad to action than the uncertain possibilities of future gain. One possible exception, and a partial one at best, is the use as a signal of the time it takes an actor to modify his position.

The marathon negotiations common in the Cold War have accustomed us to this usage. Stalemates in which each side merely restates its position are taken for granted. Just because a state refuses to make concessions over a period of weeks or even months does not mean it will not change over an even longer length of time. This seems so natural that it is easy to forget that there were times when prolonging the negotiations for this purpose was generally not done. Thus in the Portsmith negotiations that ended the Russo-Japanese war the participants believed that if agreement could not be reached shortly after both sides had made clear their views this would signify that negotiations were useless until the balance in the war had shifted—and the adoption of these norms made this belief true. Soon only two points remained in dispute—whether Russia would pay an indemnity and who would own the island of Sakhalin. In what the participants felt would be the last meeting,

---

[21] Dyck, *Weimar Germany* . . . , 205. Emphasis in the original.

[22] This point is underlined by the difficulties of finding a place where Johnson and Kosygin could meet in 1967 without seeming to thereby confirm the substantive position of either side on the Middle East issue. For Johnson to come to New York, where Kosygin had gone to a session of the UN General Assembly which had been convoked at Soviet request, could be seen as supporting the Russian view of the need to restore the 1949 borders in the Middle East which the June 1967 Arab-Israeli war had altered. To meet in Washington could be interpreted to mean that Kosygin was willing to consider broad cooperation with the United States without an American commitment to the 1949 boundaries.

Komura, the chief Japanese negotiator, "stated that Japan would withdraw the indemnity claims if Russia would recognize her occupation of Sakhalin . . . Whitte [the chief Russian delegate] refused this. Then Komura stated that Japan would return the northern portion of the island if Russia would recognize the 50th parallel as the boundary . . . Whitte approved this."[23] It is unimaginable that in international conflict today the refusal of a major concession would lead *immediately* to another concession without any attempt to "wait the other fellow out." Today the speed with which the second concession was offered would probably lead the other side to refuse it in the belief that a still more favorable offer would be forthcoming. The changed convention on the speed of concessions probably helps some states relative to others, but it makes cooperation harder to realize because prolonged negotiations delay agreement and often entail behavior that deepens the conflict.

Trying to "outwait" the other becomes an index if waiting is costly and if patience is thought to indicate behavior in areas unrelated to the case in dispute. And, of course, waiting is more than a signal when one actor remains in possession of a value his adversary is trying to gain. However, refusing to make concessions quickly is also partly a signal because the implications drawn from this behavior are underpinned by somewhat artificially established expectations. Each side has an incentive to hold to its position longer because it knows it is possible that the other, although willing to give in, is trying to see if it cannot prevail by being patient. If actors believed that stalemates would not be employed as signals the utility of waiting would fall. No actor could be sure that it would be in his interest to try to stand firm in negotiations to wear the other down. Although if his last offer is preferred by his adversary to breaking off negotiations he will secure a favorable out-

[23] White, *The Diplomacy of the Russo-Japanese War*, 309. Similarly, British concessions in negotiations with America to end the War of 1812 followed one another very quickly. (Perkins, *Castlereagh and Adams*, 80-90.)

come, if his last offer is not acceptable his adversary will believe no agreement is possible without changing the balance of forces and will end the negotiations. Since the actor can rarely be sure that his last offer is adequate, he is apt to be very cautious about giving the impression that any offer is absolutely his last unless outwaiting is part of the signaling system.

Unilateral Decoupling

Only when there is strongly felt common interest will states join in multilateral decoupling. When one state has greater incentives or resources for decoupling, or when decoupling is in the interest of only one state, attempts will have to be unilateral. Compared to multilateral decoupling, these efforts are usually costlier and entail a higher risk of unintended and undesired consequences. But they also may yield higher payoffs. If successful, states can attach to behavior meanings that will increase their overall power or give them a better chance of prevailing in a given dispute.

Only broad guidelines can be given on the general question of how an actor convinces another not to take something as a signal. The exact tactics depend on the identity of the actors, their theories about each other and about general conflict behavior, and the details of the specific situation. In general, an actor trying to remove the signaling implications from an incident can do such things as announcing his actions ahead of time and explicitly denying any signaling intent, isolating the incident from wider issues, and taking other actions that contradict the undesired impression. For example, an actor could announce that a given issue he wished to decouple should not be taken as a signal of resolve, retreat on that issue, and then stand very firm on the main dispute. Doing this a few times could purchase a good deal of decoupling credibility, and the actor could then decouple other signals at lower cost (i.e. would not have to subsequently take a tougher stand than usual to make the adversary believe a given behavior was not a signal).

152

Decoupling may seem like an odd notion because so many of the connections provided by signals are taken for granted. Thus it is easy to overlook the fact that the interpretations drawn from many behaviors depend on conventions and beliefs that can be altered. For centuries it seemed "natural" for the ranking of Ambassadors to be linked to the standing of the states. Throughout much of history it seemed obvious that a state's power and prestige was partly judged by its ability to protect its nationals abroad with little regard as to the merits of disputes in which they might be involved. Decision-makers in these periods might have found it hard to imagine that in other times these behaviors might not be used to draw inferences about states. While some of the changes can be related to basic alterations in states' political and social systems, others are more within the control of decision-makers.

It should be noted that decoupling is more apt to be successful if the actor indicates his position at the beginning of the interaction and acts accordingly. If instead he first acts as though the incident were important and then tries to decouple and retreat, he is apt to pay a high price. For once there has been a significant conflict over an issue the other side may take the actor's behavior not as a signal, but as an index to his general resolve.

The degree to which actor A can decouple a signal depends in large part on B's perceptions of A's perceptions of his own success. State B will not draw undesired inferences from A's failure to respond in what was previously considered the expected manner if B believes A feels he has demonstrated that he no longer considers it a signal. The belief that decoupling has succeeded helps make it succeed. To make this concrete, assume that the United States feels it gains nothing by retaliating against Soviet moves against American diplomats. It may then want to end the practice of expelling Soviet diplomats whenever Americans are expelled and restricting the travel of Soviet officials in response to Soviet restrictions. However the United States might be willing to do this only if the Russians would

153

not take the change of policy as a signal of American willingness to make concessions on important issues. If, after careful preparation and explanation, the United States adopted this policy the Soviets would not take it as a signal if they believed that the American explanations accurately portrayed American beliefs, including the belief that Russia would not regard the actions as a signal.

In some cases the expenditure of significant resources will not be needed and decoupling can be accomplished simply by announcing that the other side would be incorrect to interpret a given behavior as a signal. Such a declaration will be especially effective in decoupling signals that rest on explicit conventions, since in these cases a disavowal of signaling intent cuts to the heart of the inference to be drawn from the behavior. This would mean, for example, that if the United States were to decide that withholding recognition from certain regimes has significant costs (e.g. by having to later give recognition even if the regime does not change, as was the case with Peru in 1962, and by diverting the time and energy of decision-makers) and does not produce proportionate results, it might be relatively easy for the United States to decouple recognition from the meaning now attributed to it.

Recognition by the United States is now considered important because the United States does not grant recognition to new governments it vehemently opposes, and recognition is thus a signal about the American attitude and future policy. Decoupling could be at least partially accomplished by announcing that henceforth recognition would be given to all governments that controlled the relevant territory and would not signal anything about the American attitude toward the regime. Since there would be no reason for the United States to make such a claim were it not true, the announcement would probably be quite effective. Further reinforcement for decoupling could be provided by America's taking strong action against a regime it had just recognized. By saying it disapproved of the new government, withholding aid, and even supporting internal oppo-

154

sition to it, the United States could show that recognition did not signal that its policy would be friendly or even neutral.

Decoupling is made less difficult by two factors. First, decoupling is not an all-or-none phenomenon. If an actor cannot completely convince another not to regard an incident as a signal he may at least be able to create doubt in the other's mind. The other will then not be able to draw a firm conclusion from the incident and the damage to the first actor's image will be correspondingly reduced. Second, the ambiguity and noise discussed earlier make it more difficult for actors to be sure what others are trying to communicate and make more plausible an actor's claims that others had misinterpreted his signals.

However, the possibilities of decoupling are of course limited. The actor's attempts at decoupling are only one of the factors influencing the interpretations others make. Traditions may have grown up that are difficult to alter quickly, especially when others do not want them altered. Or the signals may seem so natural that the idea of decoupling may not even appear. But this should not lead us to ignore the conventional nature of the ties between signals and the inferences drawn and the consequent leeway actors have in altering these relationships. Furthermore, this amount of freedom may be greater than is generally realized.

DECOUPLING AND DECOMMITTING

An important application of decoupling is in helping an actor get out of a commitment. A great deal of attention has been paid to the advantages and techniques of commitment, but relatively little has been said about what an actor can do to reduce the damage to his signaling reputation if he finds it in his interest to renege on a pledge. Schelling's argument that "one cannot get out of [a commitment] with cheap words,"[24] while largely correct, should be modified. In many cases the actor may be able to decouple his earlier

[24] Schelling, *Arms and Influence*, 65.

signals by claiming he had been misunderstood and that he is not committed—or at least not committed to a specific course of action. It should be stressed that if the commitment the actor had made were an empty threat decoupling would only protect the actor's signaling reputation. The actor would still lose the object he had pledged himself to protect, and his inaction could still be taken as an index of the degree to which and the objects for which he was willing to run risks. Thus while his signaling reputation would not be tarnished, his total image could still be damaged.

The prospects for decommitting in this way are enhanced by two factors. First, since decoupling is not an all-or-none affair an actor able to partially decouple can at least reduce the cost of decommitting even when he cannot avoid this cost altogether. Second, the actor need only decouple his previous signals on any one of three points: *what* he said he would do to *whom* under what *conditions*.[25] The last point in turn provides two ways to decouple. There may be ambiguity about the conditions the actor said would invoke his commitment, and about whether these conditions have been met.

The threats and promises actors make are often vague. Often a country will say it will aid another in a venture or project, but exactly how much support and in what form may be left unspecified. Similarly, threats often do not detail exactly what will be done if the other takes an undesired action. In these cases the actors can often partially fulfill their pledges and plausibly claim that that was all they had previously signaled they would do. For example, after the German *Anschluss* with Austria Neville Chamberlain pointed out in the House of Commons that "We were under no commitment to take action *vis-à-vis* Austria, but we were pledged to consultation with the French and Italian Governments in the event of action being taken which affected Austrian independence and integrity. . . . We have fully discharged [this] pledge of consulta-

[25] See Iklé, *How Nations Negotiate*, 78-79, for a somewhat similar three-fold distinction.

tion. . . ."[26] However, even if this tactic partially protects the actor's signaling reputation, he will probably have to be more specific in his future pledges since others will tend to believe he will place a similarly restricted interpretation on his signals.

On some occasions it may be unclear who the actor has pledged himself to retaliate against. When a state tries to deter an opposing bloc that consists of a major power and several satellites, and one of the satellites makes a "forbidden" move, appropriate reinterpretations of his signals may allow the actor to preserve his signaling reputation by retaliating against the satellite even if others had originally believed he was committed to attack the opposing major power. Similarly, an actor may be able to convince others that he has fulfilled his pledge when he attacks insurgents even though others had originally thought he was committed to attack the guerrillas' sponsors.

Probably the easiest way to decommit is by convincing others that the conditions under which you said you would carry out your pledge have not been fulfilled. Not only are the actor's statements about necessary and/or sufficient conditions often ambiguous, but even if others are sure they knew what the actor said, it may be very hard to determine whether the actual events constitute a meeting of those conditions. In March 1939 Neville Chamberlain was able to argue that British passivity in the face of the destruction of Czechoslovakia did not violate the "moral guarantee" to that country promised after Munich because the Slovak Diet's declaration of independence before the German move had, in Chamberlain's words, "put an end by internal disruption to the State whose frontiers we had proposed to guarantee, and, accordingly, the condition of affairs [which formed a necessary condition for the guarantee] . . . has now ceased to exist, and His Majesty's Government cannot accordingly hold themselves any longer bound by this obligation."[27]

[26] Quoted in Neville Chamberlain, *The Struggle for Peace* (London: Hutchinson and Co., 1939), 127.

[27] William Rock, *Appeasement on Trial* (Hamden, Conn.: Archon, 1966), 203-4.

Indeed, the basic facts about the events may be unclear. Thus if a state pledges itself to protect another against aggression and subsequently the other is faced with infiltration and subversion, the state may be able to renege on its commitment by claiming that it had only pledged itself to react in case of direct aggression (i.e. armed attack of large-scale units across borders). Thus in November 1938 Chamberlain claimed that the "moral guarantee" given Czechoslovakia was limited: "We never guaranteed the frontiers [of Czechoslovakia] as they existed. What we did was to guarantee against unprovoked aggression—quite a different thing."[28] Or, if the state had previously included protection against indirect aggression in its pledge, it could claim that a low level of infiltration did not constitute indirect aggression. And if, as is often the case, it is hard to be sure whether the subversives were sent across the border by a hostile power or are local rebels, the actor can claim that although infiltration planned and actively supported by another country would indeed be indirect aggression and call his pledge into operation, such infiltration was not occurring.

Of course such decommitting is difficult or impossible to carry out if events are unambiguous and the actor has clearly spelled out what it will take to activate his pledge. But often promises and prohibitions are fairly general. A state may say it will not allow its vital interests in an area to be compromised, or that it will protect another's territorial integrity and sovereignty. But it is often difficult to tell whether these things have happened, and even more difficult for others to be sure when the actor who has given the pledge believes they have happened. This is the key point, since the actor needs to convince others not that the conditions that should have activated his commitment have not occurred, but only that he thinks they have not occurred.

This process of decoupling by reinterpreting signals about the conditions which would activate a pledge is op-

[28] *Ibid.*, 198.

erating when an actor says he is making a final offer and will do something his opponent wants only if certain concessions are made. If it seems unlikely the opponent will comply the actor may want to strike a bargain without sacrificing his reputation. Decommitment may be possible by any of three approaches: by convincing the other that you believe he has fulfilled your original demands, by convincing him that you hold a certain interpretation of his moves, or by convincing him that you hold a certain interpretation of his motives.

Obviously it is easier to claim he has fulfilled your demands if your original signals were ambiguous and your opponent's behavior cannot be easily measured against them. If an automobile salesman demands $5,000 for a car and a buyer says he will only pay less than that, there is no way to make the deal without a sacrifice of bargaining reputation. But if the buyer offers not only money, but a used car whose value cannot be determined exactly, either party can decommit himself by claiming he has received new information that alters his estimate of the value of the used car. In international relations commitments and behavior are often ambiguous enough to permit the use of similar tactics. To take a hypothetical example, if an actor has pledged to take steps on a matter only if "reasonable progress" is made in an unrelated set of negotiations, there are apt to be many points at which he can convincingly claim to believe that such progress has been accomplished.

This tactic may have been used in Vietnam when the United States said it would not totally stop bombing North Vietnam until the North reduced or promised to reduce its military activity.[29] The United States perhaps came to

[29] While it is impossible to determine the extent of the concessions made by North Vietnam to obtain a bombing halt, it seems quite possible that the existence of the kinds of ambiguity discussed below facilitated American decommitment. The *New York Times* stated in an editorial that the North did not make any concessions or promises to limit military activity, but even if this assertion is correct it is wrong to argue that the Administration's claim to have lived up to its previous commitments served mainly "as a means of veiling from

159

believe North Vietnam would not make such a concession and felt it would be worthwhile to stop bombing if negotiations could be expected to follow and if such a move would not damage the American signaling reputation. In that case the United States would have wanted to decommit itself, and one of the methods with the greatest chance of success would be to claim that certain North Vietnamese actions— e.g. lack of aggressiveness on the part of main line North Vietnam units, a reduced infiltration rate, or even an end to the increase in the rate of infiltration—constituted fulfillment of the American conditions for stopping the bombing, although when the commitment was made it had meant to imply that greater North Vietnamese concessions were needed. Even if Hanoi suspected the Americans had backed down on a pledge, it would have to seriously consider the possibility that it had misread the original American demands and that the United States had not bluffed.

In this case, unlike many others, not only the pledges actors have made, but also the actions they have undertaken, are so ambiguous that this tactic can be carried one step further. Actors can misrepresent their perceptions of what the other actually has done and thus convince others that they believe the adversary has taken the actions demanded of it. Thus even if North Vietnam had not reduced its infiltration and military activities in the South, the United States might plausibly claim that it believed the North had done so. This could be done as long as the North Vietnamese believed the intelligence and reconnaissance

---

American opinion [the Johnson administration's] diplomatic retreat on the bombing issue" and that "Washington will be much freer from irrational pressures if it strips away the inherited doubletalk on the mythical agreement." ("That Vietnam 'Understanding'" *New York Times*, March 1, 1969, p. 30.) If the United States had convinced the North that it thought the North had made promises in return for a bombing halt, not only would the United States have protected its signaling reputation, but it also would have given the North greater incentives to limit its military activities. For if the North did not do so, its signaling reputation in America's eyes would be damaged.

problems are great enough so that the Americans might have inaccurate information.[30]

However decommitting by misrepresenting one's perceptions of the adversary's actions may involve more difficulties than decommitting by misrepresenting one's views about the conditions specified in one's original signals. Efforts of the former type will involve cost to the adversary if, as will frequently be the case, they imply the adversary has defaulted on his pledge. In this case Hanoi has said that it will not make concessions to gain a bombing halt, and if the United States were to believe that Hanoi had done so, the latter's signaling reputation, at least in America's eyes, would be damaged. Thus the process of decoupling in this way will necessarily be costly to one side only if one actor has pledged himself not to do X until the other does Y (or to do Z if the other does B), while the other side has committed itself not to do Y (or to do B). But if the other side has not made a pledge that contradicts that of the first actor, the first actor's reputation can be preserved without damaging the adversary's.

In some cases the actor would not have to be concerned with the motives that produced the behavior it is claiming met its conditions. But in the example of Vietnam this is not so. The implications of a reduction of North Vietnamese military activity that came about because the North was unable to maintain its forces at full strength due to the American bombing are very different from those that would follow if the reduction was ordered by Hanoi as a political

[30] Schelling argues that it is apt to be difficult to demand that specified results be reached rather than that the adversary take specified actions because "results are more a matter of interpretation than deeds usually are. Whenever a recipient of foreign aid, for example, is told that it must eliminate domestic corruption, improve its balance of payments, or raise the quality of its civil service, the results tend to be uncertain, protracted, and hard to attribute. The country may try to comply and fail; with luck it may succeed without trying; it may have indifferent success that is hard to judge; in any case compliance is usually arguable and often visible only in retrospect." (*Arms and Influence*, 85.) For these reasons, an actor who has made his demands in terms of results may find it easier to decommit.

161

measure to obtain a bombing halt. In this case ambiguity attaches not only to the demands made and the degree to which the other side's action fulfilled those demands, but also to the intent behind the activities. To decommit itself the United States had to attribute certain motives to the North Vietnamese behavior; it had to claim, whether it believed it or not, that the reduction was meant to be the reciprocation the United States had said was a necessary condition for a total halt to the bombing.[31]

It should be remembered that these tactics, like any attempts at decommitment by other means, entail a retreat on the substantive issue.[32] Thus in this example the United States would not receive all the benefits originally sought (e.g. a total cessation of North Vietnam aid to the Viet Cong and a displayed index of American resolve), but it could avoid giving the impression that the United States engages in bluffs.

Of course any stated perceptions of fact or motive may be rebutted by the other side. State A may not want to let B decommit because it thinks it can force B to publicly retreat. Or A may object to the substance of B's interpretation. Both these considerations could operate in this case. Hanoi could believe that the American position was so weak that the United States would soon have to halt the bombing even if in doing so it had to admit it was defaulting on an earlier commitment. Second, the implicit admission by the North that it had made concessions to gain a

---

[31] During the 1967 Tet truce and the lull in the fighting in the summer of 1968, the United States made the opposite interpretation and claimed the reductions in North Vietnam's support were caused by the efficacy of the bombing and therefore should not be regarded as reason—or excuse—for calling off the bombing. Of course this does not mean the American policy was unwise, since apparently the government did not want to decommit itself.

[32] However, an actor can not only protect his signaling reputation but also get his adversary to make a concession if he not only decommits himself but commits his adversary by claiming to believe that the latter has signaled that concessions will be forthcoming. This process of commitment by coupling will be discussed in the next section of this chapter.

bombing halt could damage its relations with China and the Viet Cong. It would also, as mentioned previously, damage its signaling reputation with the United States, since if the Americans thought North Vietnam had reneged on this issue it would be harder for the North to make other credible threats and pledges. In cases like this, where the actors cannot easily admit the other's version of the events is correct, both sides might be willing to go to the conference table after having announced their conflicting interpretations and the reasons the other side wants a different version accepted. This is a specific application of the common diplomatic practice of both sides publicly announcing contradicting interpretations of an agreement.

In the example being considered here an alternative solution could be reached because the incompatibility of the views of reality the actors want accepted was not complete. Hanoi wanted China and the Viet Cong to believe that it did not make concessions, and the United States wanted others to believe that it thought Hanoi did concede. If the North did not care strongly about gaining the added advantage of damaging America's signaling reputation and was willing to accept some damage to its own reputation in America's eyes, Hanoi could try to persuade its allies that it had stood firm while not disputing the American claim that it believed its conditions for the halting of the bombing had been met.

An actor trying to make it easier for his adversary to retreat can employ similar tactics to decouple the latter's signals of commitment.[33] Actor A may try to get B to agree to a proposal B had previously staked his reputation on not accepting by convincing B that he (A) never understood B to issue such a signal. There are two necessary conditions for such an attempt to succeed. First, A must be able to make a plausible case. This implies that B's commitment must not have been transmitted well, frequently, or forcefully. Or A must produce special reasons why he thought

[33] For a similar argument, see Schelling, *The Strategy of Conflict*, 34-35.

163

B's commitment was not genuine (e.g. it did not come through normal channels). Second, B's statements must have been threats and not warnings. That is, the proposal itself must seem to B worth accepting if it can be disentangled from previous commitments. Thus President Kennedy's statement that the United States would not tolerate offensive missiles in Cuba was a warning, and even if later Soviet attempts to decommit the President by convincing him that they thought he was referring to the purpose for which the weapons were installed and not their physical type had been successful, the President would not have been willing to allow the missiles to remain.

The first requirement is made easier to meet by the fact that an actor can explain what proposals he feels the adversary has made. The actor can refuse a demand made and accept a demand not made and yet claim the latter was really what was demanded. This was done by President Kennedy at the end of the Cuban missile crisis when he said he accepted Khrushchev's proposals "as I understand them" and then outlined what he had reason to believe was an acceptable solution—but one that Khrushchev had not formally proposed. Of course there are limits to the use of this tactic. Unless the other side's demands are ambiguous (e.g. to an "equitable solution") the actor cannot claim to have understood a version substantially different from the one sent to him. However the leeway is often significant.

Furthermore, this leeway can be enlarged and decoupling in general can be facilitated if there is ambiguity as to the ends the adversary is seeking. In this case the actor can claim that the adversary's commitment is not to a specific policy, but to a higher goal that can be reached in a mutually satisfactory manner. Thus the United States did not vigorously dispute Khrushchev's claim that the Soviets had placed missiles in Cuba to protect that island, a commitment that had been met because the Soviet policy had led to an American promise not to invade Cuba.[34] To the extent

[34] This pledge, in fact, was conditional on inspection of Cuba to

164

that it was believed that this, rather than the alteration of the strategic balance, was the goal of the Soviet policy, the removal of the missiles constituted less of a defeat for the Soviets.

COUPLING

As we noted earlier, to discourage adversaries from doing or saying something, actors may try to couple other's signals by claiming certain behavior will be taken as a signal of hostility. But the more common use of coupling, and the one we will be concerned with here, occurs when an actor tries to convince his adversary that he believes the latter has signaled he will grant a concession or in other ways act in accord with the actor's desires. If the adversary believes this claim he is more likely to live up to the signals he actually never sent for two reasons. First, not doing so involves the cost of damaging his signaling reputation. Second, the adversary will place a higher probability on the actor's standing firm because the adversary will believe that the actor expects him to live up to his signals and make concessions. And, in an application of the familiar he-thinks-that-I-think-that-he-thinks cycle, the adversary will think the actor is even more likely to stand firm if he believes the actor believes he believes the actor is expecting concessions. It is for these reasons that after the Yalta conference both Russia and the West not only gave differing interpretations of the agreements they had signed, but insisted that the other side had at the time accepted its interpretation.

If one actor actively exploits the possibility of coupling while the adversary remains passive, the latter is apt to find he is appearing to project an undesired image. Unless the adversary can seem to remain totally unaware that the actor is claiming he has sent certain signals, which is extremely difficult to do, the longer the coupling goes on and the more convincing the case the actor can develop, the

---

provide assurance that the missiles had been removed. Since Cuba refused to allow inspection, the pledge never took effect.

harder will it be for the adversary to alter his image. A good example of this is provided by the consequences of the 1958 Conference of Experts which discussed methods of detecting nuclear tests. The American delegation contained only scientists and received almost no political instructions from Washington. They were claimed to be, and were, independent of the government. The Soviet delegation, on the other hand, included Semen Tsarapkin, a leading diplomat, and clearly operated under political instructions.[35] Either of two courses could have been in the American interest. Either the meetings could have openly contained a large political element on both sides, in which case the positions of the delegations would be based not only on scientific findings but also on official governmental policy; or the members on both sides would be free from political instructions, and, more importantly, neither side would make inferences about what the other considered politically acceptable from the behavior of the scientists. The latter position was probably best for the United States since it would have permitted maximum exploration of the scientific problems and alternative agreements.

But by not being fully aware of the ambiguous status of the conference the United States got the worst of both worlds. Not only was it drawn into having uninstructed delegates pass judgments on questions with large political elements, but the Soviets were later able to claim they believed the views of the experts represented not the best scientific opinions of the available data, but commitments of the governments. Because the United States made only minor efforts to convince the Soviets that the American experts' behavior was not a signal and that the United States would therefore not be bound by the conference report, the Americans tacitly accepted the Russian view.

This coupling harmed the United States in several ways. Not only did it become difficult to examine the key political

[35] This gave the United States the relatively minor advantage of learning what positions were politically acceptable to the USSR. (Jacobson and Stein, *Diplomats* . . . , 75-76.)

question of how much confidence in the control system each side required, but even purely technical questions were no longer easily open to discussion. The United States discovered this when it presented evidence from new theories and experiments that indicated that underground tests were harder to detect than had been believed when the Conference of Experts designed its control system. This meant, the United States claimed, that more controls were needed to meet the same requirements the experts had set forth. The Russians resisted any changes in the recommendations of the 1958 Conference by claiming that the report had committed the governments.

Furthermore, even if the political assumptions of the experts were acceptable and no new information had developed, acquiescence to the Soviet interpretation of the status of the report decreased the actors' flexibility and made it more difficult for them to explore alternative ways of reaching the goal of preventing cheating. This was against the American, and possibly the Soviet, interest. As Jacobson and Stein point out, "Any control system is composed of variable elements. . . . All of these elements are interrelated, and changes in one area can be compensated for by adjustments in another. For example, one can compensate for a smaller number of on-site inspections by having a greater number of control posts. Similarly, one might also compensate for less efficient or trustworthy operating personnel by having a greater number of control posts. The ability to make such trade-offs, however, was greatly reduced as long as the Report of the Conference of Experts remained the immutable basis for the nuclear test ban negotiations. . . ."[36]

Another incident in the test ban negotiations provides an example of a partially successful Soviet attempt to couple American signals and commit the United States to a position it did not want to take even though the American officials realized it was against their interest to permit this. In late October 1962, when the negotiations were dead-

[36] *Ibid.*, 489.

locked over the number of on-site inspections to be permitted, Jerome Wiesner, Kennedy's science advisor, met "privately with Soviet scientist Fedorov . . . , a friend from his Pugwash days. Trying to get the USSR to modify its position so that negotiations would again be possible, Wiesner told Fedorov that if the Soviet Union would come back to its earlier position and accept a small number of inspections, he felt confident that the United States would be able to reduce the number which it would ask for. Till that point the minimum American demand had been for 12." A little later Arthur Dean told Soviet Deputy Foreign Minister Kuznetsov that the United States might settle for eight to ten inspections.[37] However in a letter sent to Kennedy in December Khrushchev claimed that Dean had stated "that in the opinion of the United States Government 2-4 on-site inspections a year in the territory of the Soviet Union would be sufficient."[38] When the 18-Nation Disarmament Committee reconvened in February, "Soviet delegates reiterated their version of the Dean-Kuznetsov conversations, and maintained that in the private conversations in January Mr. Foster [head of the Arms Control and Disarmament Agency] had been very cautious in denying this. . . . Soviet delegates also stated that in the second half of October, 1962, Jerome B. Wiesner [in his talks with Federov had said that] . . . a small quota of two to three inspections annually would open the way to an agreement. The USSR held that by now insisting on more than three on-site inspections the West was acting in bad faith."[39] Although there seems to be a high probability that Soviet officials honestly misunderstood the remarks of Dean and Wiesner, it is also possible that they consciously misrepresented their understanding of the offers in order to commit the United

[37] *Ibid.*, 426.

[38] Quoted in *ibid.*, 431.

[39] *Ibid.*, 439. For a similar account of this incident, see Arthur Dean, *Test Ban and Disarmament* (New York: Harper and Row, 1966), 41-44.

States' signaling reputation to a position it knew the United States had never taken.[40]

The attempt to couple an actor's signals and commit him has occurred on the most important issues of international politics. The French used this tactic on several occasions before World War I to increase Britain's commitment to aid her. In 1905, shortly after the Entente had been formed, the British Foreign Secretary told the French Ambassador the two governments should keep in closest contact and should "discuss in advance any contingencies by which they might in the course of events find themselves confronted."[41] On the basis of this promise, the French Ambassador reported that Britain was ready to support France in the event of a German attack. The ambassador also sent the British Foreign Secretary a copy of his understanding of the conversation, and the British leader quickly sent the ambassador a letter to set him straight. However this was unsuccessful, and the ambassador continued to believe—or claim to be-

[40] In either case the United States should have made greater efforts to convince the Soviet Union and third audiences that it had never offered to settle for three on-site inspections. The United States ignored Khrushchev's interpretation of the Dean-Kuznetsov conversation quoted above because it felt the "error" was attributable to "hasty composition." (Jacobson and Stein, *Diplomats* . . . , 431.) Not surprisingly, "the American failure and inability to deny the Soviet accounts of the Wiesner-Federov conversations damaged its case before the eight new members of the [18-Nation Disarmament] Committee." (*Ibid.*, 439.)

In the immediate postwar period the Russians tried to couple American signals to commit the United States to the Soviet position on such issues as reparations, the veto on procedural matters in the U.N. Security Council, and the Oder-Neisse line. [Herbert Feis, *Between War and Peace* (Princeton: Princeton University Press, 1960), 59, 118, 223, 226.]

In 1949 the Russians said that the United States had promised that, in return for the lifting of the Berlin blockade, the West would temporarily cease preparations for the formation of a West German government. The United States quickly rebuffed this claim and the Soviets let it drop. [Dean Acheson, *Present at the Creation* (New York: Norton, 1969), 273.]

[41] Quoted in George Monger, *The End of Isolation* (London: Nelson and Sons, 1963), 197.

lieve—the British had promised support against a German attack. Furthermore, over the next nine years the French periodically invoked the British "commitment," and, as British memories of the incident blurred, the French interpretation was at least partially accepted.

In this case it is not certain whether the French honestly misunderstood the British or whether they were fully aware of what they were doing. In a later incident it is clear that the French were consciously employing the tactic of misrepresenting their beliefs about what the British had pledged. In 1912 the British and French unilaterally, but with knowledge of each other's actions, altered the dispositions of their fleets. The British concentrated their ships in the English Channel and North Sea, and the French moved almost all their ships to the Mediterranean, thus leaving their Northern coast undefended. Although the French hoped that British support in any war with Germany would protect her coast, the new fleet arrangements were thought to be the best possible even if Britain remained neutral. However, later, when Britain and France were negotiating a naval agreement, the French tried to insert a clause saying that the previous fleet dispositions had arisen out of conversations between the governments. The British, and particularly First Lord of the Admiralty Winston Churchill, vigorously and successfully objected, pointing out that this would imply that Britain had incurred an obligation to protect the French coast in the event of war.[42]

The two governments were finally able to compromise on a preamble to the agreement that stated that in case of the threat of war they would consult with each other. The British Prime Minister said this formulation "is almost a platitude." One scholar has argued that the British made a great error because what to them seemed insignificant was felt to be a great victory by the French.[43] But the

[42] Williamson, *Anglo-French* . . . , 569-77. For another instance of this tactic in a different situation, see Kennan, *Russia Leaves the War,* 338.
[43] Williamson, 586.

French feelings were only justified if they could convince Britain that they felt that the British were now more committed to their defense. And to the extent that the British Prime Minister could convey to the French his view that the preamble was merely "a platitude," he was able to neutralize the French attempts at coupling. If the Prime Minister believed his interpretation had been conveyed to the French it would be self-fulfilling, since he and his successors would not feel bound by the "commitment."

States have also tried to raise the price an adversary would have to pay for taking hostile action by claiming that the latter had forsworn aggression. Thus in 1938 Czechoslovakia claimed that a reassuring German message received during the take-over of Austria was a general pledge of nonaggression. Germany denied this and argued that their pledge applied only during the *Anschluss* crisis. Similarly, an associate of Chamberlain has said that the Prime Minister was not, as is commonly believed, convinced that the Munich agreement had brought "peace in our time." Rather, "he hoped but was not deluded. He deliberately gave publicity to the document . . . , first because he thought it might help Hitler to keep his word, and secondly because if he broke it, the public here and in America would see clearly the kind of man he was."[44]

In this light we should re-evaluate the common claim that one manifestation of American idealism and lack of understanding of the importance of power in international relations is provided by the fact that the United States has often claimed that others have pledged themselves to act in a way America desires and has professed to believe these states will act accordingly. The two best-known examples are the open-door policy[45] and the pledges exacted from

[44] Quoted in Laurence Thompson, *The Greatest Treason* (New York: Morrow, 1968), 258-59. For the Czech attempt at coupling, see *ibid.*, 43.

[45] See George Kennan's famous critique of this policy as the archetypical case of America's ignoring the realities of power and interest. [*American Diplomacy 1900-1950* (New York: New American Library, 1951), 23-37.]

171

the Soviets at Yalta that the East European governments would be democratic. In the former case the United States even exaggerated the assent of the other powers to the American doctrine, as well as the possibility that they would actually live up to it. In the latter case, "the American Government clutched at this wan promise to support freely elected governments in liberated areas as though it were a strong obligation."[46] Similarly, when in turning over disputed areas of Germany to Poland, the Soviets, to avoid violating the Yalta agreements, said the areas were not being ceded to Poland but were only being put under Polish administration until the powers could decide on the permanent disposition of the territory. The United States not only acknowledged the Russian pledge, but claimed it was only acquiescing in the Soviet action because of it.[47] These policies may not have been naive. Even though they were largely unsuccessful because the stakes to the other powers were much greater than their signaling reputations, there was little else a country unwilling to expend more substantial resources could have done. Indeed, almost no policy could have succeeded in reaching America's goals in these instances, and the attempt at coupling probably was as effective as more costly policies would have been.

An actor can initiate the coupling process not only by announcing that he is attaching a given signaling significance to his adversary's behavior but also by announcing that he is treating as an index certain of his adversary's actions that are manipulatable. As I discussed in Chapter 3, once it is generally known that an easily controlled aspect of an actor's behavior is being used as an index, the behavior is apt to either cease entirely or become a signal. The United States may have tried to accomplish this kind of coupling when it announced that one "straw in the wind" that indicated some progress in the Paris negotiations with the North Vietnamese was that the coffee breaks during the negotiating sessions—with their attendant in-

[46] Feis, *Between War and Peace*, 62.
[47] *Ibid.*, 36-37.

formal discussions—were growing longer. Since either side could cut these breaks short the American announcement meant it could no longer consider the length of the breaks as an index. However, the announcement also implied that the Americans would now take the length of the break as a signal. Given the fact that the North did not adopt the readily available response of taking only short breaks and refusing to talk informally to the Americans during them, the United States could claim to expect the North to make at least minor concessions in the negotiations.[48]

[48] See above, 102-4 for a discussion of the impact of the failure to undertake behavior that is both easy to do and convincing.

CHAPTER SEVEN

Coupling and
Decoupling of Indices

AFFECTING THE INTERPRETATION OF INDICES

THE coupling and decoupling of indices involves attempts by an actor to convince his adversary to accept a given explanation of his behavior or to convince him that he (the actor) holds a given interpretation of the adversary's behavior.[1] This is usually accomplished by an actor's giving a convincing explanation of why he acted as he did. Diplomatic historians have generally ignored or denied the possible benefits to a state of getting others to adopt a desired interpretation of its motives. For example, Thomas Bailey claims that "a diplomatist should refrain from publicly giving his reasons for some action, unless circumstances demand such a statement. If he delays publishing his reasons, he may think of better ones later."[2] While decision-makers rarely accept at face value others' accounts of the motives, goals, calculations, and perceptions that led to their decisions, this data is almost never ignored. This is true not only because actors to some degree stake their reputation for issuing accurate signals on their statements about their actions, but also because these statements often seem plausible. Given the fact that many different theories can usually explain the state's behavior, and the difficulty in determining whether the other believes what he says, it often seems wise to give at least some weight to these explanations of indices. Furthermore, the actor's explanation may present a pattern into which others can satisfactorily

[1] While decoupling and manipulation both involve the use of indices to project a desired image, the two processes are quite different. In manipulation the actor behaves in a way he knows others will take as indices of desired characteristics. Behavior is tailored to give a certain impression. In coupling and decoupling the actor tries to alter the inferences being drawn from indices by giving explanations. The indices are not themselves manipulated, rather interpretations of them are used to influence the image.

[2] *The Art of Diplomacy* (New York: Appleton-Century-Crofts, 1968), 162.

put much of its behavior. Were the explanation not given, no coherent pattern, or a less desirable one, might seem the most convincing. Thus Daniel Elsberg points out that "words can suggest hypotheses which might not have occurred to the person otherwise, or focus attention on these hypotheses, which can be tested much more precisely."[3]

Actors can use the fact that explanations can alter the inferences drawn from indices to project desired images. What you say about your goals, motives, and calculations is apt to be easier to control cheaply than what you actually do and may produce a relatively large pay-off in terms of the interpretations others make. Kenneth Waltz's argument that the President's opinion has a great deal to do with whether or not the American public believes the government "stood firm"[4] in a conflict can be applied with reduced force to other audiences. Decision-makers take their cues partly from each other. A large number of interactions are ambiguous not only in terms of who won and who lost, but also in terms of why the actors behaved as they did. In these situations the actor who quickly, confidently, and consistently defines the situation in a given way can often convince the other that this picture is an accurate representation of the interaction, or at least that this is the situation as it appears to the actor, which is frequently all he needs to accomplish.

Thus when the United States ordered a military alert during the tense days of the abortive summit conference in May 1960, the Soviets, rather than responding in kind, indicated that they did not take the American action as an index of high American resolve and indeed felt their own decision not to stage an alert was evidence that they were confident they could hold firm. As Khrushchev put it: "We have not declared an alert and will not declare one. Our nerves are strong."[5] Even if this did not lead the United States to

[3] Daniel Elsberg in Kathleen Archibald, ed., *Strategic Interaction and Conflict* (Berkeley: Institute of International Studies, 1966), 213.
[4] Waltz, *Foreign Policy* . . . , 296.
[5] Quoted in Hans Speier, *Divided Berlin* (New York: Praeger,

revise upward its estimate of Soviet resolve, it would make it difficult for the United States to feel the American alert had impressed the Soviets, and the American bargaining power would therefore be somewhat decreased.[6]

One might ask, in this connection, why the West, which possessed a larger and more versatile navy than the Soviet bloc, has not more frequently used naval demonstrations as indices of resolve in Cold War disputes. One of the reasons is that Russia, which until recently lacked a naval force which could easily be used for these purposes, convinced others that she would not consider such displays as indicative of future action. Vagts notes that demonstrations took their significance from "the belief that the demonstrating Power was nearing the end of its patience and was contemplating serious measures. The Soviets declined to share this view, or fiction. From all external appearances, they refused to be impressed by short-of-war moves and gestures, because they are persuaded that their adversaries are not going to war even if they demonstrate, or are least ready to go to war when they demonstrate."[7] As the Soviet Union develops naval forces capable of being used for demonstrations, she may try to use them as indices of resolve (e.g. the sending of a squadron to Alexandria after

---

1961), 109. Similarly, in January 1970 Egypt tried to reduce the impact of Israeli demonstration air strikes against targets on the outskirts of Cairo by declaring that the attacks provided "clear proof that Israel is laboring under a severe state of nervous tension," (presumably caused by the American peace proposal which Israel strongly opposed). (Raymond Anderson, "U.A.R. Scorns Israeli Raids Near Cairo," *New York Times*, January 15, 1970, p. 3.)

[6] It should be noted that the American move was designed to gain much of its effect by impressing the Russians. If it succeeded in doing that even if the United States did not know that it succeeded, the United States would still receive significant benefits. The Soviet decoupling could only hold down the advantage to the United States by not allowing America to know that it was safe to press harder because the Soviets had a more favorable image of America's resolve.

[7] Vagts, *Defense and Diplomacy*, 259. Naval demonstrations are signals as well as indices and much of the discussion in the preceding chapter applies to decoupling them.

the Arab-Israeli war of 1967) and may thus allow the West to similarly employ its navy.

The importance of coupling and thereby getting others to accept a desired interpretation of an event can be seen by the fact that, except when indices directly affect major values, the outcomes of events and interactions are usually less important for the immediate and concrete gains and losses they produce than for their impact on the actors' images of each other. Thus, as was discussed in Chapter 1, Hitler's seizing of the non-German portions of Czechoslovakia caused a change in British foreign policy all out of proportion to the value of the land seized. A less dramatic example can illustrate that the acceptability of an outcome to an actor may largely depend on how he thinks other actors will interpret it. An actor may support a proposal to show that it is not directed against him. Of course this can most easily be done when the other's policy is largely verbal. Thus a member of the American UN delegation explained that the United States voted for a "fuzzily worded resolution on non-intervention [which was] not the sort of resolution we'd [usually] draft or support. . . . It was introduced by the Soviet Union and was interpreted to mean an attack on our Vietnam policy. . . . [We voted for it because] if the United States votes for the resolution it can't mean Vietnam."[8]

[8] Quoted in Beichman, *The 'Other' State Department*, 52.

There are similar instances in the American legislative process. Congressional intent often has to be estimated by the executive in deciding how to apply the law and by the courts in passing on its constitutionality. Intent is established partly by the legislative history of the bill and by the interpretations Congressmen gave when they supported it. Thus Congressmen can affect the enforcement of a law by their discussion of it. This is illustrated by the recent debate and vote in the House of Representatives on an amendment to the Civil Rights Act of 1964 that would require that the school desegregation provisions of that law be applied uniformly throughout the country. It is more likely that the executive and the courts will interpret the bill in the way desired by liberal Congressmen because many of the liberals who originally opposed the amendment said at the conclusion of the debate that the explanations given had convinced them that the amendment would not hinder the desegregation of Southern

177

An aspect of the Cuban missile crisis illustrates both the importance to the actor of the interpretations made about an interaction rather than the concrete outcomes and the looseness of the relation between outcomes and interpretations. American decision-makers quickly saw the possibility that Khrushchev would demand that the United States dismantle its missile bases in Turkey in return for removing the missiles from Cuba. Although Kennedy had previously decided that those weapons created a risk and a burden out of proportion to their contribution to security and had unsuccessfully tried to have them removed, he decided that to withdraw them in such a bargain would adversely affect the Russian and allied image of the United States. The NATO countries and presumably the USSR understood that these weapons had little value and probably knew that the United States was planning to dismantle them. Thus to grant the substance of the Soviet demand was hardly a concession at all. What mattered was that others would interpret such a move as an index of the willingness of the United States to retreat under pressure even

---

schools. They showed their belief in this interpretation by voting for the provision (which would have passed anyway). If they had denounced the amendment as an effort to curb desegregation and had voted against it, the provision might be construed very differently. Thus the liberals may have changed the law by their attitude and behavior toward it. Indeed, influencing the interpretations of votes, proposals, and laws is one of the most important functions of political debates. Whether a vote is or is not seen as a test of strength, whether a proposal is taken as a defeat for one side, whether a position is believed to be moderate or extreme, usually depends in part on what each side chooses to say. In a related way, Woodrow Wilson was able to remove the anti-administration implications of the drive for national military preparedness in 1914-1917 by adopting the program as his own. [Robert Osgood, *Ideals and Self-interest in America's Foreign Relations* (Chicago: University of Chicago Press, 1953), 205.] These tactics can also be seen in the light of William Riker's argument that the smallest possible winning coalition is of maximum value to its members. Members of larger coalitions may thus try to expel some of the other members of the coalition. (Riker, *The Theory of Political Coalitions*, 54-76.) An appropriate counter-tactic at times will be for those members to refuse to leave, as the cases cited here illustrate.

178

though the substance of the Soviet demand was almost completely irrelevant. If the Russians had asked the United States to change the color of its postage stamps the problem would have been essentially the same. The United States seemed to assume that the interpretations that would be made were unalterable givens. While it is probably true that there would be *some* undesired inferences drawn from any American concessions, it is not clear that there was nothing that could have been done to minimize this. Kennedy could have publicly explained that the bases were obsolete and their removal represented such a slight loss that this did not show that the United States would sacrifice significant values under Soviet pressure. The fact that the decision to dismantle these bases had been made previously could have been stressed and the hesitancy of the bureaucracy to carry out Kennedy's original decision could have been pointed to as another example of the problem, familiar to all great powers, of maintaining central control over the details of policy. That the American decision-makers were unwilling to consider such action when it was believed it provided a way out of an extremely dangerous situation shows on the one hand the high price states are willing to pay to have a given interpretation of an interaction accepted even if the substance is unimportant and, on the other hand, the lack of consideration given to alternative means of affecting interpretations.

Coupling and Decoupling of Signals and Indices

Although there are important differences between the coupling and decoupling of indices and the coupling and decoupling of signals,[9] the two processes serve many of the same purposes and have a great deal in common. Actors can make substantial probes while protecting their images in the event that others react in undesired ways; actors can discourage others from taking certain actions by claiming that such behavior will unfavorably alter the actor's image of the other; and they create or avoid challenges.

[9] See below, 183-85.

179

Actors can use the possibility of decoupling to supply some protection when they take actions that may be seen as contradicting the image they desire. And, as in signaling, they may choose a course of action partly because they will be able to influence the interpretations made about it after others' initial reactions are observed. An aggressive state that wishes to launch an armed probe into a neighboring territory may first encourage others to believe its military is not under complete control. If the probe is thrown back or other nations seem ready to take actions not in the first state's interest (e.g. vast increases in defense budget, strengthening of alliances, retaliation) the first state can plausibly claim the attack was the result of unauthorized action by a segment of the military. If, on the other hand, it succeeds it can be acknowledged as under official control. Thus in 1932 it was easier for the Peruvian government to allow a private military force to seize a piece of Colombian territory claimed by Peru than it would have been to have ordered the Peruvian army to take this action.[10] Today the Arab governments do not carry out raids against Israel with their armies but rather utilize civilian groups the governments can claim they do not, and indeed cannot, control. Labor unions similarly try to utilize wildcat strikes. Defining the situation in this way makes retreats less costly and makes it less likely that others will see the actor as aggressive.[11]

[10] Bryce Wood, *The United States and Latin American Wars* (New York: Columbia University Press, 1966), 175-76. However, as the Peruvians learned, there is a possible cost involved here aside from the obvious one that others may see the actor as so weak that no bargains with him are possible. Secretary of State Stimson apparently believed the Peruvian claim that the government was not supporting the armed band and thus his "first moves were less cautiously made than if he had anticipated that a serious international dispute might arise." (*Ibid.,* 183.)

[11] An additional advantage to the state of having its adversary believe a military expedition is not under government control is that the adversary is less likely to believe that sanctions against the actor will be effective. This, plus the fact that the adversary will be seen as escalating the conflict if he employs official violence, decreases the probability of retaliation. However, decoupling by offering this ex-

Alternatively, the state may offer special, limited reasons for undertaking hostile actions that might otherwise be seen to have far-reaching implications. To the extent that these explanations are plausible others will resist the state's initiatives less because they will not fear they are a prelude to further undesired actions and that conceding will be taken as an index of weakness. Furthermore, if others do resist, the state will be able to retreat with less damage to its image. It is probably for these reasons that when the Russians began the blockade of Berlin they did not claim they intended to drive the Allies from the city, but rather that "technical difficulties" necessitated the closing of the autobahn and railways. They even drilled holes in a bridge to demonstrate the need for closing the autobahn.[12] "They announced that, following an investigation, two high-ranking German railway officials had been fired for allowing the right-of-way to fall into a state of disrepair."[13] Similarly, during the harassment preceding the blockade "interference with freight was usually justified by 'technical reasons' or on the grounds that shipments were improperly labelled; individual Germans were prevented from traveling through the Soviet zone because allegedly their interzonal passes were not in order or they were engaging in 'speculation.' "[14] When the Soviet representatives walked out of the four-power Kommandatura that governed Berlin "they did so allegedly because Colonel Howley [the American representative whose deputy had remained in the meeting] had departed first. These justifications were often trivial or even ridiculous, but they left the way open for retreat without sacrifice of principle, if retreat should be desirable."[15]

---

planation makes it easier for the adversary to move directly against the "unofficial" groups that have initiated the violence.

[12] *Documented Chronology on Political Developments Regarding Germany* (U.S. Office of Military Government for Germany, 1949), xvii. I am grateful to William R. Harris for calling this to my attention.

[13] W. Phillips Davison, *The Berlin Blockade* (Princeton: Princeton University Press, 1958) 127.

[14] *Ibid.*, 65.   [15] *Ibid.*, 71.

These attempts to limit others' resistance and leave open an avenue of retreat by providing explanations of your actions that minimize the chances they will be seen as indices of undesired intentions should be distinguished from the related tactic of dividing a major action up into small steps. Each step is less apt to call forth violent opposition and, if need be, the actor can stop at any point and leave others in doubt as to whether he had ever intended to proceed further. Thus in the months before the Berlin Wall was erected, East Germany gradually restricted travel between the two halves of Berlin.[16] Although the East Germans probed cautiously, proceeding step by step, they generally did not offer special and limited explanations for each of their actions. Thus they did not attempt to gain the added influence and protection provided by getting the adversary to accept a desired interpretation of these indices.[17]

As in the decoupling of signals, it is easy to characterize these efforts as a desire to "save face." But the purpose of these tactics is to project or protect an image at variance with possible and undesired interpretations of the actor's behavior. If the results of these tactics are only to reduce embarrassment by not openly acknowledging an interpretation of an actor's behavior that others are making, then the predictions others make will not be affected and little of value will have been accomplished.

The actor's desire to have his adversary accept his interpretation of indices should also not be confused with attempts to score propaganda victories with uncommitted audiences. Often there are conflicts between the images

[16] Jean Edward Smith, *The Defense of Berlin* (Baltimore: Johns Hopkins Press, 1963), 258-59.

[17] One exception occurred in early August when "the East German Ministry of Health officially requested the government to suspend all travel between East and West Germany, including West Berlin, because of what it contended was a polio epidemic then raging in West Germany. With complete seriousness the Health Ministry suggested that West Germany's other neighbors were about to do likewise and that such a move was necessary to insure the well-being of the GDR." (*Ibid.*, 260.)

182

required for these two goals. For example, a state may gain some public acclaim if it is believed that it was the "protector of the peace" in a crisis. But the state may want to disavow that title in order to convince others that it was and is willing to go to war rather than make concessions.

The desire to score propaganda victories may also conflict with the perception you wish your adversary to have of your interpretation of his behavior. Thus after the USSR broke the moratorium on nuclear tests in September 1961, the United States in effect had to decide what image of its interpretations of the Soviet action it wanted to project to the Soviets. If the Americans felt that because of the dangers of Soviet exploitation and domestic opposition it could not enter into another moratorium, it should have made definite efforts to forestall the possibility that the Russians would, as indeed they later did, try to obtain consent to other moratoriums. To do this the United States would have had to stress that it now felt that moratoriums did not sufficiently commit a state's reputation. It could have argued that there were great differences between a treaty and a moratorium in this respect. Otherwise the arguments against another moratorium (i.e. that the Soviet action showed that she could not be trusted) could be used with equal validity against entering into a treaty with her, a goal the United States presumably still sought. To make the largest propaganda gains, on the other hand, the United States would have had to stress how deceitful Russia had been. This would have meant arguing that she had broken an extremely important pledge, one little different from a formal treaty. In fact, the United States seems to have followed no carefully thought-out policy about what images of its interpretations it wanted accepted and the Russians were able to create difficulties for the United States by continuing to argue and win support for further moratoriums.

Compared with signals, the coupling and decoupling of indices involves greater rewards and difficulties. Coupling and decoupling of indices provides a higher payoff if successful because it involves the attaching or detaching of motives and explanations to an actor's behavior in such a way that he can influence others' perceptions of the most important aspects of his image (e.g. whether he is aggressive, has high resolve, etc.). The coupling and decoupling of signals, on the other hand, influences the actors' signaling reputations or uses these reputations to induce desired behavior. Thus when an actor decouples as he retreats from a previous commitment, he can at best see to it that his adversary does not doubt his word any more than he has in the past. But the actor cannot stop the adversary from taking this new position as an index to how he will act in the future. However if the actor could decouple the index, his adversary would not draw any undesired conclusions from his behavior. For example, even if America was able to decouple its signals about the reciprocation required before the bombing would be stopped in Vietnam by convincing others that it had never demanded an end to high rates of infiltration, Hanoi could still take the American willingness to stop the bombing without such a major reciprocation as an index to its intention of being conciliatory on the main issues in the war. To do more than save its signaling reputation the United States would have to convince the North that a willingness to halt the bombing without getting much in return was not typical of how it would act in the future.

The coupling of indices also changes the incentives to and pressures on the actor differently than does the coupling of signals. Actor A can alter B's behavior if A can convince him that certain of his actions are indices to characteristics and intentions he does not want A to think he has. Here A does not claim he believes B has given a signal or that B necessarily wants to convey an impression, but rather that he would see the action as part of a wider pattern of B's increasing hostility and that he would therefore have to reply in kind. Thus in the summer of 1968 the United

States tried to convince the USSR that undertaking large-scale deployment of advanced ICBMs would be seen by the United States as an index showing that the Soviets had no real interest in an agreement on missile limitation.[18]

[18] William Beecher, "U.S. Aides Eager on Missile Talks," *New York Times*, July 3, 1968, p. 12. Interestingly enough, Secretary of Defense Clifford denied that the Soviets would be justified in taking a continued American program to build a missile defense system as an index that the United States was not serious about negotiating a missile freeze. (Joseph Loftus, "Clifford to Meet Saigon's Leaders," *New York Times*, July 12, 1968, p. 7). When the question of deployment was reopened in the early months of the Nixon Administration, the head of the Arms Control and Disarmament Agency repeated this claim, bolstering it with the argument that since the Soviets had not objected to the initial American announcement of the intention to deploy the system, there was no reason "to think that a decision to resume such deployment . . . would . . . prejudice the prospects of strategic arms limitation talks." (John Finney, "Nixon Aide Denies Sentinel Imperils Atom Arms Talks," *New York Times*, March 7, 1969, p. 2). Six days later, however, the Soviet government warned that deployment of the ABM might hamper arms control talks. (Bernard Gwertzman, "Moscow Suggests Sentinel Could Hamper Arms Talk," *New York Times*, March 13, 1969.)

The American position is especially ironic since while the Soviets have been insisting that ABM's would not destabilize the strategic balance and have opposed limitations of these "defensive" weapons, they have deployed them only around Moscow. The United States has argued that ABM's are more destabilizing than ICBM's, has urged that both sides refrain from building them, and has plans to install a larger system. In early 1969 the United States government claimed this odd Soviet behavior was explained by purely technical considerations—i.e. the desire to procure a more effective system that led the Soviets to delay deployment until new radars and missiles were ready.

While there is no evidence as to what inferences the Soviets would draw from the American deployment, it is interesting that several Senators have said that they would take a decision by the Nixon Administration as an index to the President's general orientation toward the arms race and the balance between domestic and foreign policy needs. Thus Senator Mansfield said that a decision to deploy an ABM system "can only be seen as a continuance of the practices and priorities of the past [and would mean that] we are not going to shift gears despite the serious inner difficulties which loom ahead." (John Finney, "Congress Awaits Key Nixon Choice on ABM This Week," *New York Times*, March 10, 1969, p. 25.) Senator Kennedy made a similar claim at hearings on the Sentinel by arguing that "we are at a crossroads in foreign and domestic policy." (John Finney, "Nixon is Delaying Missile Decision; Opposition Rises," *New*

It should be noted that while it is easier for A to make a plausible case that he sees B's action as an index (whether he actually does or not) if the action has some direct impact on both actors, the value of the action to B must not be as great as continued good relations with A or else it will be seen as worth taking regardless of the possible deleterious effects to B's image. An example of a successful coupling of this kind is provided by an incident during the discussions in the 1920s between Germany and the USSR about problems resulting partly from Soviet support of the German Communist party. "*Pravda* warned that any inclination by Germany to identify the Comintern with the Soviet government, as the British had [before they broke off relations], would be judged a sign that Germany was closing ranks against the USSR."[19] Germany found this plausible and did not risk pressing the issue.

Coupling of indices of the adversary's behavior will have less payoff than coupling of signals when the actor performs these operations to convince his adversary that he believes the adversary will soon make a concession. When signals are successfully coupled for this purpose the adversary not only believes the actor is apt to stand firm in the expectation that the adversary will offer a concession, but the adversary will feel he will damage his signaling reputation by not offering one. When indices are coupled the reputation for living up to one's word is not involved, and the only added pressure on the adversary to give in is created by the belief that the actor will be more likely to stand firm in the expectation that a concession is forthcoming. When an actor wants to try to get the other side to act in a given way by coupling indices he will be able to exert pressure if the adversary believes the actor would see the desired behavior as an index of the other side's friendship.

York Times, March 12, 1969, p. 2.) This stance clearly seems to have been designed to increase the domestic political costs to the Nixon Administration of deciding to proceed with the ABM system.

[19] Dyck, *Weimar Germany* . . . , 200.

Coupling and decoupling of indices is usually more difficult than coupling and decoupling of signals because while signals derive their meanings from conventions that can be broken by either party, indices have meanings regardless of whether the actors are trying to convey a message. However only in some cases will an actor be completely sure an aspect of the other's behavior is an index, and what conclusions to draw from it. Only a few major actions, such as the launching of an all-out attack, are completely self-explanatory. In many other cases, ambiguity is high and the actor may be uncertain as to what inferences to draw. Are another state's military preparations offensive or defensive? Will state A's takeover of area B leave it sated or are future aggressions to be expected? Does the fact that state C refused to defend state D mean it will stand aside in the future? The answers to these questions are an important determinant of states' foreign policies, and they are rarely easy for decision-makers to arrive at.

The Likelihood of Successful Coupling and Decoupling

The timing, the objects, and the direction of the coupling and decoupling affect the room for maneuvering. First, decoupling will be more likely to succeed if the actor starts trying to influence the interpretations the other is making of his behavior in a specific incident quite early, before the other has firmly arrived at his own view of the situation. If the actor quickly and consistently puts forth his version of the events, others may come to see this as the natural and obvious explanation. However if the others have an opportunity to first arrive at their own conclusions, the actor's view will have to compete with an established image that will be difficult to dislodge. Speed and consistency are especially important in decoupling when the actor wants to make his adversary believe he does not feel a given issue on which he is retreating is important. It is hard for an actor who first resists making a concession to later claim that he gave up nothing of significance.

187

If he succumbs to the temptation of first spending a significant amount of resources on the issue in the hope that the other side will retreat and then tries to disengage when the costs become disproportionate to the specific dispute, he may gain the worst of both worlds. The actor will have difficulty convincing his opponent that his behavior is not related to his resolve on other, more important, questions. However a stark refusal to become involved in an issue may convincingly be claimed to show that the actor regards it as distinctly separate from the other matters. Challenges ignored from the start may thus have little impact on the actor's image.

Second, coupling and decoupling will be easier when the actor needs only to persuade the other that he believes the version of events he sets forth, rather than persuading the other that the version is objectively correct. Thus it is usually easier for X to convince Y that X believes Y acted out of certain motives or that X believes Y's actions had certain impact than for X to convince Y that certain events actually occurred. Thus the United States might be able to convince the Soviets that it had certain motives in deploying an ABM system, but would not be able to convince them that an ABM system had been deployed when in fact it had not been, or vice versa. The fact that in most cases the actor need only convince others that he holds a certain view of the situation often makes coupling and decoupling viable strategies.

Third, it is easier to couple and decouple if the evidence is ambiguous. If an actor wants to claim he believes he won a conflict, others are more apt to believe the actor thinks this, and that it is correct, if the outcome was not overwhelmingly against him. A state that wants to ignore the challenge presented by another's interference in its internal affairs can more easily do this if the interference is subtle and carefully disguised than if it is obvious. Since the evidence about motivation is usually especially ambiguous, this is a frequent target for coupling and decoupling.

Fourth, coupling and decoupling work best when the

188

effect is to preserve, rather than change, the other's image of the actor. In these cases the attempts to influence interpretations will be reinforced instead of counteracted by the strong pressures toward maintenance of images. In circumstances like the Cold War in which the actors have a healthy respect for each others' resolve, it is often possible, as I will discuss in greater detail in the next section, to couple and decouple indices in a way that permits the great powers to avoid challenges without greatly damaging their images.

However, even under the most favorable circumstances the use of these techniques involves risks and uncertainties because of the difficulties in knowing how the other perceives what the actor is doing and what the unintended consequences of the actor's conscious attempts to influence this image will be. This is true partly because the explanations given by the actors, however plausible, are but one of the factors that influence the interpretations of indices others make. A great deal is out of the control of the actor trying to project the desired image. Indices often seem to point mainly in one direction and basic modifications cannot be produced by explanations. A state that attacks several of its neighbors will be thought to be aggressive, and a state that consistently avoids taking firm stands will not be able to convince others it really has great resolve. The interpretations of behavior on issues clearly considered important by both sides cannot be basically altered. For example, the United States could not hope to decouple a retreat from Germany under Soviet pressure from others' image of American resolve and values.

Although bounds on the possibilities of influencing interpretations of indices cannot be clearly established in general, these limits are ultimately set by the difficulty of affecting—and even of knowing about—the processes by which others draw inferences about an actor's behavior. The actor must always set his policies in this area by his estimates of what the others' perceptions are and how these perceptions can be influenced by the actor's behavior and explanations.

189

If an actor believes others will take his behavior as an index to a certain undesired intention and that he cannot alter this interpretation, he can only abstain from the behavior or project the undesired image. Furthermore, if others think he realizes this, his attempts at decoupling are even less likely to succeed. Thus the claim made by the Iraqi delegate to the UN, who resigned shortly after the international furor caused by his country's hanging alleged spies, that he had resigned for personal reasons, not as a protest, may be viewed skeptically by observers.[20] They will be especially apt not to believe his claims if they think that he took his action knowing that he probably would not be believed. In that case he probably would not resign unless he were willing to have others see his action as a protest.

However, the costs and limits of coupling and decoupling should not lead us to ignore the degree of leeway actors have or the possibilities of furthering their interests by affecting the inferences others draw from their actions. Since most scholars seem to assume that this leeway does not exist, it seems appropriate here to focus on the possibilities rather than on the limits.

Decoupling and Avoiding Challenges

One of the most interesting and important aspects of decoupling is the possibility it provides for avoiding challenges. Schelling argues this cannot be done: "unlike those sociable games it takes two to play, with chicken it takes two *not* to play. If you are . . . invited to play chicken and say you would rather not, you have just played."[21] This is often true. If state A indicates it will take B's action, or

[20] Drew Middleton, "Iraq's Delegate at U.N. Resigns," *New York Times*, January 30, 1969. President Johnson's decision to remove General Westmoreland from command in Vietnam and make him Army Chief of Staff, coming as it did in the middle of what was known to the public to be a major internal debate on Vietnam policy, can be interpreted similarly. See the discussion in Hedrick Smith et al., "The Vietnam Policy Reversal of '68-II," *New York Times*, March 7, 1969, p. 14.

[21] Schelling, *Arms and Influence*, 118. Emphasis in the original.

190

inaction, in a given situation as an index and B makes no effort to convince A not to draw such inferences, it indeed cannot avoid the game. However, B may be able to persuade A not to attribute the original meaning to B's behavior, or even not to draw any inferences at all from the action. If it can do this, it can "opt out" of the challenge aspects of the situation.

As we pointed out earlier in this chapter, decoupling is more apt to succeed if attempted from the start. This is especially true with efforts to avoid a challenge. Only if the actor is careful not to begin to take up the challenge are his later efforts at decoupling apt to seem something other than an obvious misrepresentation of the actor's actual views. The West, for example, does not seem to have suffered from its failure to aid Tibet from the Chinese attack in the fall of 1950. And if the United States was willing in 1968 to apologize to North Korea to secure the release of the Pueblo's crew and thought that such a step would be effective, it could have lowered the price of doing so by making the apology almost immediately, before it came to be seen as a major issue. The apology would then probably have been seen as the natural and expected thing a compassionate state would do to protect its captured men, not as a retreat on a meaningful question. Furthermore, the explanations offered by the United States for its apology could have influenced the inferences drawn. By stressing the not unreasonable view that it was merely doing what any sensible state would do in this situation, the United States could have made it less likely that issuing the apology would damage its image. Since the United States resisted giving an apology for a considerable length of time, the alternative tactic of repudiating the apology as it was being given was necessary.

However Boulding's argument that an actor challenged to chicken can go blithely "off on a side road" and "refuse to play the game"[22] cannot be accepted without serious

[22] Anthony de Reuck and Julie Knight, eds., *Conflict in Society* (Boston: Little, Brown, 1966), 298.

191

qualifications. The actor must always estimate the impact of his behavior on other actors' images of him, a point which Boulding, ironically enough the author of a book entitled *The Image*, slights. Thus it should be realized that decoupling will not successfully avoid challenges under all circumstances, and that it almost always involves significant risks and costs. Especially when faced with an adversary who will continually try to create challenges, these costs may outweigh the potential gains of decoupling. But if a series of challenges is not expected, or if the test is posed on an issue that places the actor at a relative disadvantage, decoupling may be appropriate.

Many of the specific tactics for avoiding challenges by decoupling can also be used to reach other goals, and so they will be discussed later rather than being singled out for attention in this context. What is important here is the general point that an actor can avoid playing chicken by convincing the other that he has not heard the invitation, that his car is not working, or that he does not care about the game and that his refusal does not indicate anything about how he will behave in matters he feels are important. In the teenage subculture that actually plays chicken, the latter may be impossible since how one plays the game is automatically taken as an index of the important qualities. In international relations, however, the linkages between many challenges and a state's vital interests are less clear and immutable. By advancing their versions of their own motives and perceptions of others' behavior, it is often within the power of actors to control whether disputes are taken as indices of resolve and predictors of behavior on a wide range of important issues.

From this perspective we can see the United States may have been able to reduce the degree to which its failure to come to the aid of the Pueblo was taken as an index of general American unwillingness to use force against provocation by claiming that the only airplanes within range of the ship were armed with nuclear weapons and thus were clearly unsuited for combat. The armament could not be changed quickly enough to permit an attack that could have saved the Pueblo, but it could be changed quickly enough to allow response to any future North Korean move. Thus the United States can imply that it is indeed willing to play chicken, but that its car was not working at the time of the last challenge. A somewhat more unfavorable image would accrue if it was believed that although some of the available aircraft were conventionally armed the United States knew these would have been overwhelmed by the larger North Korean air force. Failure to rise to the challenge under these conditions might make the adversary believe he could succeed in further adventures as long as he retained military superiority. However, by increasing its air force in Korea (as has in fact been done), the United States could decrease the number of instances in which the North Koreans could expect to repeat the balance of forces that prevailed in the Pueblo incident. The most damaging image of the United States would have been produced if it were believed that the American failure to respond was based not on calculations of the probable outcome of an air battle, but rather on the fear of escalation. Under these circumstances the United States would have been seen to refuse to play chicken because of general lack of resolve and there would be no reason for others to believe that, even if the local balance of forces were altered, the Americans would play in the future. Thus the American claims that it had only a few planes available, and those few armed with nuclear weapons, served an important function. Indeed a country that thought its adversary might engage in limited provocations to which it did not want to respond could try to decrease the damage to its image by making sure that it was physically not able to react.

In other cases actors can avoid challenges by deciding where lines will be drawn and how ambiguous these lines will be. While actors will draw firm lines if they think it will deter their opponents, they will avoid doing this if they believe deterrence may be ineffective and do not want to have to pay the price of fulfilling their threats. Thus one

193

reason English leaders did not want to reach a formal agreement with Russia in the 1880s on the boundaries of Russia's territory in Central Asia was that "the danger of conflict would actually be increased [by such an agreement] since the violation of a fixed and recognized border could not be lightly ignored."[23]

When actors engage in disputes over matters of low intrinsic value to them they are apt to create "tests of strength" in which their behavior will be taken as an index to their capability and resolve. An actor who wishes to avoid such a test, for example because he feels raising tensions will make solutions on the major issues harder to reach or because he is better able to stand firm on the major issue, can attempt to decouple the minor issue. When the test ban negotiations opened "it took an informal, off-the-record meeting lasting three hours . . . to achieve agreement on the title of the conference. Even after that the parties disputed the meaning of the title, 'The Conference on the Discontinuance of Nuclear Weapons Tests.' The United States held that discontinuance meant 'suspension' while the Soviet Union interpreted it as meaning essentially 'cessation.' There was more to the dispute than mere semantics, a basic issue was at stake, the question of whether a test cessation would or would not be permanent and unconditional, and both sides sought to have the title reflect their position."[24] While the issue clearly was real, the connection between the title of the conference and each side's image of the other's intentions and resolve—which presumably would influence the outcome—is not so clear. Either actor might have been able to prevent the other from drawing unwanted inferences from a retreat on this question by announcing that any title was acceptable because it would bear no relation to the matters to be discussed or the substantive concessions the actor would make.

It may also be possible to decouple the disputes about agenda common in East-West negotiations. The United

[23] Greaves, *Persia and the Defence of India*, 104.
[24] Jacobson and Stein, *Diplomats . . .* , 116-17.

States might publicly declare a policy of making maximum concessions on the agenda consistent with allowing discussion of matters of importance to it. Even if the Soviet Union at first continued to treat this as an index, the United States might produce decoupling if in several meetings there were great disparities between these agenda concessions and American tenacity on substantive issues. A state may similarly be able to decouple the acceptance of a proposal "as a basis for discussion" from its final position. This would allow the actor to get to the substance of the issues without damaging his image.

Since there is apt to be significant conflict in these cases, opposition to decoupling will be frequent. The actor who is taking certain behavior as an index (or who wishes to claim he is) can refuse to acknowledge the other's tactics and imply that he is still attributing special meaning to the behavior. Each side will then be faced with the problem of how to act in the situation and what inferences to draw from the other's behavior. For example, assume the United States has tried the tactics mentioned above in connection with the Soviet demand to include certain items on the agenda of conferences. When this issue arises at any given meeting the United States has to decide whether its decoupling campaign has been successful. For if it has not, and if the United States plans to stand firm on the more important issues, it would be unwise to comply with the Soviet demand. If the United States acquiesces, the Russians then have to judge whether the action has implications for future American behavior. They have to decide whether the American disavowals were misleading, and, as we saw in connection with the decoupling of signals, this in turn depends partly on whether they think the United States thought its decoupling was successful. The United States, of course, presumably would have based its action on how it believed the Russians would trace through this elusive calculation.

The conflict over whether a bit of behavior should be considered an index can continue after the behavior is over,

195

with both sides proclaiming their contradicting interpretations. As was pointed out in the discussion of the functions of ambiguity, except for the rare cases in which an actor makes a major decision on the basis of his first analysis of the other's behavior, what matters are the relatively final, or at least delayed, inferences the actor draws. Thus the adversary is apt to try to convince the actor that he did not believe the latter's decoupling claims and that the behavior was seen as an index that the actor would make concessions on the substantive issues. If the adversary believes this he will be more apt to stand firm, and if the actor believes that the adversary believes it, the actor will be more likely to make greater concessions.

Avoiding a game of chicken is often part of the process of an actor's defining for others, and perhaps for himself, what he sees as areas of vital interest. While some matters will seem to be clearly included or excluded because of past behavior or expectations about how any state in a particular situation will act, for many issues the actor's claims are one of the most important factors determining whether others believe the actor sees the issue as important and whether they take his behavior concerning it as an index to the way he will act on other issues. For example, although the American willingness to allow its adversaries to construct the Berlin Wall and end almost all aspects of four-power control in East Berlin presumably lowered the Soviet perception of American resolve,[25] the American efforts to decouple the fate of East Berlin from that of West Berlin probably decreased the damage that was done. As one commentator notes, "during the latter part of July and early August, the Western powers had been exceptionally careful to identify their position in the former German capital only

[25] It is commonly believed that this incident contributed to Khrushchev's belief that the United States would not resist a Soviet attempt to put missiles in Cuba. While this argument is certainly plausible, there is little direct evidence supporting it. Several events in 1961, including the Bay of Pigs, the retreat in Laos, the Vienna Summit Conference, and the Berlin Wall probably all helped develop this image.

with its western sectors."[26] In his major address of July 25, President Kennedy referred not to the defense of Western rights in Berlin, but to the protection of West Berlin.[27] Major figures in the Administration, including the President, referred to the problems the flow of refugees was creating for East Germany and the USSR without implying that an attempt to close the Berlin border would be seen as an infringement on the four-power agreements and thus as affecting important American interests. After the Wall was constructed, the Allies' protests were late and mild. The United States told its adversaries and allies that the "heart of the matter" (the phrase is Rusk's) was free access to West Berlin, the right to keep Western troops there, and the economic and political viability of the city.[28] Critics have charged, with some validity, that this definition of our interests invited the Communists to seal off the Eastern sector. However if the United States believed the pressures on the Soviets to carry out such a move were very great and that they might do it even if the West tried to deter them, the United States could have felt that it should trade a degree of protection of the four-power rights in the East to decouple the fates of the two halves of the city. To the extent the Soviets believed American statements reflected its definition of its own interests, they would be less likely to take American passivity to the building of the Wall as an index to American unwillingness to fight for West Berlin. By making the plausible claim that the flow of refugees was not included in the "heart of the matter" the United States reduced the costs of a retreat on the former question.

Alternative Explanations for Retreats

When challenges cannot be avoided an actor who would rather make concessions than play chicken can mitigate the effect on his image by influencing others' interpretations of his behavior and convincing them not to take his retreat as

[26] Smith, *The Defense of Berlin*, 265.
[27] *Ibid.*, 250.   [28] *Ibid.*, 293, 297, 300-1.

197

an index to his lack of resolve. Four specific kinds of claims can be made to accomplish this goal. When none of them can be plausibly made, the actor still has a choice as to the underlying factors to which he will attribute his behavior. First, he can try to limit the inferences drawn by isolating his behavior from other issues by claiming that special circumstances explain his actions. This could be related to unusual features of the international situation (e.g. the state's being taken by surprise, the pressing need of allies to avoid a conflict). Alternatively, special domestic factors may be claimed to have caused the behavior. Thus the state could explain that the concessions either were not authorized at the highest levels[29] (but would not be retracted lest the actor seem guilty of bad faith) or were the result of a temporary internal coalition. However, the state not only has to present convincing evidence that its explanation is correct, but also has to show that these special circumstances would not be apt to recur. Thus if the domestic factors mentioned above had been asserted to have been responsible for the retreat in one case, the people responsible for the "unauthorized" actions would have to be demoted and, in the other case, there would have to be a reshuffling of high level officials to show that the coalition that had made the concessions no longer was in control.

Second, sometimes an actor can claim to have made a major concession only because he expected his adversary to reciprocate in the future, thus eventually establishing a fair trade. The actor may then even exaggerate the value of the concession he has made. This occurs most frequently in structured negotiations that are influenced by norms holding that neither side should have to make all, or nearly all, the concessions. But when the actor has retreated in a particular conflict (e.g. withdrawn a claim to a disputed territory) rather than reduced a demand in negotiations, it will usually be hard to claim to expect later reciproca-

[29] For related examples, see any discussion of the Hoar-Laval Agreement and the case cited in Herbert Feis, *Three International Episodes* (New York: W. W. Norton, 1946), 245.

198

tion unless some ambiguous hints have been given by the other side.

Third, when an actor retreats on an issue that has not been a major source of conflict over an extended period of time, he may be able to decouple his action as an index to his power and resolve by explaining that he never regarded the issue as particularly important, did not realize that the other side felt strongly about the matter, and was not trying to engage in a test of wills. However, the actor must be able to provide criteria that differentiate the issue he retreated on from other issues lest his adversary infer that he does not care about them either.

The fourth type of claim the actor can make is that he retreated because he had a certain image of the adversary (e.g. that he thought this was the last demand the adversary would make). Claims of this sort will be discussed in greater detail later because not only are they useful for reaching goals other than covering retreats, but because they reveal a further important range of choice a state has in portraying its view of the world and its reasons for acting as it did.

When none of these tactics can be used, the actor will have to imply that he made the concessions because of the justice of the other side's case or because of the relative power positions of the actors. It can be argued on the one hand that the former explanation saves face and can be used to build generally agreed-upon principles or, on the other hand, that this is usually hypocritical and that states should rather acknowledge the "realistic" determinants of international behavior lest they forget the importance of power and place their faith in insubstantial instruments. But these considerations are apt to be less important to the decision-maker than the image of his state he wants others to hold. What the substance of this image will be depends largely on his goals and his analysis of the international situation. If he feels he cannot easily alter the distribution of power or resolve, and if the dispute in which he made his retreat is clearly different from other issues about which he feels strongly, he will probably want to convince others that he acted largely out of his beliefs about the merits of the case. He will claim not to have made a concession, but to have acted justly. Others are then less apt to believe his concessions indicate he will retreat under pressure in other cases involving different principles. Thus, before the construction of the Berlin Wall Senator Fulbright claimed that allowing the Communists to halt the refugee flow would not be an index of American weakness, but would merely be following a recognized principle—and one which had no other applications against American interest. "I don't understand why the East Germans don't close their border because I think they have a right to close it. So why is this a great concession?"[30] In this light it can be seen that those Englishmen who in the debate over Munich argued that Britain had acted as she did not because of the legitimacy of the German demands but because of her weakness may have had the unfortunate effect of reinforcing in the Germans' minds the belief that Britain would not fight to prevent Nazi domination of Europe.[31] Of course the adversary in this situation may make opposite claims. If B thinks that A thinks that B behaved as he did because of the pressure A was exerting, B will be more apt to believe that A will stand firm in future disputes in the belief that B will repeat his behavior pattern.[32] Thus when Cornell University sold its stock in banks that lent money to the Union of South Africa, an action which militant students had demanded, the stu-

[30] Quoted in Smith, *The Defense of Berlin*, 260.

[31] This is not to claim that anything could have basically altered Hitler's image of Britain at this late date. Furthermore, to have had Hitler believe that Britain thought his demands on Czechoslovakia were just would have been a mixed blessing. He might have been deterred from attacks on non-German territory, but would have been encouraged to expect Britain's cooperation in regaining Danzig and the Polish corridor.

[32] Indeed when B acts in accord with A's desires, A is in fact likely to overestimate the degree to which his actions caused B's response (Jervis, "Hypotheses on Misperception," 476-7) and if B realizes this he will be more likely to believe that A's claim is an accurate representation of his perceptions.

dents denied the university's claim that this transaction was based on "purely financial" considerations and said they had won a "clear victory." While the desire to gain prestige may be partly responsible for the competing claims, the outcome of future confrontations is apt to be influenced by the degree to which each side can convince the other that it believes its version of the events.[33]

If, on the other hand, the actor who retreated feels he can increase his power or resolve and if it is very difficult to distinguish the substance of the issue on which he retreated from a number of others on which he hopes to prevail, he should argue that he only made concessions because he had to and should deny the justice of his adversary's demand. Thus in the future when he has rectified the distribution of power and resolve others will be more likely to believe that he will stand firm.

Victory Claims

In those cases when the outcome is not clear, an actor may claim he has won a victory whether or not he actually believes this to be true. Although the desire to impress domestic audiences, allies, and neutrals is well-known, we are here concerned only with the effects on the adversary. The actor often will want his opponent to think that he thinks he won because the opponent is then more apt to believe the actor will behave similarly in the future. This impression will deter the adversary if the actor's actions had exacted a high price from him in the previous interaction.

This is an application of the well-known bargaining tactic of misrepresenting the gains and losses an actor feels will accrue from alternative policies. If actor A can convince B

[33] "Cornell Head Learns a Bit Late of Sale of Controversial Stock," *New York Times*, March 10, 1969, p. 37. It should be noted that since only the University can know the reasons for its decisions, it could believe it acted on purely economic considerations and simultaneously think the militants believed it had given in to their pressure. The students, however, could not believe their version of the events and still believe the University believed its version.

that if B adopts a certain policy, A will believe it in his interest to respond in a way that exacts a high price from B, B may be deterred from undertaking that policy. This makes it in A's interest to claim he feels that the last time he made a similar response the gains outweighed the losses. Thus, for example, even if the Soviets felt their invasion of Czechoslovakia was a mistake it would be in their interest to make the opposite assertion to deter other East European countries from trying to assert their independence. And the American habit of claiming as victories what are actually defeats may not be a national delusion.[34]

On the other hand, convincing the other side that one regards what is really a defeat as a victory entails a danger. The other side may then believe that the first will accept resolutions of other disputes along the lines of the previous settlement rather than engage in a mutually costly conflict. Thus a union might decrease its bargaining position for the next round of negotiations if after a strike in which it agreed to a much smaller raise than it had expected, it convinced management that it regarded this settlement as a victory. For then management could plausibly expect that labor would accept a similar raise without a strike when the contract was renegotiated and labor would find it difficult to lead management to believe that it would strike unless it received a better offer.

Claims of victory wildly at variance with the facts will usually be thought to be merely an attempt to "save face." Alternatively, those actors not involved in the agreement may suspect that it is a "cover" for another part of the bargain which is being kept secret. This will be true even if the actor really believed he received adequate concessions for what he gave up. For example, when "Germany exchanged part of her African possessions for the Island of Helgoland .... [nobody] in Europe could believe that such a bad bargain had actually been made in good faith [as it really

---

[34] For such a claim, see the remarks of Daniel Ellsberg in Richard Pfeffer, ed., *No More Vietnams?* (New York: Harper and Row, 1968), 113.

was]; everyone assumed that England had secretly agreed to join the Triple Alliance."[35]

Furthermore, when acting as he did has involved a high cost to a third party the actor may not be able to forthrightly claim that he will behave similarly in the future. For example, if after a few years the Viet Cong is completely beaten but South Vietnam is crippled, the United States might not find it profitable to claim that it will use the same tactics in case of guerrilla wars in other states since those states could feel that the cure was worse than the disease. The United States would then want to project an ambiguous image of its perceptions of the previous war, hoping that the insurgents and their sponsors would be deterred by the possibility of a similar reaction but that the target countries would not be frightened into accommodations with the native or foreign Communists against American interests.

Irrespective of his intentions, an actor who cannot claim a defeat to be a victory will try to discourage others from drawing wide-ranging conclusions about his power and resolve from the interaction, and will try to lead others to treat the incident as isolated. By contrast, the winner of a confrontation has a wider choice of images he may want to project and his desires will depend partly on his intentions. He will usually want his adversary to believe he is willing to run high risks and pay high costs for certain goals, but there can be variety in the type and range of goals for which he will want others to think he is willing to do this.

Three illustrations will show that different intentions can lead the actor to want his adversary to believe his behavior foreshadows what he will do in infrequent cases, a moderate number of cases, or a great many cases. If the actor is aggressive and wishes to lull the other side he, like an actor who has been forced to retreat, will claim to have been motivated by particular details of the issue and will not want others to think his behavior is part of a pattern. Thus

[35] Reiners, *The Lamps Went Out in Europe*, 24.

after his triumphs Hitler did not publicly argue that he won because he was strong and the other side weak, although that was, in fact, what he believed. Second, when a defensive state pledged to sustain certain aspects of the international status quo wins a confrontation, it will want the other side to believe the event predicts the way it will behave if certain other areas are challenged, but it may not want the other to think *all* of its ambitions to change the status quo will elicit a similar reaction. An aggressor trying to impress and intimidate others without frightening them into forming a coalition against him will try to project an analogous image. Third, a defensive power committed to preventing the other side from making changes by the use or threat of force will, if it makes the other side retreat, want its adversaries to draw the most general inferences and believe the conflict can be used to accurately predict the state's resolve in all cases of aggression. And an aggressive actor willing to sacrifice the remnants of a peaceful image in order to maximize intimidation will adopt a similar policy.

Claims About Images of Others

An important aspect of an actor's reasons for behaving as he does usually lies in his image of other actors. A portion of the explanations he gives thus often includes reference to these images. This means that an actor can use the image he claims he has of the other to justify certain actions that otherwise would lead the other to adopt an undesired image of him. By convincing others that he holds a certain image of them he can influence their behavior. If the image is undesired, the chances that the other will act to change it will be increased. Or if the image is desired the other may be inhibited from acting to discredit it. Thus state A may want B to think it believes B is hostile in the expectation that B will feel the need to demonstrate its friendship by making concessions. Or A may use the pretended belief in the threat posed by B to reduce opposition to its own aggressive program. For example, in July 1961,

President Kennedy made a major speech about the growing tension concerning Berlin. He stressed both America's determination not to sacrifice that city and a willingness to negotiate. However, Schlesinger reports, "Khrushchev read it, or affected to read it," solely as a belligerent speech. He claimed to feel that "the United States had declared preliminary war on the Soviet Union. It had presented an ultimatum and clearly intended hostilities."[36] It was in Russia's interest to have the United States believe they interpreted Kennedy's speech in this way, for in that case the United States would be more apt to see the construction of the Berlin Wall the next month as a defensive reaction to a perceived American threat. The United States would be less likely to feel that the Soviet action was an index of future aggression in Berlin and Germany and indeed might believe that rather than stressing its own firmness it was more important to be friendly to show the Russians the United States was peaceful. Hitler, with his masterful timing, was often able to use this technique. He withdrew from the Disarmament Conference and the League of Nations only after it was clear that France was not going to live up to her promises to disarm. He announced his intention to break the Treaty of Versailles by reintroducing conscription and establishing a large army four days after France, to compensate for the reduced birth-rate in 1914-18, had announced a doubling of the period of service of her soldiers. He marched into the Rhineland a week after France ratified the Franco-Soviet treaty which, Hitler claimed, was incompatible with the Locarno Pact.[37] These claims had an effect on British decision-makers predisposed to believe the degree of security demanded by France was unreasonable in the face of a Germany that understandably feared France and wanted only limited and legitimate changes in the status quo.

In other less frequent circumstances state A will want B to incorrectly think it thinks B is not aggressive. For exam-

[36] Schlesinger, A Thousand Days, 392.
[37] Bullock, Hitler, 321-22, 332-33, 341-43.

205

ple, if A withdraws some of the costly protection that it has been supplying to area C against attack by state B, it will probably want to convince B it is doing this not because it is unwilling to pay a high price to defend its allies or because its resolve is weak, but rather because it no longer feels state B is a threat. Thus it would protect its own image as an actor who will fight to defend important interests. Furthermore B might not take advantage of the weakening of the defenses of C since B would believe that an attack would lead A to unfavorably change its image of B, and to consequently oppose many of B's actions and policies.

Alternatively, if state A wishes to increase its arms to protect against hostility from state B, but does not want to publicly admit this for fear of further embittering relations with B, it may claim to be arming out of fear of state C. Bismarck, for example, used this tactic when he wished to restrain Russia without alienating her.

Munich and the policy of appeasement illustrate the importance of the actor's projecting a given image of his image of his adversary. Chamberlain neglected the possibility of influencing Hitler's behavior by accurately conveying to him the image of Germany that lay behind his policy of appeasement. He could have tried to show Hitler that he was acting as he was largely because he believed Germany sought only legitimate revisions of the Treaty of Versailles and that if he found this image was incorrect and Hitler had wider ambitions he would go to war. Instead he did little to contradict Hitler's belief that England was at least partially aware of Germany's commitment to dominate the Continent and gave Hitler few grounds for believing England would react any differently to threats against Poland than she had to threats against Austria and Czechoslovakia.

Similarly, an actor may want others to accept certain beliefs about his image of a situation and his views about what has happened in the past. A state that does not want to take up a challenge may, in ambiguous cases, be able to deny aggression has taken place. Or it may claim to believe the situation is such as not to fall within the realm of its vital interests. Thus at the outbreak of the Korean War the Soviets responded to President Truman's plea that they help restore the *status quo ante* by claiming that South Korea was the aggressor. This version of events gave them at least an excuse for not restraining the North Koreans. If the United States believed the Russians believed this, the American image of Russia would not be significantly affected by the war. In this case, the events seemed too unambiguous for the United States to even contemplate that the Russians might believe the view they were espousing. But, what is more important in this context, once the United States intervened with military force, this version of the Soviets' beliefs had grave drawbacks. It implied that they now thought an innocent friendly regime was being attacked by the Americans. If the Soviets did not go to their aid it would seem that they were publicly admitting their unwillingness to prevent imperialist aggression. Furthermore, for this reason the Americans might fear Soviet intervention and thus be tempted to pre-empt. To avoid this situation the Russians altered their version of how they saw events in Korea. They quickly claimed that because the conflict was a civil war they would not intervene.[38] To the extent others believed this represented actual Soviet perceptions, they would not fear immediate Soviet intervention (which of course also meant the Russians would sacrifice possible deterrence of further American involvement in the war) and would not take Soviet inaction as an index to her willingness to allow other of her allies to be attacked.

Challenges Avoided or Created by Claims About One's Own Motives

The other side of this coin is that since the concessions actor B is willing to make to A are related to B's image of A and his beliefs about how A will react to alternative poli-

---

[38] Max Beloff, *Soviet Policy in the Far East* (London: Oxford University Press, 1953), 185-86. Similarly, during the Quemoy and Matsu crisis of 1958 the Soviet Union stressed the degree to which the conflict was a civil war. [Oran Young, *The Politics of Force* (Princeton: Princeton University Press, 1968), 225-26.]

cies, challenges can often be created or avoided by the motives A attributes to his own actions. This is partly because these attributions directly influence B's image of A and partly because they influence the interpretations A can plausibly claim to have drawn from B's behavior. If B claims to act on the assumption that A's signals about his motives were accurate, A will be likely to believe that if he later acts inconsistently he will not only damage his signaling reputation, but B can be expected to react differently. Unlike some of the strategies discussed previously, these attempts to influence the interpretations others are making occur before or during, rather than after, the outcome of a particular interaction since they are designed to influence this outcome as well as the actors' images.

An obvious application of this principle is involved when A tries to make it more likely that B will make concessions by convincing B that he (A) is acting on narrow grounds that will not apply in many other situations. Even if B does not believe A he may retreat and accept A's public explanation in the belief that it will be more difficult for A to later make credible threats based on motives that contradict this explanation.[39] President Johnson seems to have employed this tactic on a number of occasions. Instead of issuing a ringing challenge to his opponent and relating his behavior to a wide range of disputes, Johnson often chose to place the narrowest construction on his actions. Thus while President Kennedy successfully forced the steel industry to rescind a price increase by relating the increase to the general problem of inflation, focusing public attention on the issue, and involving his own reputation in the dispute, Johnson used different tactics to get the aluminum companies to cancel their price increase. While dumping aluminum from government stockpiles onto the market, he

[39] However, if, after the actor has claimed that his motives were limited, his adversary retreats, the actor may then claim his and his adversary's behavior were indices to behavior on many other issues. While such a strategy has high payoffs, it is difficult to carry out. For further discussion of this topic with special reference to the Cold War, see Chapter 8.

"insisted that the dumping had nothing whatsoever to do with the [price] increase" in the hope of a "quick and quiet retreat by the industry."[40] Similarly, it has been claimed that one reason Johnson began the bombing of North Vietnam and the commitment of combat troops to the South without public announcement of what was planned was the belief that such an announcement would have constituted "a direct and formidable challenge" to the Russians and Chinese.[41]

In general, then, when an actor undertakes behavior clearly against another's self-interest and wants to minimize the other's opposition, he will try to provide convincing explanations showing that the issue is special, that he will not draw wide-ranging inferences from the other side's retreating, and that his own behavior is not an index to his general hostility toward the other. Just as an actor who retreats on an issue usually tries to explain that this behavior is not typical,[42] an actor who wants to make it easier for his adversary to make a concession tries to explain he also views the situation as atypical. In both cases these explanations are designed to separate the specific question under consideration from wider issues and thus to decouple the actor's behavior from predictions of how he will act on other matters. For example, when in 1932 Peru used force to seize territory she had ceded to Colombia in a treaty several years earlier, she laid great stress on the arguments that the President of Peru who had concluded the treaty was a tyrannical dictator who, partly because of undue American pressure, had forced the agreement through Congress by coercive means.[43] To the extent that others accepted these explanations they would have less reason to fear Peru would repudiate other past or future agreements and therefore less reason to become generally hostile to Peru.

[40] Max Frankel, "Why the Gap between LBJ and the Nation?" *New York Times Sunday Magazine*, January 7, 1968, p. 44.
[41] *Ibid.*
[42] See above pp. 197-201.
[43] Wood, *The United States and Latin American Wars*, 32-42, 186-88.

The Russian stance in bargaining over Berlin also illustrates this principle. The Russians, who are trying to force the United States to make concessions and who therefore want the issue seen as local to minimize the cost of retreating to the United States, have generally avoided linking Berlin to broader issues of world politics. Rather they have tried to treat the status of the city and the access routes as an "anomaly," an isolated relic of World War II. One scholar argues that this partially explains why the Soviets did not try to exploit the American tactical weakness in Berlin during the Cuban missile crisis, as many American decision-makers feared they might. To do so would have contradicted their position that Berlin was an isolated issue and strengthened the credibility of the American claim that the question "was central and strategic."[44]

Thus the Soviet efforts to use East German authorities and personnel to carry out tasks hostile to the West reflect not only the desire to secure recognition for the East German regime, but also the wish to decouple this conflict from wider issues. During the blockade when the Russians wanted to disrupt the functioning of the Berlin government and other non-Communist institutions that exercised authority in all sectors of Berlin, they used local Communists rather than Russians.[45] Similarly, East German troops were used to seal the Berlin border in August 1961. The other side of this coin is that the West has usually stressed that the fate of Berlin rests with the great powers and that behavior on this issue will be taken as an index of Soviet intentions and American resolve. This partially accounts for the continuing American resistance to the West German desires to act on the claim that West Berlin is part of West Germany, the desire to make the Soviets display their military forces during the confrontations at Checkpoint

[44] Seyom Brown, *The Faces of Power* (New York: Columbia University Press, 1968), 260.

[45] Davison, *The Berlin Blockade*, passim. This posture was partly undercut by the attempts to assert Soviet control over all of Berlin and to claim that the Western authorities were subordinate to the Russian commander.

210

Charlie in October 1961,[46] and perhaps for the minor incident during the blockade in which the American Military Government *ordered* the Berlin Philharmonic not to play for audiences in East Berlin or to play over the Communist-controlled radio rather than merely following the wishes of the orchestra, which had already voted to this effect.[47]

Russian behavior at the onset of the Berlin blockade generally showed an awareness of the advantages of claiming their motives were limited. By arguing that "technical difficulties" and the disrepair of the railroads and autobahns were responsible for the halt in the traffic instead of making an explicit challenge to the Allies' rights to be in Berlin they made it both easier for them to retreat if the West exerted extreme pressure and less likely that the West would resist strongly. The fact that the challenge was so unambiguous that this strategy seems to have had relatively little impact should not obscure the fact that the Soviets thought it was important that they go out of their way to present these special reasons for their actions. Furthermore, even with hindsight one cannot be sure that the West would not have reacted more vigorously had the Russians chosen to claim from the start that the access agreements were void and to thus imply that a Western acquiescence in the blockade would be interpreted as an acknowledgment of the rights of the USSR to unilaterally control the flow of traffic to Berlin.[48]

When the Russians erected the Berlin Wall they were more successful in their efforts to decrease Western opposition by stressing that their dividing the city was only solidifying the borders of East Germany and not a prelude to

[46] General Clay told a press conference that "The fiction that it was the East Germans who were responsible for trying to prevent Allied access to East Berlin is now destroyed. The fact that the Soviet tanks appeared on the scene proves that the harassments which were taking place at *Friedrichstrasse* were not those of the self-styled East German government but ordered by its Soviet masters." (Smith, *The Defense of Berlin*, 323)

[47] Davison, *The Berlin Blockade*, 208.

[48] For a further discussion of this example, see p. 193.

interfering with the access routes to West Berlin.[49] Thus the Warsaw Pact communiqué released as the Wall went up stressed the need to prevent the West from undermining East Germany and explicitly assured the West that "it goes without saying, that these measures must not affect the existing order of traffic and control on the ways of communication between West Berlin and West Germany." The East German announcement similarly stated: "This decree in no way revises former decisions on transit between West Berlin and West Germany...."[50] And the Soviets waited over a month, until it was absolutely clear that the West would not challenge the Wall, before resuming even minor harassment along the access routes.

It should be noted that the actor who tries to win concessions on an issue by decoupling it from other issues often faces a dilemma. To maximize the probability that his adversary will retreat the actor must stress his high resolve and, as one important component of his resolve, how much he values the specific object at stake. But doing so may make it harder to claim that the conflict is set apart from others since it may be hard to find special aspects of the object that the actor, but not the adversary, values highly. Berlin, being the only piece of non-Communist territory within a Communist state is an issue about which the Russians can claim to feel very strongly without inadvertently defeating attempts to decouple it as an index to general Western behavior, but this configuration is uncommon. Thus the Russians would probably be unable to claim they placed especially high value on getting greater rights in Steinstuecken—the small Western enclave near Berlin—without implying they intended also to exert pressure on the wider issue of the future of Berlin. The opposite side of this coin is that an actor who wants to convince his adversary that he will fiercely resist attempts to change the status

[49] The United States made similar claims. This had the effect of decreasing the damage to America's image caused by our allowing the Soviets to construct the Wall. See above, 196-7, 200.

[50] Quoted in Smith, *The Defense of Berlin*, 268.

212

quo is aided by this factor. Usually he can without contradicting himself stress how much he values the object and how closely he sees it linked to other issues or principles. Thus the United States can claim it places a high intrinsic value on West Berlin, and that, partly for this very reason, a Western retreat there would, and should, be taken as an index of low Western resolve.

Limiting conflict by claiming the issue is isolated and that one's motives do not imply wider plans is more difficult than expanding conflict by making provocative claims about one's motives. By couching his justifications in the broadest possible terms, the actor can imply that his behavior on the specific issue is an index to the way he will act on many other matters. Doing this often involves claiming that one is committed to a principle that applies to a number of cases as well as the present one. If the actor does this and wins he will have gained much more than he would have had he tried to keep the conflict limited. Unless the other side is able to successfully decouple, the actor can take, or at least claim to take, the result of the conflict as an index of the actors' relative power and resolve on many issues. If the other side does not actively reject the actor's interpretation of the situation, the actor can claim to believe the other realized the actor had broad motives, and thus to believe the other side has knowingly shown a willingness to make concessions on a wide range of issues in the future. If the other side, by making a serious effort to prevail in the dispute, actively rises to the challenge and loses, the actor can even more plausibly make this claim. Furthermore, in this event he may actually be able to take the other's behavior as an index and can thus more safely take a firm stand in many disputes. Unless the other side is ignorant of these consequences, if it does not attempt decoupling it is apt to fight tenaciously over the issue and there will thus be conflict out of all proportion to the intrinsic value of the matter being contested.

These tactics raise the stakes of conflict by simultaneously increasing the expected costs to the other side of standing firm (because the probability is higher that since the actor sees the issue as linked to other important matters he will not retreat) and increasing the costs of backing down (because the actor has indicated he will take this as an index to the other side's behavior on a wide range of other matters). For these reasons, actors who want to keep conflicts limited have to be careful to ensure that when they become committed to a position, especially a defensive one, they do not also issue a challenge to the other side that gives the latter greater incentives to try to make the first actor retreat. Some members of Kennedy's White House staff apparently opposed certain proposed methods of strengthening the American commitment to Berlin on these grounds.[51] An actor in this position will have incentives to link the specific issue and his behavior concerning it to other issues and principles of greater value to him than to his opponent. The adversary will then have greater reason to expect the actor to stand firm and yet will not suffer especially high costs by not successfully forcing the actor to retreat. In other words, the actor may be able to couple the issue to others in ways that minimize the degree to which the payoffs are zero-sum.

An example of an actor issuing a challenge less by his actions than by his statements about his motivations is supplied by a dispute at the University of California at Berkeley in the spring of 1965 between Chancellor Meyerson and student protestors. The Chancellor refused to permit the on-campus sale of a student magazine that contained profanity and the student activists pressed Meyerson for an explanation. If he had claimed that he acted as he did because of the delicate nature of the situation, the extreme pressures of the Board of Regents, and the relatively slight restriction that his action entailed, the activists might well have made concessions and the conflict could have been kept limited. However, Meyerson chose to justify his action on the grounds that the Chancellor had the right to prevent the sale of magazines at his discretion and need not give

[51] Brown, *The Faces of Power*, 251.

reasons for doing so. The issue that was then posed to the students was not whether to agree to a minor and temporary infringement on what they considered to be their rights, but rather whether to acknowledge the authority of the administration over questions they considered vital. The activists, therefore, were unwilling to make quick concessions and when, after the expenditure of significant resources, they were forced to retreat, their losses—and Meyerson's gains—were much higher than they would have been had Meyerson given a narrower explanation of his motives.[52]

An analogous international case is provided by the conflict between Italy and Yugoslavia over the status of the people living in the Istrian Peninsula just south of the city of Trieste. At the London conference of 1954 this area was awarded to Yugoslavia and Trieste given to Italy. "To satisfy Italian feelings, the two sectors were not formally declared a part of each country, but only put under the administration of each. Thus in Istria, the residents, many of them Italian-speaking, took on all the rights of Yugoslavs, but did not technically acquire Yugoslavian citizenship."[53] Italy did not object when Yugoslavia issued identity cards to the residents of the peninsula. But when Yugoslavia defined "these cards . . . as a proof of citizenship" Italy felt that this was a challenge she could not avoid and therefore retaliated by breaking off the important negotiations then in progress with Yugoslavia on the renewal of a trade agreement.

Thus if the actor indicates he will not draw wide-ranging inferences from the other's retreating he both increases the likelihood that the other will make concessions and decreases the long-run payoffs that will accrue to him if this happens. And, conversely, behavior that indicates the opposite increases the costs the adversary will pay to stand

[52] It also should be noted that the justification was never given publicly and that the mechanism discussed here operates by influencing the actors' images of each other, not by affecting third audiences or either side's desire for prestige.

[53] Richard Eder, "Italians Reviving the Issue of Trieste, *New York Times*, March 19, 1967, p. 27.

215

firm and increases the later benefits if he is forced to retreat. This inverse relationship between the magnitude of a payoff and the difficulty of obtaining it is of course common to most bargaining situations. And the kind of image that will be of long-run benefit to the actor can be thought of as an added stake the actor can try to win if he thinks he has sufficient resources. However, unlike many other stakes, its nature prevents it from being the object of explicit bargaining and compromises. Since it involves trying to convince the other about the actor's motives and the way he sees the situation, it can rarely be introduced or withdrawn in the middle of a crisis. The decision, which is often implicit, made at the beginning of the confrontation of whether to try for the extra "image gain" is difficult to revoke.

EXPECTATIONS

Interpretations depend partly on comparisons between what was expected and what is believed to have happened. In those cases when expectations are too firmly set to be influenced, actors can adopt a strategy of manipulating their behavior so that it favorably contrasts with what was expected. For example, if an actor in a system that frowns upon having to borrow money is forced to do so, he may find it wise to borrow a little more than he needs. The marginal cost of asking for the extra sum is slight, since the main penalty is incurred for having to borrow at all. This extra money will allow the actor to repay some of the loan ahead of schedule. This will contrast with the behavior expected of a debtor and will somewhat modify the actor's unfavorable image.[54]

Once a particular kind of negatively sanctioned behavior comes to be expected from an actor, he is apt to pay relatively less cost by displaying that behavior. If Mr. Smith is known to be rude, other people's valuation of him will be lower than it would be otherwise, but each time he

[54] Great Britain's repaying ahead of schedule some of her loans from the International Monetary Fund may have had this effect.

is rude he will not pay a very high price. People will react by thinking, "Mr. Smith is being his usual, rude self," if indeed they even notice the common instances of his behavior. Similarly, a state may pay a certain price if others expect it to be unreasonable, but as others come to take this trait for granted they will not censure the state for displaying it. Rather they are not only apt to avoid criticizing the state, which they feel at best will have no impact, but also will adjust their behavior to the expectation that the state will not follow accepted standards of international politics (e.g. not use abusive language, refrain from supporting subversion and revolution in other states, show willingness to compromise on most issues). For example, for many years the neutralists assumed that the Soviet Union would not alter its position in disputes and thus put pressure on the West to make concessions so an agreement might be reached. And recent American behavior may lead other countries to see as normal certain actions they oppose (e.g. armed intervention), thus decreasing the international costs to the United States of each instance of that behavior.[55]

In many cases expectations are less firm and the actor can try not only to manipulate his behavior but also to influence the expectations. For example, to judge trends within the United States and the political gains and costs of various courses of behavior, actors and observers try to estimate the strength of contending groups. To this end they examine such indices as the number of letters written to Congressmen and newspapers, the number of advertisements in the mass media, and the number of people attending rallies and marches. However, when the activity or the circumstances are unusual, it is difficult to draw accurate inferences from the raw data. In other words, it is then difficult to determine the correlations between these indices and the movement's political strength. What inferences about the opposition to the war in Vietnam are we to draw if a well-publicized march attracts 100,000 people? How

[55] I would like to thank George Quester for pointing this out to me.

217

would this inference compare with the one we would draw if 400,000 attended the march?

The puzzle of interpretation can often be phrased as: "'only' or 'as much as'?"[56] Did the protesting group turn out "only" 100,000 people or "as many as" 100,000 people? Does a radical nationalist government "only" nationalize big foreign concerns or does it "go so far as to" nationalize them? During the Suez crisis did Russia ask Turkey to allow through the Dardanelles a naval force of "only" a cruiser and three destroyers or a force "as large as" that? The judgments made are both important and often difficult to support with careful and systematic reasoning. The actor is more apt to react with an "only" if the behavior was expected. In these cases, the strength or weakness of the organization or the behavior will be judged less by the indices alone than by comparisons between these indices and the behavior expected. And the claims of an actor, often the actor undertaking the activity, can play a large role in establishing these expectations.

Thus a protest group planning a march is often well-advised to release lower than its actual estimates of the number of people expected. And a country planning a naval demonstration should avoid sending fewer ships than expected.[57] Polsby and Wildavsky note a similar tactic used by candidates seeking the Presidential nomination who try to get others to accept favorable interpretations of primaries and balloting in the convention.[58] In primaries limits are placed on the utility of influencing expectations by the fact that relevant elites are largely concerned with trying to use the results of the primaries to estimate how well candidates would do in the general election, and these estimates are only marginally affected by their previous

[56] This is a familiar problem in the analysis of data in the social sciences. For a discussion of it in this context, see Herbert Hyman, *Survey Design and Analysis* (Glencoe, Illinois: Free Press, 1955), 126-27.

[57] Grenville, *Lord Salisbury* . . . , 29.

[58] Nelson Polsby and Aaron Wildavsky, *Presidential Elections* (New York; Scribner's, 1964), 65-67, 72-75, and 82-91.

expectations concerning the primaries (although this margin may be an important one). For example, once Kennedy had entered the West Virginia race he probably had to do very well to be nominated. The fact that he not only won, but did much better than others had been led to expect, aided him significantly. But if people had thought he would get only, say, 20% of the vote and he did twice as well he probably still would have been unable to convince the delegates he could win in November.

During the nominating convention itself there may be even more advantages to controlling expectations. Delegates wish to vote for the man who will get the nomination. Thus bandwagon effects (either for or against a candidate), which depend largely on each delegate's perception of other delegates' perceptions of which candidate will win the nomination, can be produced by expectations that, if widely held, will be self-fulfilling (e.g. if X doesn't win on the first ballot he has lost his chance, if Y can keep in the running for three ballots everyone will switch to him).

This is not to deny the important roots of these expectations beyond the power of candidates to influence. It is hard to make people believe a candidate has to win on the first ballot if he is to win at all unless there are good reasons other than expectations why delegates are not apt to choose this candidate as their second choice. However, within limits, the indices by which delegates can gauge the perceptions of other delegates and the fortunes of the candidates are rarely clear and unambiguous, and the candidates and their leading supporters in the state delegations can influence delegates' interpretations by frequent and consistent statements of their perceptions of the candidates' strategies, the delegates' perceptions, and the probable course of the convention.[59]

[59] The development of extensive polling of the delegates by the mass media makes it much more difficult for candidates to stimulate or impede first ballot bandwagons by the methods discussed here. If the delegates in the 1968 Republican convention knew of and believed the TV networks' delegate polls showing that Nixon would win on the first ballot the ambiguity that is a necessary condition for the acceptance of the competing views sponsored by Reagan and Rockefeller would be missing.

In the case of protest demonstrations, the importance of what is expected in determining how indices are interpreted operates at another level as well. People not only try to draw inferences about the movement's total strength from such things as turnout at rallies, but they also try to compare this estimated strength with a feeling of what is "normal." Even if we are able to determine the number of people opposing the war in Vietnam and the intensity with which these opinions were held we would view this against the background of beliefs about how much opposition should be "expected" in such a situation. Lacking alternative standards, the previous activities of the antiwar groups seem to be an important determinant of these beliefs about normality. If a given level of protest, even a fairly high level, is maintained, people will get accustomed to it and the protest will lose much of its impact. A protest movement must work ever harder to produce the same impression.

Thus leaders of the movement for Indian independence in the 1930s found the length of fasts had to be increased to maintain pressure on the British.[60] When the civil rights movement in the American South started, almost any protest received great publicity and exerted significant pressure. Any sit-in made national headlines and upset local leaders. As the number and scope of nonviolent protests increased, changes seem to have occurred not only in people's estimates of how dissatisfied the Southern Negroes were, but also in their beliefs about how much dissatisfaction and protest was normal. What is thought of as normal passes almost unnoticed.[61] Thus the arrest of, say, 100 people in a sit-in came to be no longer regarded as newsworthy by reporters or as threatening by local elites. Indeed, like the barking of the dog in the Sherlock Holmes story, demonstrations of this size attract most attention when they do not occur.[62]

[60] I am grateful to Gene Sharp for pointing this out to me.

[61] Thus Saul Alinsky advises protest groups to frequently change their tactics.

[62] See, for example, Paul Good, "Odyssey of a Man—and a Move-

A similar transformation occurred with campus protests in the late 1960s. Since most colleges could function without the temporary use of one or two buildings, the seizure of such buildings exerted pressure on the college largely by upsetting the administration's view of how students ought to behave and by triggering a response that increased the support for the student demands. When the administration and faculty change their outlook and treat this form of protest as the expected behavior of dissatisfied students, seizures lose their usefulness and the protestors have to develop new ways of exerting pressure, probably ones that constitute more of a direct attack on the values of their adversaries. Even events that not only are indices, but directly involve major values, lose some of their impact if they come to be expected. This may be occurring with sporadic rioting in the ghettoes. These have so far been taken to mean, among other things, that conditions in those areas are intolerable and require governmental assistance. But if rioting—confined to the ghettos—becomes more common, people may adjust to it and come to believe that rioting, like traffic jams and smog, is merely an expected aspect of our urban, industrial society.

Indeed, if it is expected that certain events will happen people may become used to them ahead of time and "discount" them in advance, thereby robbing the events of their impact. Thus all the discussion of the high probability of future ghetto riots may decrease the reactions (of various kinds) if such riots occur. Similarly the United States may not have been able to put additional pressure on North Vietnam by bombing previously spared targets because

ment," *New York Times Sunday Magazine*, June 25, 1967, pp. 5ff. This is not to imply that this process is completely nonrational. To the extent that people believed protests of a given type and size would automatically have certain consequences (e.g. violence or insurrection) that did not follow, they have less reason to pay attention to a steady level of protest. Furthermore, protests now involve less danger and cost to the participants than was the case a few years ago, and the level of protest should thus be expected to increase "naturally."

221

Hanoi may have believed such moves were inevitable and written these targets off.

If the behavior the actor initially threatens to carry out does not involve an immediate high cost for the adversary but rather exerts pressure largely through the implied danger of escalation, the adversary will reap significant advantages by discounting these actions ahead of time. By claiming they are expected and normal under the circumstances, the adversary can reduce the actor's belief that his actions will intimidate. Thus during the crisis surrounding the election of the West German President in Berlin, a West German official replied to the Soviet threat to take "grave measures" by claiming: "We are reckoning that something will happen,"[63] and indicating they had "concrete" intelligence indications that there would be Communist harassment on the access routes. A week later, when the Russians announced plans for joint troop maneuvers with the East Germans, "West Germans . . . reacted calmly to the announcement, indicating that they had expected such a move."[64]

When the immediate actions do involve significant costs to the adversary, as is the case in the Vietnam bombing and ghetto rioting examples mentioned above, it is not easy to determine whether this phenomenon helps or hinders the actor trying to exert pressure. As long as the cost to the other side is high, and as long as it believes concessions will be effective, it may concede as soon as it feels that otherwise the punishment (e.g. continued rioting or the bombing of additional areas) is certain to occur. Thus the actor may derive benefits without the costs and risks of having to make or carry out open threats or warnings. However, if the other side's experience with the first stages of the undesired outcomes shows them to be tolerable, it may adjust to the idea of bearing an objectively greater

[63] David Binder, "Reds Test Radio Jamming in Berlin's Air Corridors," *New York Times*, Feb. 15, 1969, p. 1.

[64] Henry Kamm, "Soviet Maneuvers Near Berlin Set," *New York Times*, Feb. 22, 1969.

sacrifice as something that has to be done in the normal course of events and may conceive of the costs as an accepted part of its life. Yet, if this actor had suddenly been confronted with the possibility of these losses they would have seemed great enough to call for forestalling concessions.

CONCLUSIONS

Stanley Hoffmann claims the difficulties involved in the use of force in the current international system have transformed "many of the generally accepted components of 'reality' in world affairs" and decreased the correlation

> between a state's material ingredients of power and its capacity to reach its goals. . . . When the physics of power declines, the psychology of power rises. Also, reality was usually defined in terms of who controlled what and who possessed what. The same new factors have led states to transfer their greed and expectations from physical mastery to the shaping of international milieu—from tangibles to intangibles. What constitutes success and failure in such a quest, what is "real" gain, or merely "symbolic" or "illusory" achievement is hard to say. Again, much depends on perceptions. Perhaps international politics today should be defined less as a struggle for power than as a contest for the shaping of perceptions.[65]

The arguments here partly support this view, but also suggest that the route to such traditional goals as security and power may often lie through the influencing of perceptions and interpretations of indices. While the present international system increases both the need and the opportunities for such activities, we should not overlook the existence of this element in pre-1945 eras. The main payoffs for many actions have never been direct and concrete, but rather have derived from the inferences actors drew

[65] Stanley Hoffmann, "Perceptions, Reality, and the Franco-American Conflict," *Journal of International Affairs* 21 no. 1 (1967), 58.

from these actions. In much of the maneuvering for power and position the outcomes and meanings of events were and are not so unambiguous as to exclude the opportunity for the actors to get others to accept desired interpretations.

CHAPTER EIGHT   Signals and Indices in
the Nuclear Era

IN THIS CHAPTER we shall consider some aspects of the projection of images especially common or important in the post-1945 international system. These phenomena are different only in degree and detail from those in other periods and reflect the underlying principles discussed earlier.

In the postwar world the absence of major wars, the lack of centrally controlled small ones, and the paucity of actions that directly affect either side's value position increase the difficulty of drawing inferences. In the past there were usually frequent opportunities to test whether various signals and indices were accurate predictors of behavior. In a discussion of pre-1939 deterrence Bernard Brodie calls attention to the "positive function served by the failures [of deterrence]. The very frequency with which wars occurred contributed importantly to the credibility inherent in any threat."[1] The increased difficulty in the nuclear era of validating cues to others' behavior may widen the scope for decoupling by increasing the ambiguity of behavior. Actors may look more to each other's definition of the situation to guide the inferences they draw. On the other hand, psychological research indicates that under conditions of high ambiguity actors will tend to turn inward, relying less on the other's behavior and more on their preconceived image of the other.[2]

Some writers believe that if threats are frequently made but the occasion for their use never arises they will have less impact.[3] This would make war more likely since eventually both sides would probe more vigorously. In the case of threats of all-out nuclear war, one cannot "reinvigorate"

[1] "The Anatomy of Deterrence," printed in Morton Berkowitz and P. G. Bock, eds., *American National Security* (New York: Free Press, 1965), 80.

[2] Allport, *Theories of Perception* . . . , 382.

[3] Interestingly enough, some of the people who make this argument also argue that the existence of nuclear weapons leads to tensions that may cause wars.

the signals by following them with the indicated action. The fact that signals have become more crude has been one response to this, although other factors have contributed to the trend. Subtlety and ambiguity about the punishment to be meted out, if not about the events that would trigger this, are absent in many Cold War threats. Decision-makers may feel that this explicitness will make up for the lack of empirical validation of the signals.

The ways actors draw inferences about the other side's resolve are partially validated by the few Cold War confrontations that directly affect the distribution of resources and values between the powers. Such conflicts as the Berlin blockade, the Korean War, the Bay of Pigs invasion, the Cuban missile crisis, and (if the Johnson administration's interpretation was correct) the war in Vietnam serve as means by which signals and indices can be validated. However, such incidents are still infrequent. And only the Berlin blockade and the Cuban missile crisis seemed to raise acutely the danger of nuclear war. Thus the states might not believe the other's behavior in these situations or the signals they employed are particularly relevant to how they would react in a more dangerous case.

LACK OF CAPABILITY INDICES

It is now generally agreed that stability in the nuclear balance tends to lead to instability on lower levels of violence.[4] When both sides have a second strike capability it is easier for each to take provocative and dramatic actions to convince others that it is willing to fight a major war if it has to. But by the same token, this stability makes these actions largely signals, which can be used for bluffing, and so may be discounted by other actors. This is linked to the fact that the ability to use capability indices to support signals of a willingness to resort to a major war is less than it was in the past. Although the long-run stability of the

[4] For one of the first statements of this position, see Glenn Snyder, "Balance of Power in the Missile Age," *Journal of International Affairs* 14 (1960), 21-34, especially 31.

military balance can be questioned,[5] as long as both sides have a secure second strike capability there are few capability indices available for use in most crises. Thus an examination of Herman Kahn's 44-rung "escalation ladder" shows that few of the rungs except those at the very top involve any significant change in capabilities. Rungs like 24—"unusual, provocative, and significant counter-measures"—are the exceptions. At this rung "it is possible for one side to carry out threatening maneuvers or military preparations that have the effect of shifting the balance of power by, for example, sharply increasing the other side's vulnerability to surprise attack."[6] It is easy to see the impact of any such move. However, it is hard to find examples of this partly because states realize that such vulnerabilities could be disastrous and work to eliminate them.

In the past this was not true and states could produce a wide variety of capability indices. Troop movements, arms increases, and alliances undertaken during a crisis would have had a major impact if war occurred. Diplomats often preferred capability indices to signals since, although they were more costly, they put the state in a better military position in the conflict and, partly for this reason, were more apt to be believed. For example, in 1913 the major powers wanted to put pressure on Turkey and therefore sent an international naval detachment off her shores. Lord Grey, British Foreign Secretary, disagreed, "but was willing to send ships into Besica Bay . . . from where they might intervene. . . . In that case, it would be [in Grey's words] 'no longer a naval demonstration but a measure of precaution in the case of perilous events.' "[7] The desire to buttress signals with capability indices exists among scholars as well as decision-makers. Morton Kaplan writes: "Obviously the less confidence a situation permits, the more closely the sign [used here in a sense that encompasses both signals and indices] must be linked to the physical

---

[5] See, for example, J. S. Butz, "The Myth of Technological Stalemate," and Butz, "Under the Spaceborn Eye: No Place to Hide."

[6] Kahn, *On Escalation*, 140.

[7] Vagts, *Defense and Diplomacy*, 253.

potentialities of the situation."[8] However Kaplan does not discuss how this can be done in the Cold War.

Henry Kissinger raises a similar point with reference to recent changes in weapons systems. "What threats . . . can one make with solid fuel missiles? If weapons are in an extreme state of natural readiness, how can one demonstrate the increasing preparedness that historically served as a warning? . . . During the Cuban Crisis of October 1962, we conveyed an effective warning by dispersing SAC bombers to civilian airports. What equivalent tactic can we employ when our strategic forces are composed entirely of missiles?"[9] This viewpoint seems, if not to overestimate the problems we are now facing, then to underestimate the problems we have faced. The visible operations no longer possible were more signals than indices. While they did increase American capability, they only put it at a level that would be equalled at all times by a force of hardened, ready-to-fire missiles.[10] Thus the absolute level of capability itself cannot be the key point. And the change in capability involved in dispersing the bombers could be carried out at a slight cost and risk compared with the benefits of convincing the other side that one would not back down. Thus the dispersal of the bombers was largely a signal, which could be used to bluff, and derived its impact from the degree to which it committed

[8] *Some Problems in the Strategic Analysis of International Politics* (Princeton: Center of International Studies, Research Monograph No. 2, 1959), 24.

[9] "Reflections on Power and Diplomacy," in E.A.J. Johnson, ed., *The Dimensions of Diplomacy* (Baltimore: Johns Hopkins Press, 1964), 25.

[10] It is true that the United States was in a favorable position in the mid-1960s when, because of the small size and vulnerability of the Soviet strategic forces, the United States might have been able to launch a disarming first strike. However the dispersal of bombers mentioned by Kissinger would not contribute to such an attack. The change in the military balance has made American nuclear threats less credible, but this is because the Russians have a more secure retaliatory force, not because the United States has shifted from bombers to missiles.

the United States to stand firm. Since the meaning of this action was largely conventional, it could be replaced, in principle, by any artificial device. The United States could announce that whenever it raised a flag with a mushroom pattern over a missile base this meant that it was taking an international event very seriously. Of course this does not seem the equivalent of dispersing bombers which intuitively seems more credible because it appears closely connected with the use of the weapons. But as long as both sides understand the code, the flag can convey the message as well. The Russians would have just as much—or as little— reason to believe the one as the other.[11]

The great powers can still use capability indices to convey impressions about their willingness and ability to engage in limited conflicts. Not only do the United States and the Soviet Union have significantly different limited war capabilities, but mobilizing and moving men and weapons can increase either side's ability to fight. Indeed those measures may be a necessary condition for the state to commence military action. However, a major determinant of whether a state will start a limited war is its beliefs about whether the conflict can be kept limited. In many conflicts the most important calculations involve not judging which side can prevail at the level of fighting at which the conflict begins, but rather how much escalation is apt to occur. Further discussion of escalation and the role played by risky actions must be postponed until we have considered some more general questions of military doctrine.

[11] Even the use of nuclear weapons against either the United States or USSR, at which at first seems obviously a capability index, in fact is apt to be largely a signal. Given a world in which both great powers have a secure second strike capability, neither side can disarm the other by an all-out nuclear attack. And smaller, less extreme measures, like exploding bombs high over the adversary's cities, destroying a target of value to him, or even disabling some military installations, will not significantly reduce the costs to the attacker of carrying on a major war. (See pp. 237-42 for a discussion of the conditions under which the use of nuclear weapons constitutes a different kind of index.)

DOCTRINE AND REALITY

The nuclear age has accentuated the split between defense and deterrence.[12] Now the pronouncements and doctrines about the way a war would be fought that are best for decreasing the probability of an enemy attack may not be in the state's interest to implement should the war actually occur. In the past states often made threats, but they generally involved signals about a willingness to go to war, not how they would fight if the occasion arose. This is no longer true, and thus means that military doctrine and strategy have a greater impact on peacetime bargaining than in the past. Today, for example, the United States could want the USSR to fear that a provocation would lead to all-out war, yet would want to prevent this from happening if there was a provocation.[13] If the Russians believed such American pronouncements, they would never be tested.

[12] Glenn Snyder, *Deterrence and Defense* (Princeton: Princeton University Press, 1961), passim.

[13] The arguments against a pure "massive retaliation" doctrine are well-known and persuasive. But it may still be possible and wise for the United States to imply that the possibility of massive retaliation cannot be completely ignored or to claim that escalation that would lead to the same results is probable. One argument against this is the opposite of the old claim that the threat is not credible—it might be too credible and lead the USSR to undertake all-out military action where it would have preferred to use limited and controlled force since it feels the response will be all-out war no matter what it does. Making the use of force, or the use of nuclear weapons, an all-or-none affair increases the chance that no force will be used, but also increases the probability of total war. Wars are less likely to occur, but more likely to lead to all-out war if they do occur. Whether this is in either or both sides' interest is extremely difficult to determine. A state could try to gain the best of both worlds by making its opponent believe that the probability that a provocation would lead to all-out war was high enough so that the adversary would not engage in probes, but not so high that the adversary would feel that it was wise for him to show no restraint should a war break out. Since it may only take a belief that there is a very small probability of keeping the war limited to make it rational for both sides to initially observe some limits, it may be possible, although difficult, for a state to design its part of the strategic dialogue to meet these criteria.

230

The validity of current theories about the possibility of limiting wars depends largely on what people believe to be right, and this in turn is not tightly linked to existing force configurations. That is, whether a conflict can be kept limited depends not so much on the objective situation (although mutual first strike capability makes it harder to keep conflicts limited and mutual second strike capability makes it easier) as on the actors' doctrines and beliefs about others' doctrines.[14] This is different from the familiar questions of learning more about an objective environment so it can be coped with better or of learning more about an adversary who may change his behavior if you learn enough to cope with his established tactics. Herman Kahn's argument that strategists are merely like messengers who bring news to the decision-makers is thus misleading.[15] Whether the "news" is correct depends in part on whether decision-makers on both sides accept it. The belief on both sides that a war can be kept limited is a necessary (but not a sufficient) condition for keeping it limited. The strategist who can convince both sides that limited wars are possible is not describing reality, he is changing it. Similarly, if both sides believe that although each possesses a second strike capability, the side with more missiles has more useable military power and can prevail in more situations, then the number of missiles each side has does affect the outcome of political bargains.[16] The usefulness of military

[14] For a similar argument, see Schelling, *Arms and Influence*, 158-59. This is not to argue that both sides' believing a war can be kept limited guarantees that fighting can be kept within bounds. Not only may the states find that popular pressures or the difficulties in determining what limits the other side is observing make it hard for them to exercise self-restraint, but calculated considerations may lead them to increase the amount of force they are using and expand the war.

[15] *Thinking About the Unthinkable* (New York: Horizon Press, 1962), 19.

[16] For denials of the importance of nuclear force greater than that required for a second strike capability, see Hans Morgenthau, "The Four Paradoxes of National Strategy," *American Political Science Review* 58 (March 1964), 23-35, and A.F.K. Organski, *World Politics* (New York: Knopf, 1968), 2nd edn., 300-37.

"superiority" thus cannot be determined by objective analysis of the costs and benefits of various uses of military forces without taking into account the actors' beliefs about the influence of varying military balances on political bargaining. By changing actors' beliefs about the utility of "superiority," strategic analysis can actually change this utility.

The task of the state trying to keep wars limited is more difficult than that of the state arguing the contrary position. Agreement is necessary for the keeping, but not for the breaking, of limits. For restraints to be observed both states must believe that each is willing and able to observe limits. State A must then not only convince B it feels escalation is not inevitable, but also that it believes B realizes this, or at least will realize this when actually confronted with a major crisis. If state A feels that while B really believes war can be kept limited it is taking the opposite view to obtain extra deterrence, it will have to convince B that it sees B is attempting deception. On the other hand, if state A takes the opposite view it needs merely to convince its adversary that its statement of its own position reflects how it will act. If B continues to maintain that limits will be observed, A does not face the difficult problem of convincing B that it believes B is trying to deceive it.[17]

The Strategic Dialogue and Limited War

The perspective of the projection of images can be used to examine in more detail aspects of the Soviet-American

[17] For three reasons a state that argues that limits are possible can continue to propound this thesis to an adversary whom it believes holds the contrary view. The state can think (a) the other does not really believe the "unlimited" doctrine, (b) in a crisis the other will so desire to avoid a major war that it will quickly be converted to the "limited" view, or (c) the other will slowly see the validity of the first side's argument and will openly accept its doctrine. Ideally a state should examine the likelihood of these arguments being correct before adopting a limited war strategy. The United States, however, may have done so in the belief that the new strategy was in some objective sense "correct" and that others would have to adjust to the new American position.

strategic dialogue and particularly the debate over whether wars can be kept limited, much of which can be seen as attempts to discover and influence the other side's escalation ladder. From this perspective one should be able to gain insights not only into the military strategy, but also into the political outlook of both sides, for many of the rungs are not neutral but aid or hinder certain plans. Thus the USSR has attacked and ridiculed the American doctrine of flexible response. The Soviets deny that nuclear weapons could be used as signals or that counterforce strikes would be kept limited. As Kahn points out, "Soviet strategists and political leaders have declared that Soviet forces would not recognize any such 'artificial' distinctions in a nuclear war. This position of theirs could be an accurate reflection of current Soviet strategic doctrine, but it could also be a posture publicly adopted to discourage disarming attacks on the Soviet Union and to decrease the credibility of U.S. threats. . . ."[18]

Since until recently the United States has had a much larger hardened nuclear force than the Soviets, the latter would be at a disadvantage in a counterforce war. Their statements denying the stability of these escalatory rungs can therefore be seen as in their interest. However, they have also claimed that a war in Europe could not be kept conventional, but rather would automatically lead to an all-out war between the United States and the USSR. The United States disagrees.[19] This is in some ways strange, since if the USSR really believes war in Europe could not be limited, or believes that the United States believes it,

[18] Kahn, *On Escalation*, 169. For an argument "that Communist regimes . . . have really understood the military problems arising with nuclear weapons since 1945 , . . . [and] that their seemingly unrealistic pronouncements on these subjects can be explained (and could have been predicted) as deliberate dissimulations . . . required by the strategic environment," see George Quester, "On the Identification of Real and Pretended Communist Military Doctrine," *Journal of Conflict Resolution* 10 (June 1966), 173-79.

[19] This is a reversal of the positions each side took in the mid-1950s. For a discussion of the doctrines of that period, see Raymond Garthoff, *Soviet Strategy in the Nuclear Age* (New York: Praeger, 1958), 98-107.

Russia would not start such a war (unless of course she felt she could destroy the United States—in which case she would attack both continents simultaneously). Thus the Russian statements are not easily reconciled with the view that she might launch a conventional attack on Western Europe.[20]

There are several possible explanations for this seemingly anomalous position, other than the obvious one that the Soviets have no intention of threatening Western Europe militarily. First, the Russians may believe that it is not they, but the United States, that is most apt to initiate the use of limited force throughout the world. The Bay of Pigs, the Dominican Republic, and Vietnam could lead them to see a pattern of constant American intervention supported by the doctrine that conventional wars can be kept limited.[21] Undermining this doctrine as it applies to Europe could be seen as the first step to convincing the United States that intervention in the underdeveloped areas was too risky to be undertaken. Second, the Russians may realize that it would be difficult for them to simultaneously claim that a conventional war in Europe could be kept limited, but that any use of nuclear weapons would inevitably lead to all-out war. And, as noted above, they have an interest in making the second claim. If they felt that it was much more important to protect against American counter-force strategy than to make it easier to leave open the option of engaging in a limited war in Europe, they might take what seems to be a strange position on the latter to safeguard their interest in the former. If this is the case the Soviet position on limited war is apt to change if they redress the strategic imbalance. Third, the Russians may place top priority on discouraging the West from using force, however limited, to defend Berlin or to oppose harassing tactics in the city or along the access routes. For this is the

[20] For a similar argument, see Raymond Aron, *The Great Debate* (Garden City, N.Y.: Doubleday, 1965), 152.

[21] For a report of this Soviet world view, see Marshall Shulman, "American Militancy: The Soviet View," *Survival* 9 (February 1967), 63-67.

only European area in which the West might want to initiate the use of active force.[22] Thus, in a nationwide broadcast on August 7, 1961, Khrushchev claimed that no conflict over Berlin could be kept limited. This was undoubtedly aimed at inhibiting any Western military reaction to the Berlin Wall which was soon to be erected. Similarly, the Russians could want to decrease the chance that the United States might use force to resist Soviet attempts to pacify East European states, although it seems clear, at least to American observers, that American intervention would be extremely unlikely even if the Soviets admitted that limited wars were possible. Fourth, she might not understand the implications of her statements. Although this seems implausible, the Soviets have in the past been unsophisticated about nuclear strategy. Finally, the United States may place a higher probability than do the Soviets on occurrence of incidents not under the control of either actor that could lead to war (e.g. border fighting between the two Germanies).[23] Furthermore, the United States may be generally more cautious than the Soviets and this could lead it to place a higher value on the protection against all-out war provided by a controlled response doctrine.[24]

The Russians seem to have recently modified their views and now "Soviet doctrine does not preach the 'inevitable' escalation of limited into general war."[25] This illustrates another aspect of the strategic dialogue. Each side would prefer that the other adopt its view of the escalation ladder, but the persistence of basic disagreements may be so

[22] For the argument that what is important is the decision to initiate a change in the status quo and that it does not matter who actually fires the first shot, see Bernard Brodie, *Escalation and the Nuclear Option* (Princeton: Princeton University Press, 1966), 75-84.

[23] See the discussion of the "autonomous probability" that certain events will occur in Karl Deutsch, *The Nerves of Government* (New York: Free Press, 1963), 70.

[24] This analysis, it should be noted, is not exhaustive and is merely designed to show that one should examine the relationships between the international discussion of possible rungs of the escalation ladder and wider considerations of military and political strategy.

[25] Thomas Wolfe, *Soviet Strategy at the Crossroads* (Cambridge: Harvard University Press, 1964), 123.

dangerous that each side may be willing to make concessions to reach some agreement. The existence of differing ladders makes it harder to control a conflict. If the actors believe this difference exists they will be less willing to start such conflicts. But if they do start, the existence of differing ladders makes the situation less predictable, and the knowledge that this is the case further compounds uncertainties and risks.

To avoid this danger, each side may want to leave the door open for the use of the other side's rules in the event of a major crisis even while arguing against the adequacy of the other side's position during the precrisis dialogues. This somewhat conservative strategy may make it less likely that all of the state's views on the escalation ladder will be adopted, but also may decrease the chance that during a crisis either or both sides will feel that their earlier conversations had indicated that limits and controls are not possible.

Bargaining over the restraints on a conflict in progress often presents an actor with similarly contradictory pressures. If you want to keep the conflict limited you would try to convince your adversary that any escalation is terribly dangerous. You could thus claim the rules presently governing the conflict to be inviolable. Once they were broken, you could not imagine any others. This makes infractions less likely, but increases the chances of a total war since, if the other side believes you, he will perceive this as the only alternative to the existing situation. Furthermore, if an ambiguous situation arises in which, for example, the limits are broken accidentally, there will be greater pressure for pre-emption because both sides will fear the other will see the incident as bringing the end of restraints. If this seems too risky, or if you think that you can match your adversary at reasonable cost at every level of conflict, you may indicate that you will respond in a controlled manner to his violations of the rules. This purchases a decreased chance of mutually undesired escalation, but at the price of increasing the likelihood that the adversary will not be deterred from further escalation if he believes that such action can force you to retreat.

The Transformation of the Threat
That Leaves Something to Chance

Many military preparations and actions exert pressure on the adversary not so much because they are indices or signals of a willingness to engage in a major conflict but because they are, in Schelling's words, "a threat that leaves something to chance"[26] which exerts pressure on both sides to end the confrontation. These strategies have "a random ingredient." "The key to these threats is that, though one may or may not carry them out if the threatened party fails to comply, *the final decision is not altogether under the threatener's control. . . .* [The] uncertain element in the decision. . . . is an ingredient in the situation that neither we nor the party we threaten can entirely control. An example is the threat of inadvertent war."[27] Thus a country could build a mechanism to control its nuclear missiles so that, for every day the mechanism was turned on, there would be a one percent chance that it would fire the weapons. The state could threaten to turn the machine on if the other provoked a severe crisis, and this threat could be credible when the definite threat to start a war would not be.[28] Of course it is hard to imagine a state building such a machine, but escalation and limited wars serve the same function of being "a generator of risk."[29]

These generators operated in the past, although statesmen may not have been fully aware of them. For example, the battle of Navarino in 1827 was not planned, but rather developed accidentally from a naval demonstration. The allied fleet had been created largely as a signal to Turkey and Egypt and, "in order to protest more effectively, the fleet sailed into Navarino Bay" where the Turkish-Egyptian fleet was anchored. "A shot fired by the enraged Turks

[26] *The Strategy of Conflict,* 187-203.
[27] *Ibid.,* 188, emphasis in the original.
[28] For a similar discussion see *ibid.,* 197.
[29] *Ibid.,* 190.

led to the historical battle"[30] that had not been ordered by either side. Similarly, the United States sent the *Maine* to Havana partly to reinforce diplomatic efforts and its destruction was, of course, instrumental in starting the Spanish-American War.

Because of the costs of actually employing force in the nuclear era, this "competition in risk taking," to borrow another phrase from Schelling, is now a more frequently used method of using the possibility of war to secure political values. The point of special interest from the perspective of this study is that many threats that leave something to chance are apt to be largely transformed into signals if the actors frequently discuss them. While some of these actions may automatically create some degree of risk of accidental war and may thus permanently retain their meaning of competition in risk taking, many are robbed of this significance if they are openly accepted as means of exerting limited pressure.

There are two steps to this argument. First, many actions that under some circumstances embody threats that leave something to chance can under other conditions be signals. Second, discussion of the action can be an important, and perhaps the most important, influence in such a transformation. To start with the first step, it should be noted that an action can be risky for many reasons. The other side may take it as an index to a coming all-out war. Thus the sudden evacuation of American cities, for example, could be taken by the Russians as evidence that the United States might launch an attack unless it was appeased or stopped by force. Or the other side may think the first is no longer under central control and may fear that local and/or uncoordinated decision-makers cannot be relied on to maintain limits on the demonstration and use of force. Or the action can be risky because it is unexpected and throws the other side off balance and makes it more likely that it will react in an unplanned and ill-considered way. Or the action may confuse people in the field and lead them to make inaccu-

[30] Vagts, *Defense and Diplomacy*, 233.

238

rate reports or take unauthorized actions that would increase the danger of war. Or, to cover many specific chains
of reasoning in a general formulation, the other side may
believe the first has become, or has shown itself to be, very
unpredictable. In addition, if actor B believes A realizes
the risks he is running, B will take the behavior as an index
of A's resolve and willingness to pay higher costs to gain his
objectives.

Thus in most situations threats that leave something to
chance operate through human expectations rather than
through mechanical devices. If I were to throw lighted
matches around a gas station this would automatically
create some risk. Once the matches left my hand there is
no other human action needed to produce an explosion.
But this is not the case with most of the threats that leave
something to chance in international relations. In this arena
the danger created by an incident is the possibility that
decision-makers on each side will react to the other side's
actions by increasing the level of violence, even though
neither side intended this to occur. And the bulk of this
risk is generated by the fact that neither side can with
confidence and precision know the interpretations of the
incident the other side is making or estimate the other side's
intentions and probable response.

Some actions can probably produce risk in this way
regardless of the actors' preconceptions and views of the
other. This may be true for any use of nuclear weapons.
Decision-makers can never be absolutely sure how they or
the citizens of their countries will react if nuclear bombs
were to explode even as demonstrations. They would be
even less certain of how other states would react in these
circumstances. But in many cases, perhaps even including
the limited use of nuclear weapons, if decision-makers see
the events as a standard and controlled rung of an escalation ladder, the chances are less that it will somehow lead
to an inadvertent war. Any escalation ladder is used to set
limits as well as demonstrate resolve. If both sides know,
for example, that mobilization of reserve troops indicates

239

the crisis is considered serious to a given degree, they also know that this action does not mean that an all-out attack is imminent. There will be less "reciprocal fear of surprise attack,"[31] less fear that an unplanned outbreak of shooting will automatically escalate, and less fear that the other side is acting out of uncontrollable anger or insecurity.

Actor A will then take B's behavior as a planned attempt to show A how risky the situation is. But if both actors believe this is the purpose of the action they have less reason to believe things will somehow get out of hand. Furthermore, if each side thinks the other believes it, the cost of taking these actions will be known to be very low in comparison with what can be gained if the other side can be made to back down. In other words, the actions will have largely become signals—ways of staking the actor's reputation which, under a different set of conventions, could be replaced by any number of less dramatic actions and indeed by a diplomatic note.

The second part of the argument is that this transformation can be heavily influenced by the statements of observers and actors. Since most actors try to limit the danger of inadvertent war, and are apt to believe others behave similarly, any discussion of an action that would create a significant probability of mutually unintended escalation is likely to lead the actors to guard against such escalation should the action occur. Since actors generally believe the other side is also aware of the danger, they are apt to believe it is also taking precautions.

Furthermore, when observers frequently talk of how actions previously thought to be threats that leave something to chance can bring pressure to bear on the adversary, both sides may be quick to see the actions in this new light. For example, Kahn argues that "the use of nuclear weapons would probably be more escalatory—and therefore more frightening—if, instead of being launched locally, the weapons were launched strategically, though against local

[31] Schelling, *The Strategy of Conflict*, 205-29.

targets. By using the same weapons systems that would be used in a general war, one would communicate to the enemy a willingness to disregard precedents and a likely willingness to" escalate further.[32] Similarly, Schelling claims that if one wants to emphasize the possibility of a limited war becoming all-out, "one may . . . try not to maximize the stability of new limits as one passes certain thresholds, but to pass them in a way that dramatizes and emphasizes that the engagement is a dangerous one. . . ."[33] But these statements if accepted will become self-denying prophecies.[34] Much of the reason for the fright and pressure is derived from the fact that these actions are seen as evidence that things are beginning to get out of hand. If dramatic and unprecedented actions are discussed as ways of showing intent, they lose their impact derived from the implication that things may escalate inadvertently. Once an act is brought within the "rules of the game" it loses much of its power as a generator of risk.

Thus, if no one had talked about the exemplary use of nuclear weapons and the United States, in the midst of a crisis, exploded an H-bomb over Siberia it might convince Russia that the risk of accidental war was intolerably high, that this action was an index to high American resolve, and that she should therefore end the crisis. But if this use of nuclear weapons had been discussed at length the actors would have little reason to believe there was a great danger of unplanned and undesired escalation. If the great powers can adjust to the fact that their warships can collide without leading to unintended consequences, there is reason to believe that more dramatic events can be treated in a similar way.[35]

[32] *On Escalation*, 139.

[33] Schelling, *Arms and Influence*, 107.

[34] Kahn, *Thinking About the Unthinkable*, 29.

[35] The transformation of threats that leave something to chance into signals is slowed by the fact that there is no agreed-upon escalation ladder. As Kahn says, "if there are two opponents there are in effect two escalation ladders, with all that this means in terms of confusion and ambiguities as to where each participant believes he and his opponent are on the ladder and each side's estimate of the other's estimate."

Schelling's discussion of "brinkmanship" in terms of the threat that leaves something to chance can thus be seen as partially misleading. "The brink is not . . ." he argues, "the sharp edge of a cliff where one can stand firmly, look down, and decide whether or not to plunge. The brink is a curved slope that one can stand on with some risk of slipping, the slope gets steeper and the risk of slipping greater as one moves toward the chasm. But the slope and the risk of slipping are rather irregular; neither the person standing there nor onlookers can be quite sure just how great the risk is, or how much it increases when one takes a few more steps downward."[36] While this view is correct, it should be modified by a realization that the contours of the slope are not completely objective. They are affected not only by the forces of nature but also by the way each participant thinks about them, and the way each thinks the others think about them. If each stares at the slope for a long time, and knows that others are also staring at it, its shape will change.

RISKS AND TWO WAYS TO PREVAIL IN A CRISIS

Those generators of risk that have not been or cannot be transformed into signals also are affected by each actor's perceptions of the other's beliefs about how risky the situation is, and these perceptions can be influenced by the actor's statements. To understand the ramifications of this we must distinguish between the two general paths through which a threat that leaves something to chance can make its impact. First, it can lead either actor to retreat because the danger of war, if the present situation continues, is too great. Second, either actor can retreat because he believes that the other's willingness to bring about or tolerate so

---

(Kahn, *On Escalation*, 217). But some agreement on the ladder has been reached and the changes from the first to the second edition of Marshall Sokolovskii's *Military Strategy* indicate an increasing area of consensus. (Thomas Wolfe, "Shifts in Soviet Strategic Thought," *Foreign Affairs* 42 [April 1964], 475-86.)

[36] *The Strategy of Conflict*, 199.

risky a condition is an index to his willingness to pay a high price rather than back down. Although both of these mechanisms may operate simultaneously, this does not have to be the case. An actor may believe that while a situation is objectively risky, the other side does not realize it.[37] In this case the actor will have no reason to expect that the other side will cease its risky behavior, unless the actor retreats. Indeed the other side may do something even more risky if the situation continues, since it will not be restrained by the perception that it is running high risks. On the other hand it is possible, but less likely, that the actor may think that while the other's behavior actually does not increase the risk of war, the other actor believes it does and thus this behavior is an index revealing that the other actor will run risks.

In any given crisis these two ways of exerting pressure partially conflict and the actor will have to choose which to stress. Actor A may hope to prevail by making B believe the risky behavior is an index to A's resolve. This is best done by showing B that A is fully aware of the risks he is running. Indeed, he may exaggerate his perceptions of risk. If B believes A is consciously running a high risk, he may judge that A will be willing to maintain or even increase the risk unless B backs down. But this tactic has a major drawback—B may feel he can hold out longer than A, since he will believe the perceived risk of inadvertent war weighs at least as heavily on A as it does on him.

On the other hand, A can act in a way that increases the chance of inadvertent war while claiming not to believe the situation is risky. This claim can plausibly be made because judgments of risk are rarely easy to make and actors have in the past created situations much riskier than they had anticipated (e.g., Russia's placing offensive missiles in Cuba). If A's claims are believed most of the pressure to retreat will be on B since he believes A regards

[37] This follows from Schelling's argument that the threat of inadvertent war "may exist whether we realize it or not." *Ibid.*, 189.

the situation as safe and therefore has little reason to back down.

While the latter technique probably increases the chances of prevailing in a single crisis, the long-run advantages for the actor may be less than if he had won by showing he was consciously running a high risk. Resolve is a relatively consistent determinant of an actor's behavior. If a state is shown to have high resolve in one situation others are apt to infer that it will stand firm on other issues. Thus the American actions in October 1962 may have convinced the Soviet Union that America would stand firm in Berlin. In contrast, raising the risks and yet convincing the other that you think the situation is still safe may not help you in future conflicts since you have not convinced others that you will consciously run risks. Others will have no reason to believe you will stand firm when you are aware the situation is dangerous. Only if you can make others believe your behavior indicates you generally act in risky ways without realizing it will you gain a reputation that will aid you in the future, and it is difficult to maintain a façade of calm if your adversary makes concerted efforts to show that certain kinds of behavior are dangerous. Similarly, while a person can win a game of chicken by showing his adversary that he is drunk, this behavior may not benefit him as much as if he had won while sober. In the latter case other drivers would assume that he would be willing to play recklessly in future contests. But if he wins by getting drunk, others may feel confident about challenging him if they can keep him away from the bottle and thus make him fully aware of the risks he is taking.

IMAGES AND "SECURITY AREAS" IN THE NUCLEAR ERA

Three characteristics of the international system are generally considered to be of great importance in understanding the superpowers' behavior. These are the essential bipolarity of the system (which exists despite erosions), the fact that the whole world is involved in the system, and the fact that both sides have a second strike capability. The

244

combination of the first two elements is usually thought to mean that in matters short of war international relations can more or less be equated with a zero-sum game. Whatever influence and control one side gains, the other side loses. Since events all over the world affect the relative power positions of the two superpowers, each must be concerned about the conflict in Yemen, strife in Guyana, and conspiracies in Zanzibar. John Herz relates this to an historical trend of the expansion of "the 'security area,' meaning the area in which whatever happened concerned the security interest of the nation in question."[38] States have come to realize "that attack upon the territorial integrity or political independence of any unit anywhere would concern every other unit in the world."[39] In a bipolar system that encompasses the whole world "the blocs touch each other everywhere, with few ways out into neutral or unoccupied ground. Whatever the security interest of one side seems to require increases the insecurity of the other side."[40]

But the links between events in these areas and the main actors' national security not only are not self-evident, but do not exist. The altered nature of technology and war means that for the first time in history the control of foreign territory either by conquest or by alliance is not directly related to the superpowers' national security. When the superpowers do not worry about invading armies crossing their borders and have much more military and economic power than any possible third states, they do not need large buffer zones. Aron argues that "the balance of forces is still approximate, equivocal," and can be "threatened . . . by a secondary unit changing camp."[41] But with the possible exception of large-scale defections in Europe, this is not true. The loss of West Europe would cut into America's

[38] *International Politics in the Atomic Age* (New York: Columbia University Press, 1959), 239.

[39] *Ibid.*, 240.

[40] *Ibid.*, 241.

[41] Raymond Aron, *Peace and War* (Garden City, N.Y.: Doubleday, 1966), 159.

245

economic strength, and the loss of East Europe could lead Russia to fear invasion, although this seems far-fetched to outside observers. But even these events, which of course are terribly unlikely, would leave the superpowers with a deterrent force that would provide more security than great powers often possessed in the past.

When we look at non-European areas the argument for the existence, let alone the expansion, of "security areas" has even less validity. Herz claims that "the more rigid the alignments, the greater the sensitivity regarding any changes or threats of changes in the existing line-up. Such sensitivity endangers world peace over the most minute of issues or incidents. . . . [The] more rigid the balance is, the greater the danger that, in the absence of countershifts and realignments, such events may sooner or later lead to that imbalance in which the more powerful can either destroy the opponent or blackmail him into submission."[42] Two things should be noted about this formulation. First, danger only occurs if there is positive feedback—i.e. "where giving way would lead to an accumulation of losses for one [side] and gains for the other."[43] But the postwar history of the underdeveloped countries indicates that this is unlikely. Guinea veered close to the Communist camp without greatly influencing its neighbors, and even without determining its own future. The former French Congo had for a period a government heavily influenced by the Chinese without leading to a chain reaction. Communism has made few gains in Latin America since Castro took power. Although part of the reason for Castro's lack of influence seems to lie in the preventive measures taken by the United States and the disillusionment of the Soviet Union,[44] it is far from certain that without these countervailing forces other

42 Herz, *International Politics* . . . , 155-56. I have omitted an entire paragraph in this quotation.
43 Kenneth Waltz, "The Stability of a Bi-Polar World," *Daedalus* 92 (Summer 1964), 903.
44 See the discussion in Herbert Dinerstein, "Soviet Policy in Latin America," *American Political Science Review* 61 (March 1967), 80-90.

countries would have followed the Cuban path. Furthermore, American decoupling could decrease the positive feedback produced by an underdeveloped country going Communist by reducing the degree to which these states believe that their futures are linked together because they are all strongly influenced by American policy. Second, even if all the underdeveloped countries became Soviet dominated, this would not directly threaten the United States. The military balance would remain essentially unchanged.

Events in the underdeveloped world could only lead to Soviet threats to the United States or Western Europe if these events drastically altered the Soviet image of American resolve. And few detailed, let alone convincing, arguments have been developed to explain how this change would come about. While it is true that the American image of resolve might be damaged if in the course of trying to prevent an underdeveloped country from going Communist the United States was forced to retreat by the threat of Soviet reaction, two caveats should be entered on this point. First, it seems unlikely that the degree of damage would be so great as to present a major threat. Second, most American defeats in third areas seem to be explained by, and understood by others in terms of, local conditions rather than dominant Soviet power and resolve. Thus even if the United States loses in Vietnam and the guerrillas in, say, Bolivia, are successful, these events may not be taken by the Russians as important indices of American resolve. In the past, the degree to which the outcome of struggles in the Third World has been taken for indices of American resolve has been increased by the American statements coupling these events, and the superpowers' behavior concerning them, to other events in the Third World and even to how the superpowers would react in other areas of conflict. But by this same token, the United States could decrease the use of such events as indices of American resolve by decoupling—by announcing it believed the fate of the underdeveloped countries was only minimally related to

American security and that the United States would therefore not extensively intervene in the Third World.[45]

It can be argued that while the events in the underdeveloped areas have little direct impact on American national security, American decision-makers believe they do.
While this is possible, the lack of clear explanations of the
security value of the underdeveloped areas given in public
or presented in presumably well-informed accounts of
American foreign policy making and the traditional strain
of idealism in American foreign policy make it plausible
that the desire for security has not been the main reason
why American decision-makers have favored involvement
in the Third World.[46] What has been more important is the
intrinsic value of these areas. Most American decision-
makers place a high value on seeing other countries independent, internally free, and on the road to economic development even if this does not contribute markedly to
American security. As President Kennedy put it in his
inaugural address: "We pledge our best efforts to help
[the underdeveloped countries] help themselves . . . not
because the Communists are doing it, not because we seek
their votes, but because it is right." A combination of egotism (the desire to have other states form in our mold)
and altruism can explain a great deal of current American
policy.

Two implications follow from this. First, many of those
who wish to decrease American involvement in the underdeveloped areas and who have been called "neo-isolation-
ists" are within the "realist" tradition of seeking mainly

[45] For similar arguments about the lack of strong feedback between
the events in one underdeveloped country and those in others and
the unimportance of these countries for American national security,
see Max Singer and Aaron Wildavsky, "A Third-World Averaging
Strategy," in Paul Seabury and Aaron Wildavsky, eds., *U.S. Foreign
Policy* (New York: McGraw-Hill, 1969); Kenneth Waltz, "The
Politics of Peace," *International Studies Quarterly* 11 (September
1967), 199-211; and Robert W. Tucker, *Nation or Empire?* (Baltimore: Johns Hopkins Press, 1968), 33-36. But see also Harry Magdoff,
The Age of Imperialism (New York: Monthly Review Press, 1969).

[46] This analysis may also apply to Soviet motives, but they are
even more difficult to determine than American motives.

national security. Those who favor wide involvement are "idealists" in the sense of being willing to pay a price for values not intimately tied to the state's vital interests. This is not to argue that the former policy is preferable. The United States is rich and powerful and is well able to defend interests wider than national security. The "tough-minded" and "realistic" defenses of world-wide involvement, however, are misleading. They masquerade what is largely altruism as what is necessary to keep Communism off American shores. Second, light can be shed on Rosecrance's discussion of two supposedly contradictory views of bipolarity presented by Kenneth Waltz. "According to one, the Soviet Union and the United States are engaged in a duel for world supremacy, or, at minimum, in a struggle to maintain their relative positions. An action by one directly affects the position of the other; all international changes are of vital significance in that they affect the balance between the two. According to the other notion of bipolarity, however, substantial territorial and/or political changes can take place in international relations without impinging on the overarching stability." Thus one or the other side can "gain" or "lose" China, Cuba, or Guinea "without appreciable impact on the balance."[47]

Even though I have argued that the second position is correct, it only contradicts the first version if we think exclusively in terms of national security. Increased Communist control of an area is a loss to America and a gain to Russia in terms of nonsecurity values,[48] and yet the stability of the system may not be affected. Rosecrance argues that under the second notion of bipolarity "immediate countervailing pressures . . . are not called forth by each change in the status quo. Imbalance may emerge."[49] But even if national security does not demand that each superpower

[47] Richard Rosecrance, "Bipolarity, Multipolarity, and the Future," *Journal of Conflict Resolution* 10 (September 1966), 316.

[48] Given fragmentation of the Communist countries the latter may not always be true, but for the purposes of this argument this question can be ignored.

[49] Rosecrance, "Bipolarity . . . ," 317.

counter the efforts of the other in all parts of the globe, the desire of each superpower to have third areas develop in its image can lead it to follow such a policy. And even if this desire wanes on one side and countervailing pressures do not develop, the imbalances that follow will primarily affect the great powers' nonsecurity interests, and will only lead to instability if they involve so much positive feedback as to eventually impinge on the most important interests of the parties. But the separation of control of most areas of the world from the superpowers' national security makes this process unlikely.

Sacrificing Values as an Index

Finally, we should note that an actor may waste money or otherwise harm himself to provide an index of his resolve. To avoid the skepticism warranted when money is spent to show one's signals are accurate,[50] a sacrifice not small in comparison to the matter in dispute must be made. For example, if you told a prospective buyer of your car who had offered $1,000 that you had made a $5,000 bet with a third party that you could get $2,000 for it he might not believe you. But if you publicly burned a $1,000 bill he would probably be persuaded, since this action would not make sense if your story were merely a bargaining ploy.[51] Since spending money in this way is a method of wasting resources or harming yourself, other techniques could be employed to reach the same goal. What would be appropriate would depend on the particular characteristic or motive about which you wish to convey information. Schelling points out that it is said that "In the early days, wealthy San Franciscans . . . conducted their 'duels' by throwing gold coins one by one into the Bay until one or the other called it quits."[52] An ancient story tells of a captured prisoner who knew he was going to be tortured and wished to

[50] See above, 92-94, for a discussion of spending money as a signal.

[51] I am indebted to Thomas Schelling for discussion on this point.

[52] "Comment" in Klaus Knorr and Thornton Read, *Limited Strategic War* (New York: Praeger, 1962), 243-44.

convince his captors that this would not make him talk. To do this he picked up a burning coal in his bare hand. Suitably impressed, the onlookers realized they could get no information from him and returned him to his own side.

The acquisition by both the United States and the USSR of a second strike capability has made this story especially relevant today. In the past there were costs attached to most kinds of international political action, but these could be outweighed by the gains. This was even true of armed conflict. In that case usually only one side lost more than it gained. Or, to put it more precisely, not more than one side lost more than it would have had it conceded rather than going to war. In Bismarck's era one could not claim war did not pay. This is no longer true. By almost any standard, both sides would suffer tremendous net losses in a major war. This also means that any act that involves a significant risk of war will entail costs greater than any but the most important stakes. In this environment it becomes more important than in the past for states to demonstrate how much given issues mean to them and how high costs they are willing to pay to prevail on them. To overstate the break with the past: before 1945 states had to demonstrate their capability to do harm to others, now the United States and Soviet Union must demonstrate their willingness to let others do harm to them.[53] In an era when the superpowers know they can inflict unlimited pain on each other, they must try to show that they can take pain. One way to do this would be to offer human sacrifices—country A could tell B, "Just to show you how tough we are we will kill 1,000 of our own people." Or, in the midst of a limited war in Europe one side might blow up one of its own cities. These actions would be indices to the state's resolve since they demonstrate a willingness to pay costs.

If spending lives is too gruesome, the state can make sacrifices of other values, such as its population's leisure, health, standard of living, etc. Money spent in support of foreign policy cannot be used to secure these other values

[53] See the discussion in *ibid.*

251

and thus can be considered to represent a sacrifice in a way not dissimilar to killing one's own population. Indeed, since the money could have been used on health programs that would have saved lives, the similarity is quite real. The maintenance of a large peacetime army and the acquisition of weapons systems, like the Atlas, whose costs outrun their military utility, may make their main contribution to national security through this mechanism.

From this perspective it is not a disadvantage that the money does not purchase military gains. Indeed, it will be a more effective display if it brings nothing in return, for then it constitutes a greater sacrifice. Instead of sending an extra division to Europe in a crisis we might want to dump a billion dollars worth of goods into the ocean to demonstrate our resolve.[54] While the Russians might see this as a "sunk cost" that would not modify our behavior if the crisis escalated, this is also essentially true for the mobilization of a division or two. Both these actions show the actor is willing to make sacrifices. The Russians may have understood this when during a Berlin crisis they added so much money to their military budget so quickly that much of it had to go to waste.[55]

Incurring diplomatic costs can similarly be employed as an index. Thus a state may seek an opportunity to offend others in order to reveal that it is willing to pay high costs to reach its goals, thereby making it less likely that others will feel they can successfully alter the first state's policy. This is illustrated by the way the USSR broke the moratorium on the testing of nuclear weapons. She resumed testing right before the Belgrade Conference of nonaligned states, did not make as elaborate excuses as she might have, and made little effort to disguise the fact that she had been planning the test series for months. Although this may have

[54] More constructively, the money might be donated to some worthy cause like helping the underdeveloped areas. But others would be prone to believe we made the donations for the same motives which underlie our foreign aid program and would not take our actions as providing evidence of our resolve.

[55] Horelick and Rush, *Strategic Power* . . . , 124.

been, on balance, unwise, it had the redeeming feature of showing others, especially the neutrals, that she would not be deflected from a policy about which she felt strongly, thus discouraging them from expecting that diplomatic pressure could sway her.

CHAPTER NINE

Application

To RECAPITULATE, actors cheaply influence the images others have of them by four basic methods. First, they use signals to commit themselves to a policy they want others to believe they will follow. Second, they manipulate indices to take advantage of the perceiver's incorrect belief that he is drawing inferences from behavior the actor cannot use, or at least is not using, to project images cheaply. Third, actors decouple signals from their usual meanings or couple them to new meanings. Finally, they influence the interpretations others make about aspects of their behavior taken to be indices.

IMAGES, SIGNALS, AND INDICES IN THE VIETNAM CONFLICT

No one interaction illustrates nearly all the aspects of signals and indices I have outlined, but enough are revealed by the war in Vietnam to make this case worth examining in this context. As I stressed in the introduction, the method of analysis used here does not claim to cover nearly all aspects of a subject or to provide answers for all questions. Thus this examination, even if it were based on all the relevant information and were greatly expanded, could not be a definitive account of the decision-making processes of the actors or the implications of the war for the international system. Rather I hope to show, as I hope the examples used throughout the text have shown, that the approach outlined in this book can lead to insights into what has happened in the past and can suggest possible policies not contemplated when more common methods of analysis are employed.

I realize a good deal of this analysis will have been outrun by events by the time it is read; indeed this has already happened to some of it since the chapter was first drafted in the spring of 1968. To the extent that the actors do adopt some of the strategies outlined below the case for my approach is strengthened. If this analysis does not help explain why the actors behaved as they did my case is obviously weakened. But I have not attempted to make specific predictions. My approach is both too unrefined and too narrow to permit this.[1] Therefore, this chapter is mostly designed to serve as an extended illustration of how actors try to project desired images in a complex interaction rather than as a definitive test of the utility of the approach.

I shall examine the war in Vietnam mainly from the viewpoint of the United States because more is known of the American goals and perspectives; with fuller information the analysis could also be done from the other side. The first thing to be noted is that the American national security goals in the war involve images almost exclusively. Strategically, South Vietnam is of little value. While the loss of this territory would make it somewhat easier for the Communists to launch new attacks, this is less important than the cost of the change in the American image that policy-makers believe a defeat would entail.[2]

American behavior involves both signals and indices. The latter aspects are probably the most important because the American actions in Vietnam have involved very high costs and seem to tap a dimension relevant to predicting future American behavior in Southeast Asia, if not throughout the world. However, it is convenient to begin by discussing the signaling aspects. One way the United States has tried to convince the Communists it will "stay the course" in Vietnam is by issuing signals to that effect. These signals gain their impact by increasing the cost to the United

[1] For a general discussion of the limitations of prediction as the test of the value of the theory, see Toulmin, *Foresight and Understanding*, 18-43.

[2] It may well be that even though the justification given by American leaders for their policies, especially since the large scale commitment of American troops in 1965, has been mostly in terms of American national security, many American decision-makers have been largely motivated by an essentially altruistic concern for the future of South Vietnam. To the extent this is true, the part of the following analysis that deals with minimizing the impact of a defeat in Vietnam is irrelevant.

For an interesting theoretical analysis of the strategic importance of underdeveloped countries, see Charles Wolf, "Some Aspects of the 'Value' of Less-Developed Countries to the United States," *World Politics* 15 (July 1963), 625-29.

States of acting in a way that contradicts them. These costs are of two types. First, as with all signals, the United States has staked its reputation on them. Indeed it has done this quite explicitly, by pointing out that it has commitments all over the world that depend on America's word being believed. Comparisons have been made with the American presence in Berlin and American decision-makers have claimed that if we do not fulfill our pledges in Vietnam there will be less reason for our adversaries to believe we will fulfill them in Europe. It is interesting to note that neither the Europeans nor the Soviets have endorsed this claim, and I shall return to this point later. Second, leaders of countries that feel directly threatened by the kind of forces attacking the South Vietnamese government (e.g. Thailand) have supported the United States on the premise that America would live up to its signals. Similarly, key individuals and groups within South Vietnam who might otherwise have tried to reach accommodations with the Viet Cong decided to support the government because of their belief that America would not abandon Vietnam without seeing that their lives and interests were adequately protected. Thus the American signals have helped to change the policies of others and so have altered the international environment. This change has not only increased support for American policy, but, what is more important here, has created a situation wherein if the United States changes its policies these allies will have to pay a high price.

In this case, as in most others, the most important cost is the first, the damage to the state's signaling reputation. Since the beginning of the Kennedy Administration the United States has sought to increase this cost in order to reassure its allies and deter the Communists. Thus if the United States decided to alter its policy and abandon Vietnam it would want to decrease the damage to its reputation by decoupling its signals. Given the fact that the American pledges have been explicit, repeated, and have contained few hedges, decoupling could not be completely successful.

256

Still, a partial success could significantly reduce the damage to the American signaling reputation.

American efforts would be made easier by the fact that the Soviets have acted as though they have not "heard" the American pledges. They have not said they believe America's word is at stake in Vietnam or implied that an American retreat would lead them to doubt American commitments in Europe. Whether or not it was Russia's purpose to make it easier for the United States to make concessions in Vietnam, her position has had this effect. However it is possible that if Russia came to believe that the United States had decided to retreat she would reverse her policy and claim that such action would undermine the American position in other parts of the world. This would increase the payoff for Russia should the United States accept a defeat, but for this reason would increase the American resolve to avoid this outcome. Thus Russia would have to face the unlikely possibility that such a tactic might lead the United States to reverse a decision to withdraw on the grounds that the costs of withdrawal were higher than previously anticipated. Decoupling would similarly be made easier by the fact that America's European allies have also generally not accepted the American argument that its word is pledged in Vietnam. These are actors who one would expect to be most sensitive to the possibility that America's signaling reputation would be damaged. Perhaps the European leaders felt from the beginning that the United States could not reach its goals and would sooner or later have to renege on its commitments to South Vietnam and therefore believed that they should try to minimize the damage by consistently rejecting the American claim that not acting according to her signals in Southeast Asia would affect her image in the European context.[3]

[3] Less likely, the European leaders may have thought that if they undercut the American attempts at commitment the United States would doubt its ability to make the Communists think it would stand firm and would therefore decide not to send troops to Vietnam, a venture many Europeans thought would divert American troops and energies away from Europe.

257

A number of claims could be made to facilitate decoupling. First, the United States could claim that it in fact had met its commitments. To make others accept this view the United States could try to return to the pre-1965 position that the American commitment is not to keep the Viet Cong from taking over the country, but rather to help the South Vietnamese help themselves. The latter claim is more restricted, for it implies that if the South Vietnamese government cannot provide a certain—and unspecified—level of military and political effort the United States is not pledged to protect it. This is a promise the United States could plausibly claim to have met even if it abandons South Vietnam. The American newspapers are filled with stories of the corruption of the South Vietnamese government, of the Swiss bank accounts of the leading generals, of the unwillingness or inability of the government to draft 18 and 19 year olds, of the disintegration of the local government in many areas during the 1968 Tet offensive, of the ineffectiveness of ARVN, and of the failure of the pacification program and accompanying efforts of the government to win the loyalty of the people. The American government has at times denied the validity of these reports, but if it decided to withdraw it could change its analysis. Since the American statements about the military and political abilities of the South Vietnamese have generally been received with skepticism, it might not be difficult to lead others to believe the United States had come to believe the South Vietnamese could not save themselves. The United States would still be faced with the problem that its pledges for the past years were generally not conditioned upon the efforts of the South Vietnamese, but the fact that the more limited commitment was made earlier and never disavowed would make decoupling easier than if the United States had to fabricate completely a pledge it could plausibly claim to have met.

The Nixon Administration's policy of "Vietnamization" of the war could contribute substantially to this kind of decoupling. And this analysis would lead us to expect that there will be more statements like that made by Hubert

Humphrey in October 1969 in which he argued that "we have succeeded in" achieving our objectives and fulfilling our commitments by having given the South time to build up its strength. "If the South Vietnamese have not used their time, that's their problem. We have done as much for a friend as a friend can be expected to do."[4]

It is interesting to note that when Britain withdrew its support from the White Russian forces in 1919-20, it claimed, with considerably more justification than can be mustered in the case of Vietnam, that the British commitment was only to supply the anti-Bolshevik forces with enough aid so they would not lose on account of lack of matériel.[5]

Second, and similar to this, the United States could capitalize on the ambiguity about whether it had promised to protect the South against all Communist forces trying to overthrow it or only against attack from the North. This familiar question of whether the conflict is a civil war or an invasion has been confused partly because of the division of Vietnam, the ambiguous status of those who went North after 1954 and returned to fight later, and the difficulty in determining what proportion of the soldiers and leaders have been infiltrated into the country from the North. This ambiguity could aid decoupling in two ways. First, the United States could minimize its perception of the participation of the North, claim that the conflict was, or had become, mainly a civil war, and reduce American intervention on the grounds that it had never pledged to fight in a civil war. At this stage such an attempt would probably be unconvincing because of the extent of North Vietnamese

[4] Philip Shabecoff, "Humphrey Says U.S. Has Met Vietnam Obligations," *New York Times*, October 23, 1969, p. 9.

[5] Richard Ullman, *Britain and the Russian Civil War* (Princeton: Princeton University Press, 1968). The reasoning behind this commitment—that once both sides in the civil war had roughly comparable arms the side with the most popular support would win—is clearly questionable. Affinity with the beliefs espoused by each side is only one of several considerations influencing each person's behavior. And variables other than popular support, such as organizational skill and the quality of leadership, affect the civil war's outcome.

involvement and the previous American position that the conflict, although containing an element of civil war, is predominantly "aggression from the North." An alternative strategy could be consistent with this position. Since Secretary of State Rusk repeatedly said that all we want is for the North "to leave her neighbors alone," the United States could stress that its commitment was to combating invasion, rather than to putting down internal unrest. By glossing over the question of the degree to which the North Vietnamese have been integrated into all elements of the Viet Cong, the administration could plausibly claim that fulfilling its commitment involved preventing the main line North Vietnamese units from overthrowing the government. The United States could then restrict its military activities to operations necessary to secure this end. If the Viet Cong were able to win military victories over ARVN, the United States could then plausibly claim that this was the result of a civil war in which it was never pledged to intervene, and could withdraw.

A third type of claim that would facilitate decoupling would be one indicating that even if the United States defaulted on its signals in Vietnam, others should not doubt its word in other areas. This could be done by playing down the importance of the commitment given, especially in comparison with others (e.g. those involving Europe). By issuing even stronger and more explicit signals about other commitments, the United States could contribute to debasing its own signals, thus making the pledges to Vietnam less important and reducing the cost of breaking them.

The importance and possibilities of decommitment can also be illustrated by the possible solutions to the dilemma in which the United States found itself in 1968 when it tried to bring North Vietnam to the negotiating table. The Communists would not open negotiations until the bombing of the North was unconditionally halted. The United States wanted to negotiate but was committed to the position that it would not stop bombing until the North promised concessions.[6] The United States apparently decided that the demands it had made were not going to be met and, as its desire for negotiations grew, became willing to accept less in return for stopping the bombing. However it desired that both allies and adversaries not believe that it was abandoning its commitments because this would lead them to expect still further concessions. Thus, to get the negotiations started the United States seems to have been willing to sacrifice some substance but wanted to save its signaling reputation, just as it might be willing to accept such a trade-off in the peace settlement.

The United States said it would stop the bombing if there were some military reciprocation by the North. An elaboration of what kind of reciprocation would be sufficient was provided by Defense Secretary Clifford's answers to the question of the Senate Armed Service Committee in which he said that the North would have to refrain from sending men and supplies south at a rate which was faster than normal.[7] The American commitment was of the general form: "We will do X when you do Y." Since the meaning of X was quite clear, decommitment must take advantage of ambiguity about what Y was and whether the adversary's behavior constituted Y.[8] Specifically, it was not

[6] Although the United States has halted the bombing since this section was written, I have not altered most of the text. While some of the verb tenses may seem awkward, it is valuable to suggest possible policies which the United States could have followed. If some of the versions of the "understanding" with North Vietnam that led to the bombing halt are correct, then the United States did in fact adopt one of the decoupling strategies discussed below by misrepresenting what it believed the North agreed to do.

[7] The United States has also said that other reciprocations would be satisfactory, and I will discuss the implications of this below.

[8] In some cases an actor can take advantage of the ambiguity of *when* certain actions will take place. But this would have only postponed the dilemma here. Even if the United States could decommit by stopping the bombing *before* the North Vietnamese had promised to make a concession and claim that it expected a reciprocation to follow, it would have been faced with the problem of how to save its signaling reputation if the North did not reciprocate. The common argument that both sides would be under pressure not to break off

clear, first, what the "normal" rates of infiltration were. The frequent American revisions of its estimates of the amount of previous infiltration indicate that knowledge of what the North Vietnamese had done in the past was not completely reliable. Second, the concept of "normal" infiltration would remain ambiguous even if we had had complete information about the previous rates. Were "normal" rates those that maintained the North Vietnamese units at their existing strengths? In this case the number of men sent south would depend on the casualties sustained by the Northern forces. If there was little fighting, there would be little "normal" infiltration. Or did "normal" mean some steady rate approximating the average rate of infiltration over the previous three years? Under this definition the North Vietnamese forces would grow if there was little fighting (and thus few losses) and shrink if battles were frequent. A lowering of the level of violence in the South coupled with "normal" rates of infiltration would then lead to an increased number of Northern troops in South Vietnam. The implications of these two points for decommitment are fairly obvious since they are further illustrations of the technique discussed above of giving an interpretation of your commitment which, while different from the interpretation you meant at the time, is plausible. Thus, the United States could give North Vietnam a figure for the "normal" rate of infiltration higher than the United States originally wanted to settle for. The North might be willing to "limit" itself to such a figure, but might not believe that the United States had previously bluffed.

Third, even if the United States knew exactly what the "normal" rate was, it was extremely difficult for it to determine how many men and supplies were being infiltrated at any particular time. Thus not only was the American commitment ambiguous, but so were the actions of the other side. The United States could not be sure whether

the negotiations once they started, although probably correct, does not deal with the central concern of this analysis of how to make concessions without damaging one's image.

the North had fulfilled the conditions the United States had laid down, and the North in turn could not be sure if the Americans believed they have fulfilled these conditions. Fourth, the United States had talked about a number of other reciprocations the North could take that could substitute for a limitation of the rate of infiltration.[9] The most prominent was a reduction in the level of violence in the South.[10] As the events of the summer of 1968 showed, it is difficult to tell exactly what would meet this requirement. American authorities debated whether the decrease in enemy activity was an index of Hanoi's attitude and would continue if the bombing were halted or whether it merely reflected the North's judgment of the wisest tactical disposition of their troops and had no political significance.

Decommitment by use of the third and fourth points of ambiguity takes advantage of the somewhat unusual difficulties in this case of determining exactly what the other side had done. Even if the United States believed North Vietnam was not limiting its infiltration, the United States could have claimed to have perceived that Hanoi was doing so. Unless the North believed that American reconnaissance and intelligence facilities were extremely good, or unless the discrepancy between the actual rate of infiltration and the rate the North thought would meet the American definition of "normal" was very high, Hanoi might well believe the American explanation. Similarly, the North could not be sure it knew what the United States would perceive as a deescalation in the South. Thus the United States could take advantage of a period when the North Vietnamese main line units were relatively unaggres-

---

[9] C. L. Sulzberger, "Foreign Affairs: The Thirteen Knocks," *New York Times*, July 17, 1968, p. 38.

[10] In fact, in the fall of 1968, the United States claimed it was totally halting the bombing of the North because of an "understanding" by which the North would reduce the violence in the South by not bombarding Southern cities and not making large-scale attacks across the DMZ. It is not yet clear whether the North actually said it would refrain from these activities or whether the United States, by pretending the North had given such a pledge, was trying both to decommit itself and to commit the North.

sive to announce that this constitutes the reciprocation it was looking for and that it would therefore halt the bombing.[11]

In some cases the actor trying to decommit does not have to be concerned with the motives behind the actions he is claiming met his conditions, or with others' beliefs about these motives. This is true in the example of decommitment from the general American pledge to defend Vietnam, but does not hold in the case of trying to escape from the demand that the bombing would not be halted unless the North promises a military reciprocation. The implications of a reduction in infiltration of military activity that came about because the North was unable to maintain its forces at full strength in the face of the American bombing are different from those that would follow if the reduction was ordered as part of a bargain with the United States. Thus the United States would have to claim to believe that the actions the North took that met the American demands were motivated by a desire to reduce the level of violence of the conflict. This would involve ignoring or overcoming the usual perception that actions of an adversary that benefit oneself are a direct effect of the pressure one is exerting on him[12] and the common desire to claim a military victory.[13]

Some of these decommitting techniques depend on the at least tacit cooperation of the North Vietnamese. For if they vehemently denied they had decreased their military support of the Viet Cong or, on the larger issue of a settle-

[11] If the United States were not willing to make further concessions to begin substantive negotiations but rather sought greater military reciprocations, it could employ tactics opposite of those discussed here—e.g., even if it believed a lull was politically inspired, it could refuse to acknowledge it. Of course, the actual determination of whether and how much fighting has subsided is far from easy and making judgments about the adversary's motivation are even more difficult.

[12] Jervis, "Hypotheses on Misperception," 476-77.

[13] For an example of such a claim made when the evidence was ambiguous, see the official American statements quoted in *I. F. Stone's Weekly*, February 20, 1967, p. 1.

ment itself, claimed that the United States had unconditionally pledged itself to preventing the South from going Communist, decommitment would be more difficult. The North might feel the need of making the former claim—whether or not it was true—to maintain its political influence over the NLF and its prestige with the Chinese and revolutionaries in other countries. In this case both sides might be content to make contradictory claims and to point out the reasons the other side is under pressure to give the explanation it is offering.[14] Decommitment would be made somewhat less effective, but the damage might not be great.

A greater problem for an American attempt to decommit by claiming that the North had promised a military reciprocation in return for a bombing halt was created by the fact that the North was committed to not making such a concession. Not wanting the United States to believe it had failed to stand by its commitment and not wanting to see its own signaling reputation damaged, the North might try to convince the United States that it had not scaled down its military efforts. In addition, the North could believe that concessions would be taken by the United States as an index showing their resolve was weakening. Because the two sides had made incompatible pledges, behavior protecting one side's signaling reputation damaged the other's. Thus there is a zero-sum element to this situation. However, the North might be willing to trade some probable damage to its image to gain negotiations without having to pay other costs. Furthermore, if the North was not sure whether the United States believed the false claim that the North had made a military concession, it might feel there was only a low probability of significant damage to its image in America's eyes, yet not be so sure that America was misrepresenting its views and defaulting on its pledge that it would greatly lower its estimation of the frequency with which the United States lived up to its signals.[15]

[14] For an example of the problems this can cause, see Freymond, *The Saar Conflict*, 178.
[15] As events turned out, North Vietnam denied it made any prom-

The North might resist allowing the United States to decommit on the larger issue of its pledge to South Vietnam if it believed America felt it was so badly defeated that it would withdraw rather than continue fighting, even if it were unable to protect its signaling reputation. However this would be a major gamble for the North Vietnamese and one they would be less likely to take because the payoff in the event they were successful would accrue to anti-American movements in general and the direct benefit to North Vietnam would not be particularly great.

Finally, it should be stressed that as in all instances of decommitment the techniques discussed here assume a willingness on the part of one of the major actors (in this case the United States) to abandon part of his goals. The United States will have made concessions it originally resisted and did not think it would have to make. However if decommitment is successful the actor will not suffer the additional cost of damaging his reputation for issuing accurate signals.

Another facet of the protection of images can help us see in a new light aspects of American, and to a lesser extent North Vietnamese, behavior that was criticized as hindering efforts at peacemaking. As noted above,[16] many people displayed impatience with the slow and indirect way each side indicated the terms on which it would enter negotiations. While these criticisms are not without some merit, they overlook the fact that an actor who wants to issue peace feelers must be careful lest his signals damage his image, and may therefore not want the adversary to be sure what he is trying to communicate. This desire for am-

---

ises in return for the American bombing halt. ("Hanoi Says Bombing Halt Doesn't Restrict Viet Cong," *New York Times*, February 27, 1969, p. 1.) However these disclaimers (or at least the public ones) were extremely mild and infrequent. Hanoi chose to allow most of the American assertions of the existence of an "understanding"—assertions themselves ambiguous as to the degree of the North Vietnamese commitment (see, for example, Peter Grose, "Challenge to Nixon," *New York Times*, Sunday, March 9, 1969, Section 4, p. 1.)—to pass unchallenged.

[16] See above, p. 129.

biguity can explain why both sides have at times chosen to issue "Delphic public signals" instead of entering into direct secret talks. Under the latter circumstances the opportunities for direct questioning and exchanges may make it too difficult to maintain ambiguity at the first, or semantic, level. This consideration may also explain why, in one of their public signals, the North chose to employ in a crucial position a word that could be translated by two different terms in English. The ambiguity was accentuated when *Pravda* translated the word one way and other sources translated it the other way, leaving the United States at a loss to know whether it had to "accept" or merely to "recognize" Hanoi's position.[17]

The desire to use the protection of ambiguity may account for aspects of the secret exchanges between Washington and Hanoi. The intermediaries chosen to convey these messages often were not of the highest reliability— many were not skilled diplomats and lacked a reputation for accurate and perceptive reporting. The frequent North Vietnamese "desire . . . to deal through volunteers rather than professionals"[18] may have been rooted in the knowledge that if both sides can be positive that the intermediary is transmitting without distortion the position of the adversary, the use of the third party will provide no protection for the actors' images. While some American officials seem to have regretted this use of "nonprofessionals," one saw that such intermediaries "can say things that are deniable later on if problems arise."[19] On one occasion when an exchange took place through high officials, useful ambiguity may have been created by two factors. First, the Americans could not be sure whether the third party (the Polish for-

---

[17] David Kraslow and Stuart Lorry, *The Secret Search for Peace in Vietnam* (New York: Vintage, 1968), 152-53. Of course this may have been accidental. The Japanese response to the Potsdam declaration accidentally employed a term with two meanings. While the Japanese wanted the Allies to believe that they were withholding comment on the declaration, the term used, and the interpretations given by Japanese newspapers, led to the perception that the Japanese had rejected it.

[18] *Ibid.*, 221.   [19] *Ibid.*

eign minister) was speaking for his own government or for Hanoi.[20] Second, and presumably accidentally, neither the foreign minister nor the American ambassador with whom he was dealing were known to be articulate and straightforward.[21]

The creation of ambiguity is not without its dangers, as is shown by the effects of the Vietnam peace feelers in early 1967. High administration officials issued confusing and contradictory signals about the actions the North would have to take to get the United States to halt the bombing. The most conciliatory signal was given by the President, who said that all the United States required from the North was "just almost any step." In this same period the North Vietnamese decreased the emphasis they had placed on their four points which had previously been seen as preconditions for negotiations and signaled that they would probably agree to talks if the bombing halted. The United States did not respond positively to these signals, but instead resumed the bombing, arguing that a military reciprocation was called for. Although one can only speculate about North Vietnamese perceptions and beliefs, it is quite possible that they thought their concessions met the American demands and felt the United States had used ambiguous signals to trick them into revealing a willingness to negotiate that involved a high cost to themselves. The North, in effect, made a unilateral concession, publicly admitted a significant role in the fighting in the South, and may have thought they appeared both to their adversaries and to the Viet Cong to be lacking in resolve. If in fact they made this interpretation they will be less likely to respond to further ambiguous signals since they will place a higher probability on the chances of American deception. The effect would be substantially the same if they believed this incident was an "honest misunderstanding," for in this case they would believe that they must wait for clearer signals before responding lest they repeat their earlier misinterpretation.

[20] *Ibid.*, 62. [21] *Ibid.*, 61.

The war in Vietnam of course involves indices as well as signals. The American government argues that the results of the war in Vietnam will heavily influence whether similar wars in the area are started and the strength with which they are resisted, and claims that if Southeast Asia falls to Communist subversion and aggression American national security will be significantly decreased. This rests on the belief that both America's adversaries and the potential victims of aggression will take the events in Vietnam as an index of America's ability and willingness to protect others against guerrilla warfare. Without here challenging the basic assumptions behind these beliefs[22] it can be noted that what is important to the United States are the inferences others draw from the outcome of the war. The links between the outcome of the war and the interpretations may not be as clear and immutable as many people seem to believe.

First of all, to make it less likely that others will start new "wars of national liberation" the United States does not have to show that such wars cannot be successful, but only that the costs of waging them outweigh the gains. Of course we must answer the question of who pays the costs and reaps the benefits, and again we can follow the government's analysis and argue that these wars generally have a sponsor (e.g. the Chinese Communists and the North Vietnamese) whose support is a vital ingredient in their success. Thus if the costs to the sponsor are greater than the gains, the sponsor will be willing to halt or prevent the war. Since the conflict between the United States and the war's sponsors is not zero-sum, the United States can win the war in Vietnam and yet the gains to the sponsor can be greater than the costs he has paid, in which case he would be tempted to start other wars. Alternatively, the United States could lose the war and yet impose high enough costs on the sponsor to deter him from repeating his perform-

[22] See above, pp. 244-50, for a critical analysis of the belief that American national security is linked to the fate of the underdeveloped areas.

ance. Specifically, the Chinese and North Vietnamese sponsorship could be repeated even if they lost the war in the South if they believed American involvement in Vietnam has helped the Communist movement all over the world by (1) wasting valuable American resources, (2) creating conflict between the United States and its NATO allies, (3) heightening internal divisions within the United States, (4) damaging the American image in the eyes of the uncommitted nations, and (5) arousing revolutionary fervor in areas ripe for revolt. Alternatively, they would not repeat their behavior even if it had led to victory in Vietnam if they had paid a high price they believed would similarly be exacted in the future. Thus the bombing of the North, even if it can neither prevent supplies from reaching the South nor coerce the North into entering meaningful negotiations, could convince the potential sponsors of other revolutionary wars that the costs of such efforts are prohibitively high. And if the United States decided it could not win in Vietnam it might take advantage of this fact and, rather than follow the commonly advocated position of stopping the bombing as a step toward withdrawal, could instead bomb the North very heavily (perhaps even hitting the dikes) before it withdrew, thus substantially increasing the price the North had paid for its victory.

Of course the past gains and losses to the war's Communist sponsors are only relevant to future decisions if they believe the costs and benefits involved in future conflicts would be similar to those in this conflict. The Communists thus have to make difficult judgments as to how the United States would react to other guerrilla wars, and this involves an assessment of how the war in Vietnam has affected American public and elite opinion. Since the United States government cannot control the mass media that reflect, interpret, and mold public opinion and cannot be sure what the principles are that guide the interpretations the Communists make, the possibilities for manipulation and decoupling are limited. Furthermore, the domestic reaction may be so unambiguous as to permit only one interpretation. The rapid growth of neo-isolationism that some policy-makers and scholars believe may well occur if the United States clearly loses the war could lead sponsors of guerrilla wars to predict that American intervention in the future would be unlikely. Indeed, even if the United States won the war such a domestic reaction might be believed to have occurred, in which case the victory in Vietnam would prove to be Pyrrhic.

If the domestic reaction is not so extreme as to lead the Communists to believe the elite will have no freedom of action, the American leaders could influence the Communists' beliefs about how the United States would act in the future by giving certain interpretations about the war and its outcome. First, if the results were ambiguous decision-makers could claim they have won a victory at an acceptable cost. For even if the sponsors thought the United States had suffered a net loss, if they believed the United States calculated otherwise they would have to attach a fairly high probability to future American interventions. Indeed such a consideration may partly explain Senator Aiken's suggestion that the United States announce it had won and withdraw its troops.

Second, if the South was clearly taken over by the Communists and the United States could not plausibly claim to believe it won the war it could still claim that its gains outweighed its losses. Specifically, it could argue that its struggle exacted a high price from the Communists and decreased their potential for violence in other countries. Related to this, the United States could argue that the war had bought valuable time in which other Asian countries had become stronger—e.g. Thailand built up its army and police force and undertook important reforms, Indonesia destroyed the Communist movement which seemed certain to gain control, Japan started emerging from her isolation to play a larger role in Asian affairs. Third, it could be argued (with considerable justice) that the hardest place to defeat a revolutionary war was in South Vietnam, a divided country that was the successor to a colonial regime

271

defeated by the Communists. Thus the American leaders could point out that a loss in Vietnam would not mean the United States would lose in other countries, or even that a high price would have to be paid for victory.

It should also be noted that if the Communists cared enough about the outcome of the war in Vietnam for its own sake they might be willing to sacrifice some of the advantages of victory in terms of images to make it more likely that the United States would withdraw. In this case they could help the United States decouple by publicly and privately claiming Vietnam was not the prototype of wars of national liberation and that what happened there was not representative of a wider class of events.

American actions in Vietnam may also be taken as an index to its general resolve and may thus influence how others think it will behave in other geographical areas, such as Europe. However, several factors reduce the degree to which this is apt to injure the United States. First, if the decoupling outlined above succeeds, the Soviet image might be unaffected by the retreat. Second, if America's adversaries and allies regard the outcome of the war as mainly a product of indigenous forces and believe it was almost impossible for any outside force to prevent the victory of the Viet Cong, retreat will similarly do little damage to America's image of resolve. Third, others are apt to believe that the value the United States places on Western Europe is vastly different from the value it places on Vietnam and thus may not conclude that a willingness to suffer a defeat in the latter country is an index to a lack of willingness to stand firm in Europe. Fourth, others may be more impressed by the fact that the United States was willing to expend a large amount of blood and treasure to defend a small and relatively unimportant country than they are influenced by the outcome of the war. If the United States will do so much for Vietnam, others may feel, it is apt to do much more than had been previously assumed to defend Europe. As we have seen, the willingness to waste resources can be taken as index to resolve. The American attitude can increase the impact of these factors, especially the last two. The United States could stress that it knew what others had consistently claimed—that it would be terribly difficult to win the war and that the effect of the outcome on world politics would be relatively slight. For if the United States was willing to fight for what seemed like an unimportant and losing cause, it would be even more willing to fight when the need and chances for victory were greater, as they probably would be in a limited confrontation around Berlin.

The continuation of the war, as well as its conclusion, provides opportunities and incentives for the decoupling and manipulation of indices. While the war goes on, each side may at times want to exert pressure on the other by making the other believe it is going to escalate. The most obvious way to do this is to use threats—i.e. to signal and so stake one's signaling reputation on the message. But if the states do not plan to carry out the threats and do not want to run the risk of being caught in a bluff, or if they fear the reaction of other audiences to their threats, or if they wish to supplement a threat, they can try to manipulate indices. The United States, for example, could mobilize large numbers of reserves. However, this would entail domestic political costs and if it were not followed fairly quickly by the deployment of many more troops to Vietnam (the very action it was designed to forestall) it would soon be seen to be deceptive. The United States could also try to manipulate indices to make the Communists think it was seriously considering the use of tactical nuclear weapons. Thus the government could send experts on the use of these weapons to Vietnam, although of course not announcing this was being done, and let the news of this move leak to the press.[23] Simultaneously, special troops could be given

[23] Thus in February 1968 a team of American researchers including an expert on the possible uses of tactical nuclear weapons was sent to Vietnam. This fact was leaked to critics of the Administration, who claimed that the employment of these weapons was being seriously considered. The government denied these charges, but the effect, if not the purpose, of this incident may have been to increase the Com-

additional training in the use of nuclear weapons. Supplies that would be needed if these weapons were employed could be stockpiled in Vietnam. It must be stressed that the United States would have to act as though it were trying to keep these moves completely secret. If they were announced publicly they would be mostly signals since the North Vietnamese and Chinese would realize they were cheap actions taken to impress them. The leaks would have to be arranged to appear genuine, since the manipulation would lose much of its value if the North Vietnamese suspected the United States were using the indices in this way.

The Chinese could similarly try to manipulate indices to deceive the United States into judging Chinese intervention to be more probable. First, they could engage in behavior like that discussed in the preceding paragraph. China could send military logistic and planning experts into North Vietnam, stockpile war material either in North Vietnam or close to the border, and take other cheap measures that would be apt to be taken by a power seriously contemplating military intervention.

In addition, China could take advantage of the fact that the Americans, taken by surprise by the Chinese intervention in Korea, have tried to see what signals and indices they missed in the earlier case. Specifically, Alan Whiting's thorough and imaginative study revealed the existence of a number of indices of China's intentions, for example the shifting line taken in the messages of the domestic mass media.[24] Unlike China's signals—e.g. the explicit message sent through the Indian ambassador—these were not meant to alert the United States (although China may not have cared if they had this effect) but rather were designed to prepare their own people for the coming conflict. Had this study been prepared but not released to the public and the Chinese, the United States could presumably with some confidence draw inferences from the presence or absence of

munists' perception of the likelihood that America would use nuclear weapons rather than suffer a major defeat.

[24] Whiting, *China Crosses the Yalu*, 50-58, 79-87, 98-112.

these indices in current Chinese behavior. Even though the Chinese know we are apt to be watching these indices, the United States could still rely on them if it was believed the shift in domestic propaganda served such important functions that it would still take place if, and only if, the Chinese were planning to intervene despite the Chinese leaders' knowledge that this behavior supplied the United States with extremely valuable information. On the other hand, if the Chinese could change their propaganda line without incurring high domestic costs in terms of getting their people to prepare for a war that is not coming and so diverting resources and reducing their credibility with their own population, they could manipulate this index so that it matched the pattern Whiting saw as indicating they would enter the Korean War. They could do this with relatively great confidence that the United States would be watching these indices because Whiting was until recently one of the leading American officials responsible for observing and evaluating Chinese behavior.[25]

In conclusion, it should be stressed that the treatment of the conflict in Vietnam in terms of signals and indices is not meant to fully cover this conflict. There are many ways of looking at the war, and the one suggested here is meant as an addition to, not a substitute for, those with which we are familiar. By looking at the world in the way outlined here we are able to see that what is at stake in many conflicts is more the interpretation of events and the images of the actors than the intrinsic value of pieces of territory or degrees of influence over third countries. We have seen

[25] If the Chinese wished to launch a surprise attack in Vietnam they could follow the reverse of this policy and avoid the behaviors Whiting had taken to be indices. But it seems more likely that the Chinese would want to get political advantages from their military position by leading the United States to overestimate the chances of Chinese intervention than that they would try to lull the United States into believing they were not going to intervene in order to gain the military benefits of surprise. In Korea the Chinese first seemed to try to warn the United States that they would intervene and then, when it seemed certain the deterrence had failed, they tried (successfully) to keep their military preparations secret.

that the interpretations and images that result from an interaction, while clearly not totally independent of major events, are not linked as tightly to them as has often been believed. Not only is lying possible, but indices can be manipulated and signals and indices can be decoupled to at least partially protect images while actions are taken that would otherwise seem to contradict those images.

Index

ABM, 185, 188
Acheson, Dean, 169
Aiken, George, 116, 271
Alinsky, Saul, 220
Allport, Floyd, 132, 225
Anderson, Raymond, 176
Anglo-French Entente, 101, 111, 169-70
Arab-Israeli conflict, 96, 103, 150, 176, 180
Archibald, Kathleen, 51
Aron, Raymond, 234, 245
Ash, Solomon, 27
Aspaturian, Vernon, 70
Austin, J. L., 37

Bailey, Thomas, 174
Bay of Pigs, 196, 226, 234
Beecher, William, 185
Beichman, Arnold, 138, 177
Belgrade Conference, 252
Beloff, Max, 207
Bennis, Warren, 125
Berkeley, University of California at, 214
Berlin, 20, 23, 43, 93, 109, 210-13, 222, 234, 249, 252, 273; blockade of, 115, 138, 169, 181, 197, 210-11, 226; wall, 182, 205, 211
Bethe, Hans, 67
Bethmann-Hollweg, Theobald von, 19
Binder, David, 109, 222
Bismarck, Otto von, 6, 87, 126, 134, 206, 251
Blake, Robert, 137
Blumer, Herbert, 4
Boer War, 95
Boorstein, Daniel, 3
Boulding, Kenneth, 3, 191
Bradbury, Ray, 69
Brehm, Jack, 77
Brodie, Bernard, 225, 235
Brofenbrenner, Urie, 67
Brown, Seyom, 210, 214
Bullock, Alan, 46, 205
Burr, Robert, 109

Butow, Robert, 98
Butz, J. S., 90, 227
Byrnes, James, 97-98

Castro, Fidel, 246
Chamberlain, Neville, 157-58, 171, 206
Chi, Hsi-sheng, 12
chicken, game of, 190, 192, 196
Chile, 109
China, 55, 56, 106, 122, 133, 149, 163, 191, 209, 269-70, 274
Churchill, Winston, 170
Clifford, Clark, 185, 261
Coan, John, 77
Colombia, 209
Colvin, Ian, 46
Compton, James, 32
Congress, 74, 75, 177-78
Congress of Vienna, see Vienna
Cornell University, 200-1
Coulondre, Robert, 36
counterforce strategy, 233
Cuban missile crisis, 5, 6, 22, 43, 92, 164, 178, 196, 210, 226, 228, 243
Czechoslovakia, 5, 35, 157, 158, 177, 200, 202, 206

Dallek, Robert, 32
Davidson, Philip, 49, 53
Davison, W. Phillips, 115, 181, 210, 211
Dean, Arthur, 168
decommitting, 83, 155-65
DeConde, Alexander, 68
Deutsch, Karl, 71, 235
Dien Bien Phu, 30
Diesing, Paul, 94
Dinerstein, Herbert, 246
diplomatic language, 113, 139
Dodd, William, 32
Dominican Republic, 234
Douglas, 34, 115
Downs, Anthony, 17, 72-73
Dulles, Allen, 22, 47-48
Dyck, Harvey, 109, 150, 186

INDEX

Eden, Richard, 215
Eisenhower, Dwight David, 103
Ellsberg, Daniel, 175, 202
Enemy Below, The, 55
Estonia, 47

Fashoda, 21
Fearing, Franklin, 4
Feigl, Herbert, 24
Feis, Herbert, 106, 169, 172, 198
Feld, Maury, 37
Feldman, Sandor, 56-57, 95
Feron, James, 116
Festinger, Leon, 77
Finney, John, 105, 185
first strike, 38, 89, 231
Fischer, Louis, 47
Fisher, Roger, 142
flexible response, 233
FOBS (Fractional Orbiting
Bombardment System), 31-32
Ford, Franklin, 36, 97
Fox, Annette Baker, 7, 86
François-Poncet, André, 32
Franke, Winfried, 12
Frankel, Max, 209
Freymond, Jacques, 117, 265
Fulbright, J. William, 200

Garner, William, 12
Garthoff, Raymond, 233
George, Alexander, 26, 45, 85
Gilbert, Felix, 42, 106
Glass, Robert, 49, 53
Gleason, S. Everett, 67
Goffman, Erving, 2, 11, 18-19,
41, 43, 65-67, 96, 107, 110,
117, 124, 146
Goldiamond, Israel, 132
Good, Paul, 220
good will, 7
Greaves, Rose Louise, 84, 194
Greenstein, Fred, 9
Grenville, J.A.S., 21, 68, 96, 218
Gresham's Law, 57
Grey, Lord, 227
Grose, Peter, 266
Gross, Feliks, 136
Groth, Alexander, 33
Grump, R., 65
Gurtov, Melvin, 22

Guyana, 245
Gwertzman, Bernard, 185

Haas, Ernst, 11, 111
Harris, William R., 181
Hawkins, William, 132
Herz, John, 245-46
Heymont, Irving, 65
Hinsley, F. H., 7
Hitler, Adolf, 7, 9, 14, 26, 45,
103, 106, 177, 200, 204-6
Hoag, Malcolm, 128
Hoar-Laval agreement, 198
Hoffmann, Stanley, 223
Horelick, Arnold, 68, 93, 252
hot line, 91
Howley, Colonel, 181
Humphrey, Hubert, 258-59
Hyman, Herbert, 218

Iklé, Fred, 44, 81, 84, 87, 128,
145, 156
implicit personality theories, 27
indices, 18, 26
instability, 89
International Monetary Fund, 216
Israel, 75, 180
Italy, 215

Jacobson, Harold, 149, 166-69,
194
Jakobson, Max, 34, 114
James, Robert, 51
Japanese decision to surrender,
97-99, 101, 267
Jervis, Robert, 9, 14, 132, 200, 264
Johnson, Lyndon, 78, 150, 160,
209, 226

Kahn, Herman, 39, 72, 74, 80,
92, 141, 227, 231, 233, 240-42
Kamm, Henry, 222
Kaplan, Abraham, 9
Kaplan, Morton, 12, 85, 227
Kaufmann, William W., 39, 92
Kennan, George, 128, 133, 171
Kennedy, Edward, 185
Kennedy, John, 22, 25, 92, 164,
178, 197, 205, 208, 219, 248
Kennedy, Robert, 63, 219

278

Khrushchev, Nikita, 23, 93, 164, 178, 205
Kissinger, Henry, 228
Knightley, Philip, 47
Korea, 10, 56, 59, 85, 104, 128, 133, 191, 193, 207, 226, 275
Kosygin, Aleksei, 150
Kraslow, David, 267-68
Kuhn, Thomas, 16

labor-management relations, 33, 52, 73, 114, 131, 142, 147, 180
Lacroix, Victor-Leopold de, 35
Laing, R. D., 57
Langer, William, 67, 132
Laos, 196
League of Nations, 104, 205
Lee, A. R., 57
Leighton, Richard, 94
Leitch, David, 47
Leites, Nathan, 12, 70, 85
Liska, George, 87
Locarno Pact, 104, 205
Loftus, Joseph, 185
Lorry, Stuart, 267-68
Lowe, J. C., 104
Lowi, Theodore, 75

MacArthur, Douglas, 133
McEwan, William, 121
McFarland, Andrew, 149
Magdoff, Harry, 248
McKersie, Robert, 52, 79, 103, 117, 131
McNamara, Robert, 39, 92-93
Manning, C.A.W., 139
Marshall, Charles Burton, 132
Marshall, George C., 31
Mattingly, Garrett, 61
May, Ernest, 85
Mead, George Herbert, 11
Merton, Robert, 122
Meyerson, Martin, 214
Middleton, Drew, 190
Monger, George, 169
Montagu, Ewan, 11, 50
Morgenthau, Hans, 71, 231
Mowat, Robert, 117
multilateral force, 78

NATO, 108, 178, 270

naval demonstrations, 107, 135, 176, 227
naval visits, 60, 107
Navarino, battle of, 237
Nicolson, Harold, 113, 117, 128-29, 139, 147-48
Nixon, Richard, 185, 258
Noggle, Burl, 79
non-proliferation treaty, 105
Normandy, invasion of, 48, 54, 59, 62, 94

Oder-Neisse line, 169
Olson, Mancur, 17, 73
operational codes, 12
Organski, A.F.K., 231
Osgood, Robert, 103, 178

Padover, Saul, 35
Page, Bruce, 47
Perkins, Bradford, 9, 31, 104, 151
Perkins, Dwight, 65
Perrault, Gilles, 48, 54, 59, 62
Peru, 180, 209
Peters, Edward, 73, 114, 118, 130, 140, 142, 147
Philby, Harold, 47
Phillipson, H., 57
Poland, 6, 206
Polanyi, Michael, 16, 37
Polsby, Nelson, 218
pre-emption, 91, 207, 236
prestige, 7
prisoners' dilemma, 73
prominence, 37, 141
promise, 81-82, 102, 108, 164, 169-70, 258
Pruitt, Dean, 24
psychological environment, 4, 8, 13
Pueblo, 191-93

Quester, George, 217, 233

Rapoport, Anatol, 16, 127
reassurance, 81
Reiners, Ludwig, 87, 203
Riecken, H., 77
Riker, William, 17, 178
risks, see willingness to run
Robertson, Terrence, 108

INDEX

Rock, William, 157, 158
Rosebery, Lord, 51
Rosecrance, Richard, 249
Rosenau, James, 12
Rush, Myron, 68, 93, 252
Rusk, Dean, 197, 260

Salisbury, Lord, 84, 96
saving face, 7, 125, 182, 199, 202
Schacter, S., 77
Schaff, Adam, 139
Schelling, Thomas C., 10, 19, 29,
    37, 44, 56, 59, 79, 81, 86, 89,
    102-3, 125, 140, 144, 155, 161,
    163, 190, 231, 237-38, 240-42,
    250
Schlesinger, Arthur, 23, 25, 205
Schorske, Carl, 36
Schwien, Edwin, 41
Sebeok, Thomas, 37
second strike capability, 89, 231,
    251
self-fulfilling prophecy, 219
Selznick, Philip, 76
semantic level, 24-25, 119, 127
Seneviratne, Gamini, 105
Shabecoff, Philip, 259
Sharp, Eugene E., 220
Sherwood, Robert, 98-99
Shulman, Marshall, 23-24, 234
Sicily, invasion of, 49-50, 62
Singer, J. David, 12, 29, 38
Singer, Max, 248
Smith, Hedrick, 100, 124, 190
Smith, Jean Edward, 182, 197,
    200, 211
Snyder, Glenn, 6, 104, 226, 236
Sokolvskii, Marshall, 242
Sontag, Raymond, 97, 124, 135
Sorenson, Theodore, 25, 105
Spanish-American War, 238
Speier, Hans, 175
spending money, 39, 92-97,
    250-53
Sprout, Harold, 4
Sprout, Margaret, 4
Stalin, 69
Stein, Eric, 149, 166-69, 194
Steinstuechen, 212
Stevens, Carl, 125
Stone, I. F., 264

Stone, Jeremy J., 40, 92
Strauss, Anselm, 77
Suez crisis, 108, 218
Sulzberger, C. L., 129, 263
summit conferences, 25, 175, 196
Sweeney, Walter, 55

Taylor, A.J.P., 5
test ban, 22, 67, 149, 166, 183,
    194
tests, 27
Thayer, Charles, 148
Thomas, W. I., 11
Thompson, James, 35, 121
Thompson, Laurence, 171
Tibet, 191
Toby, Jackson, 149
Toulmin, Stephen, 16, 29, 255
Trieste, 215
Truman, Harry S, 75, 207
Tuchman, Barbara, 87
Tucker, Robert W., 248
Turner, Henry Ashby, 134

Ullman, Richard, 259
ultimata, 20, 114, 205
unintended consequences, 189,
    219, 241
Union of South Africa, 200
United Nations, 137, 177, 190
unpredictability, 86, 146, 236, 239

Vagts, Alfred, 107, 127, 135,
    146, 176, 227, 238
Versailles, Treaty of, 6, 14, 205-6
Vienna, Congress of, 148
Vienna summit conference, 25,
    196
Vietnam, 87, 92, 99, 116, 124,
    159-61, 172, 184, 190, 203,
    209, 234, 247, 254, 255-76

Waley, Arthur, 133
Walton, Richard, 52, 79, 103,
    117, 131
Waltz, Kenneth, 12, 34, 75, 175,
    246, 248-49
War of 1812, 9, 104
Webb, Eugene, 65
Wheeler-Bennett, John, 6, 36
White, John Albert, 33, 151

Whiting, Alan, 59, 132, 134, 274
Wiesner, Jerome, 168
Wildavsky, Aaron, 218, 248
Williamson, Samuel, 48, 54, 170
willingness to run risks, 14, 20, 22, 191, 229, 238-39, 243
Wilson, Hugh, 32
Wilson, Woodrow, 34
Wohlstetter, Roberta, 29, 123
Wolf, Charles, 255

Wolfe, Thomas, 235, 242
Wolfers, Arnold, 13
Wood, Bryce, 180, 209

Yalta, 172
Yemen, 245
Young, Oran, 207
Yugoslavia, 215

Zanzibar, 245

DATE DUE